Islamic Fundamentalisms
and the
Gulf Crisis

ISLAMIC FUNDAMENTALISMS
AND THE
GULF CRISIS

EDITED BY JAMES PISCATORI

The Fundamentalism Project

American Academy of Arts and Sciences

The collection of essays in this volume is based on
a project conducted under the auspices of
the American Academy of Arts and Sciences
and supported by a grant from
the John D. and Catherine T. MacArthur Foundation.
The opinions expressed are those of the individual authors only,
and do not necessarily reflect the views of
the American Academy or the supporting foundation.

Inquiries may be addressed to
The Fundamentalism Project
1025 E. 58th Street
Chicago, Illinois 60637

Islamic fundamentalisms and the gulf crisis / edited by James Piscatori;
sponsored by the American Academy of Arts and Sciences.

\# 25130766

p. cm.—

ISBN 0-9629608-0-2 (alk. paper)

Library of Congress Catalog Card Number: 91-072487

This book is printed on acid-free paper.

CONTENTS

ACKNOWLEDGMENTS

Barbara A. Lockwood of The Fundamentalism Project coordinated the international exchange of ideas and flow of information from her office in Chicago. She also typed and retyped the various chapters and joined in the proofreading of the manuscript. Micah Marty designed the book and oversaw its production. Ritchie Ovendale of the University of Wales contributed the Chronology, a version of which will be published in his book *Longman Historical Companions: The Middle East Since 1914* (Longman). Patricia A. Mitchell prepared the index. The editor acknowledges his gratitude to Scott Appleby for a cheerful assistance and patience that were extraordinary.

FOREWORD

Martin E. Marty and R. Scott Appleby

During the Persian Gulf crisis of 1990–91, Islamic fundamentalist movements of North Africa, the Middle East, and South Asia faced their own internal crises in response to Saddam Hussein's call for a *jihad* (in this context, a "holy war") against the West. Movements were divided and defined by the positions they adopted toward Saddam and toward the presence of Western "infidels" and "crusaders" in the Islamic holy lands. The strength, wisdom, and political maturity of these movements were put to the test. Was this a propitious moment for the mobilization of devout Muslims and a display of fundamentalist sociopolitical influence? Given the heightened anti-Western sentiment among the populace of various nations, was this a period of intensive recruiting on the part of fundamentalist movements and a time to enhance their salience in the public order? Or did the transparent nature of Saddam's new-found Muslim faith undermine the attempts of radical fundamentalists to exploit anti-Western sentiment?

In the months before the war, during the air campaign, and again on the eve of the ground campaign in February 1991, many analysts warned that Muslim unrest threatened to destabilize governments and entire regions. Although the direst predictions proved wrong, the Gulf crisis did change the status of fundamentalist movements within their political environments and significantly affected the climate in which Islamists must operate.

In addressing these issues and in assessing the impact of the war upon Islamic movements from North Africa to South Asia, the present volume draws upon the research of an interdisciplinary cross-cultural study of modern religious fundamentalisms conducted by the American Academy of Arts and Sciences and supported by a grant from the John D. and Catherine T. MacArthur Foundation. Over a five-year period The Fundamentalism Project is holding conferences and commissioning essays on movements around the world within major religious traditions. The project directors and participants seek to comprehend the historical and contemporary contexts of fundamentalisms, the social, political, and religious character of fundamentalist movements, and the consequences which obtain when fundamentalisms come to prominence or power in a society—their impact on government and political life, economies, legislation, state security, cultural expressions, and religious organizations. The scholars who contribute to this project, many of them drawn from the various religious traditions and nations in which fundamentalist movements are found, hope to serve the cause of discriminating carefully among movements by providing accurate assessments concerning the size, motivations, and intentions of each movement, and the relationship of the movement to the historic religious tradition from which it has emerged.

Fundamentalisms Observed, the first volume of project essays published by the University of Chicago Press, examines the rise of movements within Christianity, Judaism, Islam, Hinduism, Sikhism, Buddhism, and Confucianism in the twentieth century. The title of the volume is not meant to indicate that every movement examined within it equally "qualifies" as a fundamentalism. Indeed the volume, and the entire project, is based on a hypothesis to be tested throughout the course of the inquiry—namely, that one can speak responsibly and accurately of "family resemblances" among disparate movements of religiously inspired reaction to aspects of the global processes of modernization and secularization in the twentieth century. As a genuinely open-ended inquiry, the project has not established its conclusions before its research is completed; only in the concluding phases of the project, after dozens of case studies and historical essays are finalized, will scholars from various disciplines with synthetic abilities attempt to "comprehend" the various phenomena and directly address the task of establishing coherent and definitive ways to speak of them within the framework of "comparative fundamentalisms." To make the point in another way: it may well be concluded that the term "fundamentalism," even when emptied of its specific historical content in the American Protestantism of the early twentieth century and reconstructed as an analytical lens by which to view profitably a range of religiopolitical movements, is inadequate to the comparative task and must be replaced with a number of less comprehensive terms. In any event, one important goal of the project is to avoid and even to overcome the erroneous impressions created when disparate phenomena are studied together under one nomenclature, whether it be "liberalism," "conservativism," "traditionalism" or "Marxism." Phenomena do fall roughly into these broad categories, as do these movements of religious activism under the label "fundamentalism" or some cognate. But it is the task of the scholar continually to point to the inadequacy of these necessary clusterings.

In commissioning essays on separate movements in their particularities, however, the project directors were careful to provide participating scholars with a description of the traits and elements of "religious fundamentalism" as a cross-cultural phenomenon. Those traits of the still hypothetical "family" of fundamentalisms are discussed in detail in the concluding essay to *Fundamentalisms Observed*. One of several working definitions of fundamentalism provided therein may be repeated here to give readers of this monograph a general idea of how the term is understood by contributors.

Religious fundamentalism has appeared as a tendency, a habit of mind, found within religious communities and paradigmatically embodied in certain representative individuals and movements, which manifests itself as a strategy, or set of strategies, by which beleaguered believers attempt to preserve their distinctive identity as a people or group. Feeling this identity to be at risk in the contemporary era, they fortify it by a selective retrieval of doctrines, beliefs, and practices from a sacred past. These retrieved "fundamentals" are refined, modified, and sanctioned in a spirit of shrewd pragmatism: they are to serve as a bulwark against the encroachment of outsiders who threaten to draw the believers into a syncretistic, areligious, or irreligious cultural milieu. Moreover, these fundamentals are accompanied in the new religious portfolio by unprecedented claims and doctrinal innovations. By the strength of these innovations and the new supporting doctrines, the retrieved and updated fundamentals are meant to regain the same charismatic intensity today by which they originally forged communal identity from the formative revelatory religious experiences long ago.

In this sense contemporary fundamentalism is at once both derivative and vitally original. In the effort to reclaim the efficacy of religious life, fundamentalists have more in common than not with other religious revivalists of past centuries. But fundamentalism intends neither an artificial imposition of archaic practices and life-styles nor a simple return to a golden era, a sacred past, a bygone time of origins—although nostalgia for such an era is a hallmark of fundamentalist rhetoric. Instead, religious identity thus renewed becomes the exclusive and absolute basis for a recreated political and social order that is oriented to the future rather than the past. By selecting elements of tradition and modernity, fundamentalists seek to remake the world in the service of a dual commitment to the unfolding eschatological drama (by returning all things in submission to the divine) and to self-preservation (by neutralizing the threatening

"Other"). Such an endeavor often requires charismatic and authoritarian leadership, depends upon a disciplined inner core of adherents, and promotes a rigorous sociomoral code for all followers. Boundaries are set, the enemy identified, converts sought, and institutions created and sustained in pursuit of a comprehensive reconstruction of society.

This tentative description of "fundamentalism" is necessarily couched in general terms. When one examines a particular religious tradition—in the case of the present monograph, Islam—such a description is useful in two ways. First, it may lead us to consider certain elements or emphases present within the efforts of some contemporary Muslims to establish the *Shari'a*, the code of Islamic law, within nation-states resistant or openly hostile to the introduction or reintroduction of religious law as a framework for political and legislative decisions, as well as social and cultural life. Second, a comparativist's description of "fundamentalism" may also help us to exclude certain movements from an examination of Islamic fundamentalism, or to nuance and qualify the term as it is applied to certain movements.

For example, twentieth century fundamentalisms are described as "reactive" in their original inspiration, that is, they are said initially to adopt a confrontational mode in response to what is experienced as the threat to the values and norms of a traditional way of life, whether that threat comes from a secular Westernized regime, or from modernizing agents within the religious tradition. The fundamentalist response falls into a more generalized pattern of oppositional movements which strive to create an alternative order by which to compete with, or withdraw from, a threatening external order. Specifically, fundamentalists look to religious precepts, doctrines, and laws in creating and sanctioning the new order they seek to build. This pure and whole "new order" is also intended to be comprehensive, reaching into all aspects of life; this stated intention of many modern fundamentalisms, as we shall see, also presents them with their greatest source of frustration within the irresistibly pluralist social, economic, and international contexts in which fundamentalists, as others, must operate today.

These reflections lead to two conclusions relevant to the discussion of Islamic fundamentalisms. First, Islamic fundamentalisms may share many traits of Islamic revivalisms, but the two phenomena are not identical. Fundamentalisms may indeed arise within, or in other cases lead to, a religious revival that features a general cultural and social but not explicitly political return to Islamic paradigms and juridical sources. But fundamentalisms ultimately do move toward the fundamentals, the determining principles and doctrines, not only of religious belief and practice, but especially of the polities in which they find themselves; that is, they are inherently political. Fundamentalist political expression is varied: it may be evident in the politics of the enclave seeking to preserve itself within an alien temporality; in the politics of the democrat seeking to amass popular support for Islamism from below; or, in the politics of the revolutionary seeking to impose the new/old order from above. In each of these political expressions, it must be emphasized, fundamentalisms are necessarily involved in compromise and accommodation—often to the extent that, after a time, they can hardly any longer be described as "fundamentalist" in the sense of the original exclusivist, dogmatic, and confrontational mode that was central to the formative experience of the movement. Indeed authors of this volume often use words like "pragmatist" or "accommodationist" to describe contemporary Islamic parties or groups which, while still committed to the basic fundamentalist goal of implementing Islamic law and establishing an Islamic state, have been tempered in their zeal by the exigencies of modern political processes.

This is simply a way of saying that fundamentalisms inevitably become involved in modern political life; and in so doing they participate in a common discourse about modernization, development, political structures, and economic planning. They may nuance and modify the terms of that discourse; they may successfully or unsuccessfully try to redirect or reinvent aspects of it; but they are contained within it and find any hope of even a partial return to pristine Islam, much less the construction of a "purely" Islamic form of modern polity, well out of reach.

This leads to a second consequence of considering Islamic fundamentalisms from a more generalized perspective. Fundamentalisms that have arisen or been reawakened in this century with the aim of establishing a polity based on the Shari'a do not enjoy an important advantage of what is often described as the prototypical fundamentalist state, namely, Saudi Arabia. Wahhabism originated and thrived within the framework of a traditional collaboration between the *ulama* (religious scholars) and the ruler, both of whom shared the basic goal of restoring pristine Islam. The Wahhabis were in this eighteenth century context able to retrieve and shape whole as it were a comprehensive system of jurisprudence that became a stable foundation for a conservative Islamic state. Unavoidable compromises with modernity were negotiated by a partnership of ulama and ruler. Contemporary fundamentalist movements of course have found themselves in a quite different situation. Islamists in Egypt, Algeria, Pakistan, and Jordan to a greater or lesser degree find themselves unable even to contemplate the construction of such a state; as the reports in this collection demonstrate repeatedly, they find themselves enagaged fully in a continual round of negotiations with and accommodations to both the secular state and the revived and variegated Muslim populace. They live and move within the framework of twentieth century secular rationality, even if they do not fully endorse it. Their version of political Islam is necessarily a hybrid of Shari'a and selected elements of modern political ideologies ranging from democratic capitalism to Marxism.

By virtue of their common goal of implementing the Shari'a, fundamentalist movements across the Middle East, North Africa, and South Asia are in a historic and ideological relationship to the Wahhabis—a relationship which of course has considerable financial and geopolitical implications for many of the movements in a situation such as the recent Gulf crisis. Focusing as it did upon the viability and future of the Saudi regime, threatened by a secular tyrant who cloaked himself in the garb of Islam, the crisis revealed the tensions within the relationship between the Saudis and other fundamentalist movements even as it exposed to view the limited expressions of internal dissent within the Saudi regime. In underscoring the differences between a conservative fundamentalist regime—one, in this case, defended by Western troops—and the various counter-hegemonic fundamentalist movements that it has supported, the crisis forced fundamentalist leaders from Algeria to Pakistan to decide between a policy of pragmatism (suggested by the Saudi expectation of political support) and radicalism (suggested by the anti-Western animus of the populations). The decision held important implications for the future of the Saudi-funded movements. This is one of many themes in the following reports.

These and other issues clarified or at least brought into sharper focus by the Gulf crisis are exceedingly complex, and the question of the role of religious fundamentalism is but one element in understanding them. And on this question itself much remains to be learned and reported in the months and years to come. Sufficient time has not passed for scholars responsibly to offer anything more than initial reflections on the role of Islam in the Gulf crisis and, specifically, the impact of the crisis upon the various fundamentalist organizations and movements in the Islamic world. With this in mind, our goal in commissioning the reports included in this volume was appropriately modest. We asked the authors, many of whom are at work on a larger interpretive volume for The Fundamentalism Project to be published many months hence, each to prepare a report of approximately 5,000 words containing a description of the major Islamic "fundamentalist" movement(s) now active in the nations in question; a review of the rhetorical and organizational reactions of these movements to the Gulf crisis, including a consideration of the primary institutional and organizational channels by which the movements could and did respond; and a brief assessment of how the crisis and the Islamic response affected the status and salience of each movement. By surveying seven countries on these questions we hope to provide basic information for those who may know some movements and countries quite well but might find a synoptic approach useful; and to discern patterns, if they existed, across movements in their responses to the crisis.

Scholars working on these and other aspects of Islamic fundamentalist movements were willing to interrupt momentarily that longer-term research to contribute to the present collection of reports in full awareness that events may swiftly and dramatically change circumstances—and thus the authors' tentative conclusions—even in the time it takes to print and distribute this book. Be that as it may, these reports do capture several fundamentalist movements at an important, and in some cases decisive, moment in their histories.

1

RELIGION AND REALPOLITIK: ISLAMIC RESPONSES TO THE GULF WAR

James Piscatori

In the Gulf crisis of 1990–91, Saddam Hussein confidently promised the decisive victory against the forces of Western imperialism, but he will be remembered for another uncommon, and unexpected, achievement. He brought his regime and country to the brink of complete ruin, and yet, in the process, millions of Muslims throughout the world, often to the discomfort of their own governments, acclaimed him a Muslim hero. Although his air force and army embarrassingly took flight or dissolved, he gained in stature for standing alone against the mighty, principally American, military force arrayed against him. Moreover, his Scud missile attacks on Israel, though they inflicted relatively little actual damage, earned him immense credit for widening the conflict to the Arabs' nemesis. In effect, Saddam's invasion of Kuwait on 2 August 1990 and the diplomatic and military crisis that ensued not only challenged the region's interstate stability, but also emphasized the central importance that religion has in the political crises of the Muslim world.

Saddam did not always appreciate the power that religion exercises on the minds of men. But apparently on the eve of battle, he rallied his senior commanders by emotionally invoking God as the architect of the imminent war. "It is the Lord who wanted what has happened to happen. Our role in this decision is almost zero." Warming to his theme, he

1

declared that, as the symbol of the Republican Party was the elephant, the Qur'anic story of the defeat of the forces equipped with elephants which had attacked Mecca was a portent of the Iraqi victory to come. He was moved to cite the appropriate verses: "See you not how the Lord dealt with the companions of the elephant? Did He not make their treacherous plan go astray?" A tape recording of the meeting reveals that cries could be heard from the audience, "Yes, Mr. President, how history repeats itself!" [1]

Prior to the Gulf crisis and particularly the dispatch of Western forces to Saudi Arabia, there were few in the Arab or Muslim world, except perhaps his most sycophantic supporters, who would have put Saddam in the front rank of defenders of Islam and of the pan-Islamic community (umma). Rather, the Ba'thist ideology to which he ascribed made the Arab nation the focal point and invested it with both socialist and secular meanings. The "republic of fear" which he systematically constructed in the name of these principles brooked no dissent,[2] and politicized Shi'ite groups, which could conceivably stoke the fires of open rebellion among the Shi'ite majority of Iraq, were seen as especially dangerous. It was a regime terrifyingly consistent and lacking in all subtlety: any opponent—Shi'ite or Kurd, religious leader or Ba'thist apparatchik, man or woman—who defied the whim of Saddam's regime was eliminated. Ayatollah Muhammad Baqir al-Sadr, one of the preeminent religious authorities of the Shi'ite world, and his sister were publicly hanged in April 1980. This event evoked the Shi'ite traditional sense of oppression and martyrdom and hence became an emblem of Saddam's anti-Islamic brutality.[3]

The ill-advised war with revolutionary and non-Arab Iran from 1980 to 1988 may, arguably, have added luster to Saddam's self-promoted image as defender of the Arab nation. But it also confirmed the universal view that Islam was, at best, of secondary importance to him. Referring to the celebrated battle in 637 at which Arab Muslims decisively defeated the non-Muslim Sassanid Persians, he scored a limited legitimizing point when he boasted that the battle with Iran, joined in September 1980, would soon yield another "Qadisiyya."[4] However, the war was to grind on for eight bloody years, and Iraqi Shiʻite opposition groups, such as Amatzia Baram discusses in his chapter, found natural support in the Iranian regime. While Tehran's Islamic rhetoric was as patently contrived for maximum domestic effect as was Saddam's Arabism, its demonization of Saddam fell on receptive ears in the broader Muslim world. Ayatollah Khomeini repeatedly spoke of the war as pitting faith against unbelief *(kufr),*[5] and Saddam was relegated to the disagreeable company of the Shah of Iran, Ronald Reagan, and Menachem Begin as archenemies of Islam.

Saddam's recent transformation into Muslim hero—in many, though certainly not all, Muslim circles—was thus all the more striking. A number of complex factors were at work, and, in this story, the emotional appeal of the Palestinian issue, latent anger at the arrogant, *nouveau riche* states of the Gulf which had invited foreign troops into the holy peninsula, and a lingering suspicion of Western motives all played their part. Yet there were also limitations on the ability of Muslim movements and groups to maximize their position as a result of the Gulf crisis, and it must be seen as having both provided opportunities for and imposed constraints on the political agenda of Muslim fundamentalists.

Saddam and the Political Symbolism of Islam

The prevalence of anti-Saudi and anti-Israeli allusions in the rhetoric of Saddam Hussein and his regime was not simply accidental. "Saudi Arabia" and "Palestine" are emotionally charged, interconnected symbols in the Muslim political imagination. Together they represent the holiest cities of Islam—Mecca and Medina in Saudi Arabia, and Jerusalem in Palestine—which formed the setting in which the Prophet Muhammad lived his life. Even secularized Baʻthists could not have avoided the pervasiveness of these symbols and the meanings that they convey.

Born in the Arabian trading town of Mecca around 570 A.D., Muhammad began to receive the Revelation there. Forced to leave because of the hostility of his polytheistic townsmen, he and his early followers migrated to a nearby town in 622. Renamed Medina ("the city"), it became the seat of the first, and generally archetypical, Islamic state. The year of the migration *(hijra)* is now considered the first year of the Muslim calendar. The continuing relevance of these founding events of Islam is also affirmed by the obligation that Muslims have, if at all possible, to undertake a pilgrimage *(hajj)* once in their lives to Mecca. One of the five pillars of the Islamic faith, the pilgrimage has entailed great physical and financial hardships for Muslims throughout history, and the title "Hajji" has thus carried enviable social prestige. Medina, the final resting place of the Prophet, has also become a special place of devotion, and, although doctrine does not require it, tradition encourages a visit to the Prophet's mosque.

Jerusalem is central to the Muslim worldview because it is believed to be connected to two extraordinary journeys of the Prophet. The first is the "nocturnal journey" *(isra)* when the Prophet was transported on a winged horse from Mecca to Jerusalem in one night. According to the traditions, Muhammad met there Abraham, Moses, and Jesus, and the general journey is memorialized in the Qur'an: "Glory to Him who caused His servant to journey by night from the sacred place of worship [Mecca] to the further place of worship, which We have encircled with blessings, in order that We might show him some of our signs" (xvii: i). Although the Qur'an does not specify the exact location, that "further place" is now enshrined in al-Aqsa mosque (literally, "the further mosque") in Jerusalem, on the site that Muslims call "al-Haram al-Sharif" or "the Noble Precinct" and that Jews call the "Temple Mount," where they believe Solomon's temple once stood.

4

The second journey, which in most (but not all) accounts follows immediately from this nocturnal journey, is the Prophet's ascension to heaven *(mi'raj)*. With his foot on a rock in the area of al-Haram al-Sharif, he ascended accompanied by the archangel Gabriel. Muhammad passed through the seven heavens and encountered God's earlier prophets along the way. When he reached the throne of Allah in the highest heaven, he was taught how the obligatory prayers must be performed. The Dome of the Rock, near to al-Aqsa mosque in the Haram area, stands as a visible reminder of this second journey.

Both Arabian and Palestinian lands are thus special preserves, and, because of this, they take on a wider importance, particularly in the competition for legitimacy that characterizes politics in the Middle East. The Palestinian dimension of Muslim politics is illustrative of this point.

The linkage between Arab and Muslim concern over Zionism in Palestine had existed since at least 1931 when the Jerusalem Congress, ostensibly called to revive the caliphate, attempted to put developments in Palestine on the Muslim agenda. But, after 1967 when Israel occupied Jerusalem and the West Bank, the matter assumed a far greater urgency. The religious officials *(ulama)* of al-Azhar, the venerable Islamic university in Cairo, had talked in 1956 of Israel as one of the "imperialist countries" and focused on the dangers of the Western-inspired Baghdad Pact.[6] But now with Israeli occupation of one of Islam's defining centers, the discourse reflected a decidedly Islamic concern. In 1968, an international gathering of ulama condemned Israeli activities as an attack on the very fabric of Islamic Jerusalem: "[The usurpers] tore down several Muslim sites, including mosques, schools, and homes, all of which were held by religious endowments *(awqaf)*." Even more worrisome, the Zionists had detestable "schemes" for al-Aqsa mosque, "the first holy place in Islam."[7]

When Saddam Hussein launched his "initiative" of 12 August, explicitly linking his withdrawal from Kuwait with

Israeli withdrawal from the occupied territories,[8] he was exploiting the profound sentiment which had become the Arab—and Muslim—consensus. It was, on one level, an obvious political ploy, a cost-free way of attempting to divert attention. He appeared to strike a blow for Palestinian liberation without doing a great deal to accomplish it. But by explicitly shifting focus to the Arab-Israeli conflict and restoring the question of Palestine to pride of place, he was, on another level, tapping into deep springs of Muslim concern. In the words of Shaikh Abd al-Aziz Bin Baz, the paramount religious scholar of Saudi Arabia, "the Palestinian problem is an Islamic problem first and last," and Muslims "must fight an Islamic *jihad* against the Jews until the land returns to its owners."[9] As Beverley Milton-Edwards points out in the case of Jordan, when Saddam gave expression to this consensus in his own inimitable manner, he found favour, if he had not already, on the streets of the Muslim world.[10]

But as the theology is all of a piece, so too the political symbolism of Palestine is inevitably linked to that of the Arabian peninsula. Saddam was able to argue that, like Palestine, the land containing the holy cities of Mecca and Medina had itself fallen prey to occupation. He spoke of the need to liberate Mecca, "hostage of the Americans," from troops of the Western-led coalition. "Until the voice of right rises up in the Arab world, hit their interests wherever they are and rescue holy Mecca and rescue the grave of the Prophet Muhammad in Medina."[11]

The response in the Muslim world to this call for jihad was not hesitant. A preacher at al-Aqsa mosque in Jerusalem sharply condemned the Saudi leadership before a congregation of some 10,000 worshippers: "Arab leaders are giving Moslem lands to the Americans."[12] In Jordan, the Muslim Brotherhood called on Muslims "to purge the holy land of Palestine and Najd and Hijaz [provinces of Saudi Arabia] from the Zionists and imperialists" (see Milton-Edwards, this volume). About 400 protestors shouted "shame" and "death to Fahd" outside the Saudi embassy in Belgrave Square in

London; they were disturbed by the Saudis' seeming willingness to have their country occupied by "the enemies of
Islam."[13] Even among Muslims as far away from the Arab
world as China, some believed that the dispatch of Western
troops to Saudi Arabia had violated the integrity of Muslim
territory. As a result, they felt that Islam had been insulted
and that Saddam's opposition to the foreign troops deserved
support.[14]

These criticisms of Saudi policy were the latest version of
the special derision which has been reserved for a monarchy
that has referred to itself as "custodian of the Holy Places."
In the eyes of many Muslims, the self-designation has been
sententious at best and hypocritical at worst. Indeed, from
the time in 1924 that the Saudi regime conquered Mecca, its
control of the holy places and pilgrimage exercised the concern of great numbers of Muslims throughout the world.
Many feared that Wahhabi opposition to folk practices and
especially to the veneration of the Prophet himself and Muslim saints would lead it to destroy such shrines as the
Prophet's tomb and force Shi'ite pilgrims to adopt Wahhabi
practices. In the early nineteenth century, Wahhabi ances-
tors had attacked the shrine of Imam Hussein, the Prophet's
martyred grandson, in Karbala in Iraq and destroyed a
cemetery of special Shi'ite significance outside of Mecca.[15]
Bad feelings persisted, and only gradually did the new Saudi
regime of King Abd al-Aziz (ca. 1880–1953) manage to reassure pilgrims throughout the world that it would not interfere
in their religious duty. Formerly dependent to a significant
extent on hajj revenues, the newly oil-rich Saudi regime
began to spend large amounts of money on preserving the
shrines and improving housing and sanitation conditions. In
the process, guardianship of the pilgrimage and of Mecca and
Medina became the heart of its formula for legitimacy.

Claiming in effect to be the protector of Islam, the Saudi
royal family thereby made itself vulnerable to constant
scrutiny and invited the scorn of other would-be protectors.
Muammar Qaddafi, the erratic leader of Libya, accused the

Saudis of defiling the holy places by allowing their American-made military aircraft to fly in the air space above Mecca and Medina, and called for their internationalization.[16] Since the revolution in 1979, the Iranians have seen the Saudis as their natural rival for leadership of the Muslim world, and historical antipathies have been revived. The Iranian assault has, as a consequence, been sustained and insistent. For example, Ayatollah Khomeini, in his last will and testament, mocked the efforts of the Saudis in distributing Qur'ans throughout the world and called Wahhabism an "aggressive sect" (al-madhhab al-mu'adi) that leads unsuspecting people to be controlled by the superpowers, whose aim is to destroy true Islam."[17]

The Iranians' desire to use the great cosmopolitan occasion of the pilgrimage to advance their notions of Islamic revolution naturally inspired agitation in Riyadh, and the stage was set for the often violent confrontations of the past decade. Small Iranian demonstrations occurred in the pilgrimage of 1980, but in 1981 and 1982 there were serious clashes between Iranian pilgrims and the Saudi security forces. In 1986, Iranian pilgrims who were thought to be importing arms were arrested and prevented from undertaking the hajj. The 1987 pilgrimage, however, was to prove the most violent, with 402 pilgrims killed and Saudi Arabia and Iran blaming each other. Iran convened an international conference to discuss the future of the holy places, but it accomplished little except to concentrate the anti-Saudi rhetoric that was already flowing from pro-Iranian circles in the Muslim world.[18] Although Iran formally boycotted the hajj from 1987 to 1990, there were explosions during the 1989 pilgrimage, and in 1990 the Saudi reputation for efficient management was not enhanced when over 1,400 pilgrims were crushed to death in a tunnel. Hizbullah, a radical Lebanese Shi'ite group, spoke of "a new massacre," and Iran referred darkly to a "criminal conspiracy" and called for the Saudis to be stripped of their custodianship of the holy places.[19]

Against this background Saddam Hussein levelled his attack on the Saudi regime for allowing Western, non-Muslim troops into the kingdom. Having faced a withering barrage of criticism for a considerable period of time, the Saudis were careful to secure a *fatwa* (religious ruling) from Shaikh Bin Baz, which sanctioned the presence of "diverse nationalities among the Muslims and others for the resistance of aggression and the defense of the country." The council of senior religious officials also specifically endorsed the King's decision and said that the *Shari'a* (Islamic law) required both that the Muslim ruler be prepared to defend Muslim land and that he "seek the help of whoever has the power that enables them to perform the task."[20] Another fatwa in January 1991 sanctioned the use of force against the Iraqis and declared the battle against Saddam a jihad. Non-Muslim soldiers had an important role to play in defeating "the enemy of God."[21]

But even Bin Baz's casuistic relegation of Western troops to the obscure category of "others" *(ghayhum)* could not disguise the fact that the vast majority of the half million troops on Saudi soil were not Muslim. Nor, apparently, did Saudi restrictions on the practice of Christian and Jewish religious services among the foreign troops defuse internal disquiet.[22] Some religious scholars appear to have felt that the presence of Western troops violated the moral integrity of the holy peninsula and that the foreigners harbored their own nefarious goals. For example, Safar al-Hawali, dean of Islamic studies at Umm al-Qura University in Mecca and a well-known popular preacher, has chastised his fellow Muslims for putting their trust in the United States rather than in God: "America has become your God." Citing sources as diverse as the traditions of the Prophet, the memoirs of Richard Nixon, and *Foreign Affairs,* he concluded that the Westerners had long been looking for a pretext to occupy the Muslim heartland.[23] Another scholar, Sulaiman al-Uwda, dean at the Muhammed Bin Saud University in Qasim, directed his fire closer to home. In a scarcely veiled reference to the royal family, he warned that nations decline when rulers maintain themselves in power through corruption and resist the Islamic duty of consultation with the ulama and others. Robert Fisk of the British newspaper, *The Independent,* reported on an unnamed religious official who pointedly asked him, "When are the Americans leaving?"[24] An *imam* (prayer leader) at a Riyadh mosque asked somewhat more obliquely but not impenetrably, "If a dog has come onto your land, would you invite a lion to get rid of it?"[25]

The apprehension, in fact, seemed to grow with time. According to reports, a number of ulama gave a detailed memorandum to the King on 18 May 1991 which outlined a comprehensive program of reform. It ostensibly called for the creation of a *majlis al-shura* or consultative assembly whose members would be chosen according to competence, and not according to rank or sex; "Islamization" of the judiciary, military, economy, and media; and abstention from all "non-Islamic pacts and treaties."[26] The last clearly referred to the concern that the continuing presence of Western troops on Saudi soil produced. The memorandum may have been intended to pressure King Fahd into abdicating in favor of the Crown Prince, Abdullah, who is generally more acceptable to the ulama.[27] But the most senior ulama issued a statement on 3 June which condemned the public manner in which the memorandum was presented, and pointedly reminded Saudis of the "bounty of security, stability, [and] unanimity" which the Saudi regime has presumably provided.[28] But in endorsing the Islamic principles of consultation and advice between ruler and ruled in certain circumstances, and, rather cagily, in not specifically rejecting the reforms demanded, the senior ulama failed to dispel the sense of disquiet in the kingdom which the Gulf crisis helped to create.

Saddam exploited this profound sense of unease, and when he spoke of the Saudis having sold out to the Americans, he struck a responsive chord. His natural Ba'thist predilection would have been to denounce them both in anti-imperialist terms, but to invoke now the resonant terms of "infidel" and "jihad" served the same purpose and, in the circumstances, may have been more effective. Certainly, a significant portion of the Muslim public across the world

10

was instinctively dubious of Saddam's Islamic qualifications; his brutal anti-Shi'ite policies at home were well known after all. And there is no reason to believe that the use of words like "jihad" automatically entails a social and political response; an Islamic vocabulary takes on specific meaning only in the context in which it is applied.[29] Yet the context in this case was that infidel troops on Arabian soil had exposed the Saudi monarchy to the delegitimizing charge that it was consorting with the infidels and, by extension, with their natural allies, the Zionists.

When Saddam asked why his troops should withdraw from Arab land when the Israelis remained unopposed in their occupation of Arab land, he found a sympathetic hearing. It was preeminently seen as a matter of justice and fair play, but the Muslim proprietary interest in Palestine was also at work. When he said that the Saudis, by allowing Western troops on their soil, were now effectively in league with the Israelis, he drew the two powerfully related symbols of Muslim politics together: the sanctity of both Arabia and Palestine was really at stake, and he, Saddam, was the new Saladin, the restorer of Islamic rule to the holy lands.[30]

The Muslim "Street" and the Fundamentalist Response

Despite the political symbolism, the leadership of the Islamic movement across the Muslim world faced a dilemma: on the one hand, sentiment from the rank and file of membership was clearly in favor of Saddam, yet, on the other hand, their very organizations were often financially dependent on the Gulf states, particularly Saudi Arabia and Kuwait.

Feelings from below were pronounced, partly for the reasons of political symbolism already cited. But other factors were also involved. First, the entire range of discontents that emanate from developing, inefficient, over-bureaucratized, and undemocratic societies crystallized in the illogical but no less real hope for some release. For example, Jordanians, including East Bank bedouin, had rioted as recently as April 1989, and despite the holding of parliamentary elections in November 1989, widespread discontent continued in the face of manifold and intransigent economic difficulties. Palestinians, the majority of inhabitants of Jordan, bore both the added grievance of opposition to Israeli occupation and a sense of disappointment that the *intifada,* the uprising in the occupied territories, had achieved so little in three years of near constant turmoil. Similarly in Algeria, as Hugh Roberts points out in his chapter, the perception that the socialist regime had wrought economic failure and moral bankruptcy stimulated civil unrest. Local elections in June 1990 ended in the rout of the ruling party, but, far from being appeased, popular dissatisfaction was encouraged. In such situations, Saddam's claim to be striking a blow for liberation had its distracting appeal.

Second, the popular pro-Saddam sentiment that was found in many, but not all, places was fueled by the distinct unpopularity of the Gulf monarchies. Ostentatiously wealthy and often arrogantly claiming that God had chosen them for special favor, the "Gulfis" have incurred the envy, and more often the enmity, of poorer Arabs and Muslims. Despite the vast amounts of petro-dollars that they have expended in the causes of Arab brotherhood and Muslim unity and the good works that have undeniably been accomplished as a result, the Gulf Arab regimes have become widely synonymous with corruption, insincerity, and licentious, un-Islamic conduct. Though at some remove, one observer typically commented, "We Muslims in China are twice as devout as the Saudi and Kuwaiti shaikhs who spend their money in the brothels of Southeast Asia and Bahrain."[31]

Related to this unflattering representation of the Gulf monarchies has been the mirror image of "riyalpolitik" that has developed (the riyal is the Saudi unit of currency). Rather than making gains as the result of the judicious usage of their financial resources, these states have lost influence among the Arab masses. This has occurred because of the perception that Gulf wealth, effectively subsidizing the American economy, is indirectly in turn supporting Israel. The Palestinian writer Sahar Khalifeh makes the point in her novel *Wild Thorns:*

> They were listening to the news on a transistor radio. The American Secretary of Defence had made a new statement about arms shipments to Israel. Phantom jets. More and more Phantoms. Billions of dollars flooding into Israel's treasury. The old men muttered grim prayers, praising God and invoking blessings on the people of the Prophet Muhammad. The young men cursed and blasphemed. . . . Arab oil revenue turned into Phantoms! So much for Arab unity![32]

Third, in addition to the hope of escape from pressing social and economic difficulties and the unpopularity of the Gulf monarchies, latent suspicions of Western intentions in the Muslim world played into Saddam's hand. Much has been written about the supposed antipathy of Islam and the West, and the received wisdom appeared to acquire a new vitality during the Gulf crisis. A. M. Rosenthal wrote in *The New York Times* that "somehow the passion of Muslims against the West is presented as inevitable, unstoppable, a terrifying phenomenon based on justified anger and the Koran."[33]

Such analyses, however, which build on the simplistic notion of an engrained "Muslim rage"[34] must be set against the complex history of interaction between Islam and the West. Civilizations rarely, if ever, act as monolithic entities with single-minded, doctrinally defined interests, or passions. As Islamic history demonstrates, political pluralism has been the norm within the Muslim world, and between it and the West there has been a pattern of alternating cooperation and competition, alliance and violent confrontation.[35] Moreover, Muslim identities have been influenced by a variety of social experiences—race, class, nation, ethnicity, and education, among them. Political circumstance can also be consequential, at least in the short run. As Amatzia Baram points out in his chapter, the Iraqi Shi'ites, while linking the

Zionist enemy with Western imperialism, obviously found themselves on the same side as the West during the Gulf crisis. The result was a notable absence of rhetorical assault on the West in general and the United States in particular.

Yet anti-Westernism is surely not absent from the Muslim world, and its presence contributed to Saddam's popularity. Indeed, recognition of the variableness of the relationship between Islam and the West should not obscure the fact that the common historical memory of Muslims—as gauged by their rhetoric—largely dates today, not from the distant Crusades as is often assumed, but from the beginning of this century. As Jean-François Legrain makes clear in his discussion of the Palestinian Muslims' response to the Gulf crisis, if they used the word "Crusade," they meant to signify neither whole-hearted support for Saddam, nor that any general struggle against the West was to take precedence over that for the liberation of Palestine. The memory that weighs heavily on the minds of the great generality of Muslims is of imperialist rule, Western antagonism toward Arab nationalism, the creation and fortifying of the state of Israel, and American hostility toward the Islamic revolution in Iran. The West has had its moments of a relatively benign image of course, such as the one enjoyed by the United States in the wake of its opposition to the tripartite aggression against Egypt in the Suez crisis of 1956. But these have proved to be short-lived.

Washington, as well as London and Paris, has tended to have precious little political capital of a sustained kind in the Muslim world, and it has become an often bewildering fact of life that regardless of the act, the hand of Western imperialism is seen to be behind it. In the Gulf crisis, many thought it villainous that the United States, long tolerant of Saddam, had now turned so decisively against him. Mumtaz Ahmad, in his chapter on Pakistan, quotes the influential intellectual and one of the leaders of Jamaat-i-Islami, Khurshid Ahmad: "The trap was to entangle Iraq in war so that it could provide the United States with a chance to interfere and advance its sinister design—to give an edge to Israel in the region and to control the Muslim oil." Similarly, al-Jama'a al-Islamiyya (The Islamic Group) in Morocco said the aim of the West was not to liberate Kuwait, but "to destroy the economic and military structures of Iraq which constitute an Arab force, with the goal of establishing a strong Israel and mastery over Arab oil wealth."[36] In his chapter on Egypt, Gehad Auda notes that the leader of the Jihad Organization believed that one of the American objectives was to recondition the Muslim mind to accept humiliation and the supremacy of the West. The Jordanian newspaper *al-Ra'i* spoke of the people of the United States, Britain, and France as the "real enemies" of the Arabs,[37] and a Moroccan policeman told a British reporter, "The West not only wants to destroy Iraq, but also to destabilize the whole Arab world in its interests and in those of Israel."[38]

All three factors help to explain why Saddam Hussein had a natural constituency on the Muslim streets. They also help to explain the pressure that percolated upward from "below," causing a dilemma for both governments and, ironically, their Islamic opposition. Regimes as diverse as those of Algeria, Morocco, Tunisia, Egypt, Jordan, Syria, Pakistan, Bangladesh, Indonesia, and even Britain and South Africa[39] faced demonstrations that expressed either direct popular support for Saddam Hussein or opposition to the level of destruction that the Western-led coalition was inflicting on the Iraqi people.

Despite the fact that it had contributed troops to the anti-Iraqi coalition, the Moroccan government was aware of the depth of public sentiment against the war. In February 1991, therefore, it allowed Moroccan Islamist groups, for only the third time in their history, to take part in a huge public march to express their views.[40] In Tunisia, the government began to collect blood to send to the Iraqis, and in Algeria the government newspaper, having earlier called for a mediated settlement of the conflict, became more militant: "The battle that has begun in the Gulf is not Iraq's, but that of all the

Arab and Muslim countries against the great Western powers—the United States, Britain, France, and the West's creature, Israel."[41] The then-Foreign Minister (and now Prime Minister), Sid Ahmad Ghozali, went so far as to say that Iraq and Saddam "incarnate . . . the spirit of resistance" to those who wish to humble the Arabs.[42]

The effect on the Islamic fundamentalist groups and movements was more telling. Many groups throughout the Muslim world have been supported by Saudi Arabia and Kuwait, either directly through their governments or indirectly through such agencies as the Saudi-backed World Muslim League (Rabitat al-'Alam al-Islami). The Jordanian Muslim Brotherhood is a case in point, as is the Algerian Front Islamique du Salut (FIS), both of which received Saudi financial backing. In his contribution to this volume, Jean-François Legrain points out that the Kuwaitis claimed to have given some $60 million in 1989 to HAMAS (Harakat al-Muqawama al-Islamiyya), the main Islamic group in the West Bank and Gaza Strip.

These groups would have been imprudent if they had endangered such financial links, and yet they would have been reckless if they had failed to respond to the pro-Saddam sentiments from the ranks of their membership. The result was an understandable hesitance. Hamas, for example, preferred not to dwell on the crisis and thus hoped not to divert attention from the central Palestinian problem or to alienate its Gulf supporters. Moreover, mindful that its chief rival, the Palestine Liberation Organization (PLO), had embraced Saddam, it wanted to be seen neither to be lagging in support for Iraq, nor simply to be parroting the PLO's position. Other groups like the Muslim Brotherhood in Egypt and Jordan, similarly partially dependent on Gulf patrons but with an eye also on political competitors at home, gradually asserted their opposition to the war against Iraq. As Gehad Auda and Mumtaz Ahmad point out in their chapters, some groups also felt the pressure of Muslim groups outside of their countries that had taken a more assertively anti-war position. In the particular case of Egypt, the Brotherhood hoped not to be outbid in its desire for leadership of the international Islamic movement by the Muslim Brotherhood in Sudan. In the process, although they may well have endangered medium range relations with the Saudis and Kuwaitis, they gained in the short-term by being responsive, as well as giving voice, to popular feelings at home and across the Muslim world.

It would, of course, be a mistake to accord too much significance to this sentiment from below, and Charles Krauthammer is doubtless correct to warn that opinion is rarely uniform and is inevitably controlled to some degree by the security apparatuses of the state. Yet he goes too far when he dismisses "the street" in the Arab or Muslim worlds as "an echo of the Palace."[43] The crisis in the Gulf has clearly demonstrated that Muslim opinions remain free, or at the least partially free, of government control, if not on the street, then certainly in the religious schools *(madrasas)* and the mosques. Mumtaz Ahmad points out that, even though the Pakistani government sent troops to the front, the elders of Pakistani madrasas had urged their students to regard the war as one against *kufr* (unbelief). Some 80,000 students were excused from classes and joined in the national day of protest against the war.

In the case of the mosque, many regimes try to prescribe an officially sanctioned sermon *(khutba)* in the Friday service, but even when they do, imams score political points by indirection and the well-timed invocation of metaphor. The Saudi imam, for example, would be foolhardy to launch a frontal assault on the corruption of the Saudi regime, but a subtle allusion to the probity of the Caliph Umar would not fail to impress on his audience the qualities of a Muslim ruler. Frequently, the sermon is much more direct and unnuanced:

> The great days of Islam, the nobility of the past are evoked; Koranic references support the arguments. The analysis is simplistic, the colours are black and white and the expression hyperbolic. The audience, largely rural and often illiterate, responds with passion.[44]

17

In effect, whether in Muslim demonstrations on the street, in lessons in the school, or in sermons in the mosque, "Islam" provides the arena in which political, and largely oppositional, sentiments can be expressed. In this way, the latent power of Islam was mobilized in the crisis to the advantage of Saddam Hussein—yet to the discomfort of many governments of the Muslim world, and often many Muslim fundamentalist groups themselves whose financial self-interest dictated the need for a lower profile.

Islamic Fundamentalism
Between Power and Revolution

This discernibly popular Islamic dimension to the Gulf conflict has intensified the perception in the West that, now that the Communist threat has collapsed and the Cold War has been won, the real challenge is an Islam which is at once illiberal and expansionist. Although writing before the Gulf war, Patrick J. Buchanan described Islam in threatening terms: "As the Salman Rushdie episode demonstrates, the followers of the Prophet, even in the West, have little use for the liberalism of J. S. Mill."[45] Somewhat more sympathetic to Islam, the British columnist R. W. Johnson speaks nonetheless of Islamic fundamentalism as a "creed that refuses the whole objective of 'modernization'."[46]

While the long run must remain an open question, the evidence to date, including that of the Gulf crisis of 1990–91, supports a rather less alarming conclusion. In mediating among three forces—the state, which they hope to capture; popular Muslim sentiment, which they do not always control; and Muslim patrons, on whom they are often dependent— Islamic fundamentalists must make compromises with each. Neither simply revolutionary nor merely accommodationist, these groups are preoccupied with reform within their societies and, in the process, continually adapt their thinking and strategies in ways which belie the simplicity of an "illiberal" or "angry" Islam.

One way in which they do this is the articulation of a social mission for Islam. Taking the traditional concept of *da'wa* ("call" to Islam) which formerly carried the connotation of missionary or proselytizing work among the unbelievers, Muslims have, in the present era, gradually transformed it, making its central purpose the return of nominal Muslims to the true Islamic path. In addition to the obvious emphasis on education, a social welfare network of impressive proportions has evolved as integral to this new sense of mission. Islamic hospitals and health clinics, housing cooperatives, and benevolent societies for widows and orphans operate in societies from Morocco to Indonesia, and as they do so they both attract followers to their cause and challenge the inefficient, competing institutions of the state.

The political implications of this kind of social mission are patent, and it is no surprise that President Mubarak of Egypt, to cite but one example, fears the delegitimizing impact of a rival Islamic social system.[47] He cannot simply repress the fundamentalists, for fear of radicalizing the relative moderates; nor, because of the strength of their integrity or because of limitations on his resources, can he coopt all of them. His "carrot and stick" policy must thus be calibrated to the circumstances, and the responses of the Muslim groups, ranging from confrontation to "normalization," must be equally deft.

Another instance of the ambiguity of Muslim political attitudes is the difficulty in creating consensus on foreign policy or national security issues. As Gehad Auda points out in this volume, President Mubarak, while conceding latitude to Muslim groups in the domestic debate, has insisted that politics stops at the water's edge. When it is remembered that Anwar Sadat's rule was undermined in great part because of the peace treaty that he signed with Israel, the prudence of Mubarak's policy is obvious. In the recent Gulf crisis, however, this induced cautionary approach to international matters came under severe strain as all the main Islamic groups, with varying degrees of enthusiasm, expressed opposition to

19

the deployment of Egyptian troops in the anti-Saddam coalition.

Yet, in spite of this, there was little agreement among the groups as to what the proper Islamic policy should be. Should jihad be directed only against the Western states in the coalition, as the Muslim Brotherhood came to argue, or against Saudi Arabia as well, as the Labor Party insisted? Does "unbelief" apply to Saddam as well as the Americans, and can it be extended to include those Muslims fighting on the side of the Americans? The crucial factor in the difference of approach was the relationship with the Saudis, but the common result was uncertainty as to what such important concepts as jihad and kufr meant in international politics. This vagueness on foreign policy matters and the Muslim groups' lack of success in opposing the Egyptian government's war policy have, in turn, stimulated a rethinking of the strategy to adopt in domestic politics.

In addition to these factors, the experience of participation in government has provided its own kind of equivocation. On the one hand, Muslim groups have sustained themselves by the often unmitigatingly harsh criticism of the regimes that they feel are un-Islamic. Employing the powerfully negative term for the pre-Islamic period of ignorance, fundamentalists characteristically accuse today's authorities, both religious and political, of perpetuating *jahiliyya*. Complacency would be immoral in the face of a regime "that does not apply God's rules,"[48] and there is no doubt that one's religious duty is to wage jihad against such forces of repression and injustice within the Islamic community.[49]

On the other hand, however, Muslim groups are, in several instances, becoming integrated into the political process. In Algeria, they have successfully contested local elections and intend to field a full slate of candidates in the national elections, which were promised for late June of 1991 but then postponed in the wake of serious riots early in June.[50] In Egypt, Muslim Brothers have participated in parliamentary elections and won seats, though under the banner of other legally recognized parties. In Jordan, members of the Brotherhood and others who formed the umbrella Islamic Movement won stunning successes in the parliamentary election of November 1989, the first general election in twenty-two years in Jordan and the first in which women were allowed to vote. Although King Hussein at first declined to admit Muslim Brothers to the government, five Brothers and two other Islamists were given Cabinet portfolios in January 1991 in the midst of the general agitation over the Gulf crisis. They remained in office until the government reshuffle of June 1991. In Pakistan, the governing coalition consists of three Islamic parties—Jamaat-i-Islami, Jamiyat Ulama-i-Islam, and Jamiyat Ulama-i-Pakistan.

As Milton-Edwards and Ahmad demonstrate in their chapters, Muslim groups have not been hesitant to use the political instruments at their disposal. Control of various ministerial portfolios, particularly those dealing with education and religious affairs, confers the advantage of direct influence over the young and over the religious authorities. This influence is important in stimulating mass support for their program. The activists have also found in Parliament a particularly useful instrument by which to magnify their voice and to intensify their pressure on the government. It was such pressure in Pakistan that led to the resignation of Yaqub Khan, the Foreign Minister, whose relatively pro-American sympathies had incurred the displeasure of a key partner in the Islamic ruling coalition.

If the Muslim street and the palace are now not so far removed from each other, the experience of proximity has proved as unsettling to the street as to the palace. Regimes such as those of Algeria, Pakistan, and Jordan may have felt impelled to distance themselves, in diverse ways, from criticism of Iraq. And in several countries, Daniel Brumberg points out in his concluding chapter, governments may have even gained the temporary advantage by initiating some form of liberalization of the political system, thereby putting the Islamic opposition on the defensive. But, at the same time, the Muslim participants in power have themselves felt impelled to act responsibly. For these Islamists, wishing still to reform the system and instill values in society that are consonant with the scriptural ordinances of Islam, participation in daily political life has demonstrated the efficacy of give-and-take, the value of compromise and consensus.

This is most obviously seen in the case of revolutionary Iran. As Said Arjomand indicates in his chapter, there has been, generally since 1985 and certainly since the death of Ayatollah Khomeini in June 1989, a transformation in revolutionary commitment among the elite. Although pragmatism in one sphere, such as foreign policy, has not been automatically replicated in another sphere, such as economic policy, the formalization of the revolution over the past decade has produced a relatively greater preoccupation with domestic matters and the desire to normalize Iran's diplomatic relations, and lesser concern with exporting the revolution and confronting the satanic West.

In the Gulf crisis, Iran might have been expected to fulfill its self-proclaimed Islamic mission either by confronting the West or by actively supporting the Shi'ites in southern Iraq. In fact, it did neither. President Hashemi Rafsanjani and his allies were able to outmaneuver the radicals by leading the public outrage at Israeli actions in the occupied territories—particularly the Temple Mount killings in October 1990. And, nearly simultaneously, they were able to reassure Syria and the Gulf states that Iran would not endanger its new international relationships by decisive support for Islamic revolution in Iraq. Preemption of radicals at home and reassurance of potential allies abroad were the marks of a confident, institutionalized revolution and of an "Islam" comfortable with power.

The case of the Iraqi Shi'ites is, on one level, obviously different from that of the Iranians. The Iraqis have not only been suppressed under Saddam's regime, but, when they revolted in the wake of the war in March 1991, they failed to receive any concrete outside help that would have given them the chance of seizing power. Yet, although they have thus not wielded power themselves, Iraqi Shi'ites have had, by the very fact of their weakness, to learn to deal with disparate groups, including the Communist Party, whose ideological goals differ from their own. It is entirely possible that the concessions that they have made are merely tactical, an allowance to adverse circumstance. But, as Baram suggests, the Islamic Da'wa Party's and Amal's specific endorsement of parliamentary democracy for post-Ba'thist Iraq is a notable evolution in their rhetoric. It may also represent an ideological shift of some importance, as well as signal a serious disagreement with the Supreme Assembly for the Islamic Revolution in Iraq, a group dominated by ulama committed to the establishment of an Islamic state.

As this suggests, the Islamic dimensions of the Gulf crisis were often manipulated by various groups and governments for their own political advantage, and these Islamic concerns may have even been of secondary importance in the competition for power. Roberts points out, for example, that the FIS hoped to capture the high ground of Algerian politics and thereby improve its standing relative to other political groups, particularly the ruling Front de Liberation National. The riots of June 1991, which gave the group its first "martyrs," dramatically enhanced its standing relative to other groups and parties competing for influence in Algeria. In the West Bank and Gaza, as Legrain demonstrates, Hamas hoped to circumscribe the influence of the PLO. Moreover, in Pakistan, the various Islamic parties were as outraged by the American decision to cut off all aid to Pakistan and by what was seen as an American-Soviet sell-out of the Afghan *mujahidin,* as they were by Western military action in the Gulf. Yet this kind of political thinking is, in its own way, a sign of political flexibility. Rather than being unbending dogmatists, as is often assumed, many Islamic fundamentalists are at ease with the complex political calculus of means and ends, constraints and values which we in the West assume to be the normal stuff of politics.

Future Muslim generations will not remember Saddam Hussein as one of the great heroes of Islamic history, and the Gulf crisis of 1990–91 will not rank as the beginning of a new Crusade pitting East against West. But this crisis will have highlighted the important mobilizing role that Islamic symbolism and sentiment play in the politics of Muslims. It will also have shown the degree to which rulers and opponents must weigh principle with self-interest, ideology with political advantage.

Endnotes to Chapter 1

I am grateful to my colleague, Moorhead Wright,
for his comments on a draft of this chapter.

1. A tape recording of this meeting was smuggled into Britain and revealed by *The Guardian,* 11 June 1991. The Qur'anic reference is to "Sura Fil," or the "Chapter of the Elephant," cv: 1–5. The chapter goes on to say that God sent flocks of birds which threw stones against the elephants. The authenticity of the tape recording from Baghdad has not been verified.

2. For a chilling description of Saddam's regime, see the pseudonomously published: Samir al-Khalil, *The Republic of Fear: Saddam's Iraq* (London: Hutchinson Radius, 1990).

3. For example, see *al-Masira (The Journey),* the journal of the Islamic League of Iraqi Students, no. 9 (Jumadi Thani 1402 A. H./April 1982), which commemorates the second anniversary of the execution of the "martyr" al-Baqir and has his picture on the cover.

4. For the relative uses of Arabism and Islam in Saddam's foreign policy, see Adeed Dawisha, "Invoking the Spirit of Arabism: Islam in the Foreign Policy of Saddam's Iraq," in Adeed Dawisha, ed., *Islam in Foreign Policy* (Cambridge: Cambridge University Press, 1983), pp. 112–28.

5. For example, in a speech commemorating the birthday of Imam Ali, as reported by Islamic Republic News Agency, 4 April 1985, in *Foreign Broadcast Information Service* [hereafter, *FBIS*], SAS-85-065, 4 April 1985, p. 11.

6. From a *fatwa,* or religious-legal ruling, issued on 1 January 1956. The text of this fatwa was reprinted in *al-Mujtama'* (*The Community*) 28 July 1986, pp. 17–18, on the occasion of Shimon Peres's visit to King Hasan of Morocco.

7. The text of this fatwa is reproduced in Ibid., p. 19.

8. For excerpts from this speech, see *The New York Times,* 13 August 1991. Saddam also linked the withdrawal of his forces to the withdrawal of Syrian forces from Lebanon.

9. Abd al-Aziz Bin Baz, *Majmu' Fatawa wa Maqalat Mutanawwi'a [Collection*

of Fatwas and Miscellaneous Articles] (Riyadh: al-Idara al-'Amma li'l-Tab' wa'l-Tarjama, 1408 A.H./1987), p. 271. The fatwa is not dated.

10. A central concept of Islamic political and social theory, *jihad* carries several meanings. Associated in medieval jurisprudential writing with the confrontation with polytheists, errant believers, and infidels, it was also seen to involve defense of the Islamic realm. Jihad became particularly identified in the nineteenth and twentieth centuries with anti-imperialist struggle, and thereby acquired much of its negative image in the West. This, in turn, has produced a certain defensiveness among modern Muslim thinkers, who prefer to use the generic term of "struggle" derived from the Arabic verb, *jahada,* to exert, to struggle. In this interpretation, the "greater jihad" is the general struggle against evil and for good, whereas the "lesser jihad" is armed struggle. Most Muslim writers today believe that the only legitimate use of violence is in self-defense, and, in the particular case of the Arab-Israeli conflict, since Israel is defined as the aggressor, the liberation of Palestine becomes automatically a defensive act. Despite this, it must be noted that, among radical fundamentalists, an internalization of jihad has occurred, whereby the primary target is the unjust, un-Islamic ruler.

11. Saddam's statement read on Iraqi television, 10 August 1990, as reported in *The New York Times,* 12 August 1990.

12. As reported by Associated Press, in *The Boston Globe,* 8 August 1990.

13. *The Independent,* 25 February 1991.

14. Dru C. Gladney, "Of Hearts and Minds: China's Muslims Respond to Saddam Hussein" (unpublished paper, 1991). I am grateful to the author for sharing this paper with me.

15. For an overview of Saudi-Iranian conflict over the pilgrimage, see Martin Kramer, "Tragedy in Mecca," *Orbis* (Spring 1988): 231–47.

16. *The Jordan Times,* 23 May 1982; also see BBC, *Summary of World Broadcasts* [hereafter, *SWB*], ME/7035/i, 24 May 1982. According to one Libyan publication, the Saudis know that "the Hijaz [the province where Mecca and Medina are located] is not a Saudi possession by right": *al-Zahaf al-Akhdar (The Green March), 15 October 1982,* p. 5.

17. *Nass al-Wasiyya . . . li'l-lmam al-Qa'id, Ruhollah al-Musawi al-Khomeini [Text of the Last Testament of The Commander Imam, Ruhollah al-Musawi al-Khomeini]* (Washington, D.C.: Interests Section of the Islamic Republic of Iran, Embassy of the Democratic and Popular Republic of Algeria, n.d.), p. 12. The testament, though amended several times, is dated 26 Bahman 1361/1 Jumadi al-Awwal 1403 A.H. (15 February 1983).

18. For example, Shaikh Muhammad Fadlallah, the spiritual head of Hizbullah in Lebanon, spoke of "oppressive countries . . . ruling over God's mosques" with the help of "mercenaries": Tehran domestic service, 25 November 1987, as reported in *FBIS*, NES-87-228, 27 November 1987, p. 53.

19. See *The Independent,* 5 July 1990. When Iran and Saudi Arabia reestablished diplomatic relations in April 1991, they began discussions on the return of Iranian pilgrims to the *hajj.* There were reports that they could not agree on the rules whereby the Iranians will be allowed to engage in sloganeering during the event. See Ibid., 8 May 1991. But the hajj passed peacefully and the Iranians were allowed to make a small, isolated demonstration against the "pagans." See Ibid., 20 June 1991.

20. "Kalimat al-Shaikh Abd al-Aziz Bin Abdullah Bin Baz . . . 'An Mawqif al-Shari'a al-Islamiyya min al-Ghazu al-'Iraqi li'l-Kuwait" ("Statement of Shaikh Bin Baz on the Sharia's Position on Iraq's Invasion of Kuwait") (mimeographed, n.p., n.d.), especially p. 6; "A Statement Issued by the Council of Senior Ulama of the Kingdom of Saudi Arabia" [in English] (mimeographed, n.p., n.d.), especially p. 1. Both were issued in August 1990.

21. *Al-Muslimun*, 18 January 1991. The fatwa was signed by Shaikh Bin Baz.

22. For reports on Saudi religious restrictions on non-Muslim soldiers, see *The Times,* 12 November 1990; *The Independent,* 13 November 1990; *The International Herald Tribune,* 23 November 1990; *The Guardian,* 27 December 1990. *The Independent,* 23 February 1991, reported that the Jewish festival of Purim would be celebrated among American Jewish soldiers—the first time that this would take place on Arabian soil for over 800 years. The New York-based Lubavitch Hasidic organization had apparently sent Purim packages to the 2,000 Jewish troops.

23. See Mamoun Fandy, "The Hawali Tapes," *The New York Times,* 24 November 1990.

24. *The Independent,* 29 November 1990. The sense of disquiet may have been encouraged by an attempt by 70 Saudi women—against Saudi tradition—to drive their cars in Riyadh in November 1990. See *The New York Times,* 7 and 8 November 1990.

25. Interview with a Saudi student, April 1991.

26. *The Independent,* 25 May 1991.

27. See *The Observer,* 2 June 1991.

28. The statement was signed by eighteen ulama, including Shaikh Bin Baz. Some reports had earlier suggested that he had signed the memorandum of 18 May. See *SWB,* ME/1090/A6–7, 5 June 1991, for the text of the 3 June statement.

29. For an attempt to distinguish between the language of politics (i.e., words motivate action) and the politics of language (i.e., words take on meaning in specific contexts and may motivate action), see my "The Rushdie Affair: The Politics of Ambiguity," *International Affairs* 66 (4) (Fall 1990): 769–79.

30. Salah al-Din al-Ayyubi (known in the West as Saladin) was a Kurdish general who took power in Egypt and Syria after overthrowing the Fatimid caliphate in Cairo in 1169. In 1187, he recaptured Jerusalem from the Franks, but this in turn precipitated the Third Crusade.

31. Gladney, "Of Hearts and Minds," p. 13.

32. Sahar Khalifeh, *Wild Thorns,* trans. Trevor LeGassick and Elizabeth Fernea (London: Al Saqi Books, 1985), p. 179.

33. A. M. Rosenthal, "Neither God Nor Infidel," *The New York Times,* 15 February 1991.

34. A notable exponent of this point of view is Bernard Lewis: see, for example, his "The Roots of Muslim Rage," *The Atlantic Monthly,* September 1990, pp. 47–54, 56, 59, 60.

35. For an overview of this pattern, see my *Islam in a World of Nation-States* (Cambridge: Cambridge University Press, 1986), chap. 3.

36. Cited in *al-Ittihad al-Ishtiraki (The Socialist Union),* 13 January 1991. As reported in Mohamed Tozy, "Le Mouvement Islamiste Marocain au Miroir

de la Guerre du Golfe" (unpublished paper, 1991), p. 5. I am grateful to the author for sharing this paper with me.

37. *Al-Ra'i (The Opinion)*, 25 February 1991.

38. *The Independent*, 26 February 1991.

39. For a report that South African Muslims called on President de Klerk to allow 10,000 Muslim volunteers to go to Iraq, see *The Times*, 23 January 1991. For an analysis of the importance of the small student demonstrations outside the American embassy in Jakarta and the anti-American sermons in Indonesian mosques, see *The Independent*, 16 March 1991.

40. Tozy, "Le Mouvement Islamiste Marocain," p. 5. There were between 300,000 and 700,000 participants, and of these it is believed that 40 to 70 percent belonged to the two groups, Al-Jama'a al-Islamiyya (The Islamic Group) and al-'Adl wa'l-Ihsan (Justice and Beneficence).

41. *The New York Times*, 26 January 1991, International edition. See Ibid., 13 January 1991, for a report that Syria's participation in the anti-Saddam coalition was not popular at home.

42. *Le Figaro*, 4 March 1991.

43. Charles Krauthammer, "On Getting it Wrong," *Time*, 15 April 1991, p. 70.

44. Akbar Ahmed, "Mosque Bros," *New Statesman & Society*, 24 May 1991, p. 19. For a sophisticated analysis of the institution of the mosque sermon, as practiced in Jordan, see Richard T. Antoun, *Muslim Preacher in the Modern World: A Jordanian Case Study in Comparative Perspective* (Princeton: Princeton University Press, 1989).

45. Patrick J. Buchanan, "Rising Islam May Overwhelm the West," *New Hampshire Sunday News*, 20 August 1989.

46. R. W. Johnson, "The Alarming Logic of Islam's New World Role," *The Independent on Sunday*, 10 March 1991.

47. See, for example, Yahya Sadowski, "Egypt's Islamist Movement: A New Political and Economic Force," *Middle East Insight* 5(4)(November/December 1987): 37–45.

48. See, for example, the interview with Dr. Umar Abd al-Rahman, the leader of al-Jama'at al-Islamiyya in Egypt: *al-Ahrar (The Liberals)*, 16 January 1989.

49. For a useful explanation of how the concept of jihad has been internalized in the modern period so that un-Islamic "Muslims" have become the main targets, see Emmanuel Sivan, *Radical Islam: Medieval Theology and Modern Politics* (New Haven: Yale University Press, 1985), chap. 5.

50. For reports on the Algerian unrest, see *The New York Times*, 5 June 1991; *The Times*, 6 June 1991; *The Economist*, 8 June 1991; and *The Independent on Sunday*, 9 June 1991.

2

FROM RADICALISM TO RADICAL PRAGMATISM: THE SHI'ITE FUNDAMENTALIST OPPOSITION MOVEMENTS OF IRAQ

Amatzia Baram

The Iraqi invasion of Kuwait, and the eruption of the armed revolt against Saddam Hussein in southern Iraq in the wake of the Iraqi defeat in the Gulf war, cast a bright light on the Shi'ite fundamentalist opposition to the Ba'thist regime of Iraq. Emerging from an obscurity that was partly self-imposed and partly the result of political weakness, several major, and often competing, movements shared a common delight in Saddam Hussein's difficulties. After all, he had vigorously persecuted them, and the Ba'thist ideology which he professed was the polar opposite of the Islamic, largely Shi'ite influenced, political program that they envisaged for Iraq.

At the same time, however, these Iraqi Shi'ite fundamentalists could not be seen to be inviting the destruction of Iraq, or allying themselves openly with the Western forces that they had long denounced as anti-Islamic and imperialistic. They thus found themselves in a kind of perilous high-wire act: a trade embargo and limited war against Iraq were begrudgingly acceptable, but the national integrity of Iraq must be upheld and outright confrontation with the embattled regime would be imprudent as long as it could still inflict heavy penalties on the Shi'ite population. In the search for a working consensus among the opposition, subtle and important shifts in rhetoric began to appear. The new rhetoric included, for example, a discussion of the role of democracy in a liberated state.

At the conclusion of the devastating air campaign and brief land war, the Shi'ite uprising broke out in the south of Iraq. The allies, including the Gulf states, wanted Saddam's demise, but not at any cost. They were not keen to open the Pandora's box of civil war, nor, more importantly, to stoke the fires of an Iranian-style fundamentalist state on the northern border of Saudi Arabia. The uprising failed after several weeks of fierce fighting, but the infrastructure of the Shi'ite movements outside of Iraq and, possibly inside as well, still exists. In fact, these movements remain the strongest component within the opposition to Saddam Hussein among the Arabic-speaking population of Iraq. (The Kurds, some 18 percent of the population, speak a different language, see themselves as a different nationality, and have their own separate political movements.) The majority of the Shi'ites are not religious fundamentalists. However, under a more democratic regime, many of them may give their support to the fundamentalist movement as a result of communal and political, rather than religious, identification. In a country where the majority (some 55 percent) are Shi'ite Arabs, but which has been ruled since it became a nation-state in 1920 by a Sunni Arab minority (some 23 percent), this kind of protest vote could eventually tip the scale in favor of the fundamentalists.

The Islamic Opposition to Saddam Hussein

The most important fundamentalist opposition movements of Iraq were born in the late 1950s and early 1960s, as a response to a general decline of religious life in Iraq. Two phenomena which accompanied this decline were the sharp decrease in the number of students of religion in the two biggest centers of religious studies—the holy cities of Najaf and Karbala—and the ascendancy of the Communist Party in many parts of Iraq, including the holy cities.

While the exact sizes of the various movements are difficult to gauge, their aims are clear. In essence, they all believe that Iraq should become an Islamic Republic, similar (though not necessarily identical) to Iran. This preeminently means the imposition of the *Shari'a* (Islamic law) in all walks of life. In addition, while they all preach ecumenism between Shi'ite and Sunni Muslims, there is considerable anti-Sunni sentiment in their publications, and they make it clear that they will not tolerate the continuation of traditional Sunni supremacy in Iraq. In fact, under the guise of a demand that the Islamic movements assume the leadership role in a liberated Iraq, it is often implied that as soon as they come to power they intend to turn the tables on their Sunni counterparts (all the important Islamic movements in Iraq are Shi'ite).[1] Finally, even though they accept Western science and technology, all the Shi'ite fundamentalist movements are committed to combatting Western (or "imperialist" and sometimes "Christian" or "Crusader") cultural, economic, and other influences in the region.

The Islamic Da'wa Party

The first movement to be born was The Islamic Da'wa ("Call") Party (Hizb al-Da'wa al-Islamiyya), established in October 1957 in Najaf by the now well-known Shi'ite religious authority, Ayatollah Muhammad Baqir al-Sadr (born in 1933, and executed by the Ba'thist authorities in April 1980). To date, this is one of the two most important political organizations among the fundamentalist Shi'ite opposition groups. Originally, it was led by a group of young religious scholars (*ulama*) under al-Sadr's guidance and with the financial help of the then-chief *mujtahid*,[2] Grand Ayatollah Muhsin al-Hakim. Its main activity, however, was directed toward lay intellectuals—chiefly university students and graduates and city professionals. After the death of al-Sadr and its severe repression by the Ba'th regime in the wake of the Islamic revolution in Tehran, the party lost most of its religious leaders (some were executed, others dissociated themselves from the party). Today, lay intellectuals constitute the majority of the two supreme bodies of the party—the highest body (seven to twelve people), and a subordinate one, which elects the highest body (a group of some one hundred representatives sent by the various regional branches).

Below these bodies are the regional branches that operate according to local circumstances. Inside Iraq, this work is highly clandestine due to severe repression (mere membership in the party brings with it the death penalty). When underground the movement is organized in "cells" (halaqat), underneath which there are the basic units, "families" (usar). This mold is indistinguishable from the classical Communist and Ba'thist clandestine organization. Contact between two "families" is maintained strictly through cells, and, similarly, contact between two cells is through higher bodies. In this way, the chance of exposure of all the "families" or "cells" is minimized. Outside of Iraq, the party has branches in Iran, Syria, Lebanon, Afghanistan, and Britain. Party work in all these places is not hindered (though in the first two places it is certainly monitored) by the authorities, and thus activity is relatively free. The branches in Iran and Syria, where there is no danger of assassination by Ba'thist agents from Baghdad, hold open general meetings and conduct open political, educational, and social activities.[3]

The party's spokesman is Hojjatulislam Muhammad Mahdi al-Asifi, who is also, apparently, a member of the highest body of leadership. The party's senior representatives in London are Dr. Muwaffaq al-Rubayi, a physician who works in a London hospital, and Hojjatulislam Hussein al-Sadr. Da'wa sources are reluctant to disclose the names of the members of the leading bodies, but the party press reveals some of them. In most part, however, even though their photographs are shown, they appear under noms-de-guerre. The Da'wa's most senior man in Damascus is Professor "Abu Bilal." Conspicuous among Da'wa activists in Iran are Professor Abu Mujahid al-Rikabi, Dr. "Abu Yasir," Dr. "Abu Nabugh," Dr. Abu Ahmad al-Jafari, "Abu Fatima," and al-Sayyid Hasan Shubbar. Except for al-Asifi and Hussein Sadr these are all lay intellectuals who have risen to prominent positions in the party since the late 1960s. In addition to al-Asifi and Hussein al-Sadr, among the party leadership there are a few other members of the ulama (Muhammad Baqir al-Nasiri and Ayatollah Kazim al-Husseini al-Hairi, among others, in Iran). However the ulama have no privileged position in the party.

In Europe, the movement's main activities are political and cultural, and they are aimed at the party's traditional constituency—university students and professionals. The situation is different in Iran, where the vast majority of the movement's members are Iraqi expatriates from the lower social strata. There the party has a plethora of cultural and social organizations that not only indoctrinate Iraqi refugees but also supply them with the practical necessities of life. These organizations include the Association of the Islamic Women of Iraq, the Islamic Union of Iraqi Workers, the Islamic Medical Association of Iraq, the Islamic Union of Iraqi Engineers, and traditional Shi'ite social institutions adjacent to mosques. These groups provide "supporters" (*al-ansar*) who are meant to serve as a protective shield around the hard-core cadre. Naturally, the mosques also serve as centers for events on religious occasions such as communal prayers, Qur'an study circles, religious processions, funerals, and remembrance days throughout the year. Cultural and social events are often connected with mosques that either were originally built by Iraqi exiles or became centers for Iraqi expatriate activity through a gradual takeover.

The Da'wa puts heavy stress on the process of recruitment of new members, in particular intellectuals, and on the grooming of a powerful cadre. Members are expected to dedicate all their free time to the party, even at the expense of their family life. At least from the account of a leading member, party life is democratic and people are elected to the higher bodies in branch meetings according to their piety, social influence or charisma, and religious learning, with no particular priority assigned to any of these components. The Da'wa is known to be a very tightly knit organization with a heavy stress on secrecy, even in the West where the party suffers no persecutions whatsoever. The full identity of the majority of its leading members is a well-kept secret as is the number of members. In Britain, membership probably reaches two to three hundred. As reflected in the party press in Iran, the party there has a few hundred members, and possibly two or three thousand supporters (as different from full members). The party has a number of underground cells inside of Iraq which engage occasionally in sabotage activities, but the number of activists there is impossible to gauge. It also has an unknown number of fighters organized as a regular unit within the Iranian army. Named after al-Sadr, it is stationed on the Iraqi-Iranian border.

In the early and mid-1980s party members were involved in international terrorism, but this stopped in the late 1980s. To date, the Da'wa is relatively independent of Iranian and Syrian domination, and it has occasionally even been critical of Iran. For example, it protested when the Iranians refused to negotiate with the Iraqis the return of the Iraqi exiles as a part of the postwar peace talks. Its finances apparently do not depend heavily on foreign aid: the party budget, as reported by a senior party member, comes from membership fees as well as cultural activities.

An organization that is very closely affiliated with the Da'wa is Jama'at al-Ulama al-Mujahidin (The Group of Combatant Ulama). It consists entirely of religious scholars and has no organized grassroots, but some of its members are among the Da'wa leadership and they regularly participate in political and cultural events organized by the Da'wa Party.

33

One of their functions seems to be to bestow religious legitimacy upon the latter.

The Supreme Assembly for the Islamic Revolution in Iraq (SAIRI)

This body (al-Majlis al-A'la li'l-Thawra al-Islamiyya fi'l-'Iraq) came into being in November 1982 in Tehran. At first, it served as an umbrella organization for all the various Shi'ite religious fundamentalist parties and groups that fought against the Ba'thist regime of Iraq. Eventually, however, even though it still retained a symbolic function as an umbrella organization, it began to act as a separate organization in its own right. Rather than merely coordinating the work of its member organizations and helping them with logistical matters, SAIRI conducts independent activities, separate from those of the other movements yet on parallel lines. Since its inception, SAIRI has been headed by Hojjatulislam (now Ayatollah) Muhammad Baqir al-Hakim, son of the late Grand Ayatollah Muhsin al-Hakim, one of the most distinguished religious leaders in Najaf. The second most important figure has been Hojjatulislam (now Ayatollah) Mahmud al-Hashimi. Another important figure is Hojjatulislam Sadr al-Din al-Qabanji, SAIRI's chief ideologue. Like their colleagues, the leaders of the Da'wa Party, SAIRI leadership has been based on students of religion who studied under Muhammad Baqir al-Sadr in Najaf in the 1950s and 1960s.

SAIRI's leader is regarded as the Iranian choice as the next head of the Iraqi state. According to interviews, SAIRI is heavily dependent on financial and other Iranian government support. It may also be assumed that since Muhammad Baqir al-Hakim and his brother, Abd al-Aziz, are prominent in the organization, some of the Hakim family's funds are being channelled to SAIRI activities.

These activities move along two trajectories: one military, the other, cultural and social. On the military level, since the mid-1980s SAIRI has been endeavoring to recruit Iraqi exiles and Iraqi prisoners of war to its regular army unit, a corps (*faylaq*) called either "Badr" (after an important victory of the Prophet) or simply "Number Nine." At the end of the Iran-Iraq war, the number of soldiers in that army group reached three to four thousand; the same number of soldiers is still in uniform today. SAIRI spokesmen also claim that they have many revolutionaries inside Iraq, and, according to their sources, they have inflicted heavy casualties and damage on the Ba'thist regime through heroic acts of sabotage. SAIRI sources had claimed that they could easily mobilize 50,000, even 100,000, fighters outside and inside of Iraq when the time came to strike at Saddam and his henchmen. These claims, however, were not substantiated by the evidence that emerged at the end of the Gulf war. The kind of activity which SAIRI seemed to perform effectively was military training of its regular force under Iranian supervision. However, according to a Da'wa, and therefore not unbiased, source, SAIRI failed in its pledge to Iran to mobilize a meaningful fighting force from the Iraqi exiles in Iran and, in response, the Iranian authorities reduced their subsidy for the organization. Yet SAIRI has clearly been adept at political, cultural, and social work similar to that of the Da'wa, only separately and on a larger scale. As reflected in SAIRI's press that comes out in Tehran, the organization has a few thousand civilian followers in various parts of Iran.

The major difference between the two organizations concerns secrecy. Unlike the Da'wa, SAIRI makes no secret of its leadership. The civilian leaders, almost all of them members of the ulama, use their full names and titles and the whole structure seems to be essentially open. Indeed, this issue of the Islamic legitimacy of a closely knit party organization is a bone of contention between the two movements. According to SAIRI ideologues, a party organization along the lines of Western parties is contrary to the spirit of Islam. Another bone of contention is the issue of the "rule of the jurist" (*wilayat al-faqih*), the doctrine elaborated by the late Ayatollah Khomeini which accords the religious officials learned in

Islamic law the right to govern. Whereas SAIRI, which is led almost exclusively by religious authorities, adheres fanatically to this principle and believes that it should be applied to Iraq once it is liberated from the Ba'thist yoke, the Da'wa, which is led by a majority of laymen who resent Ayatollah al-Hakim's aspirations for leadership, is opposed to this principle, even though it expresses it in a somewhat muffled manner.

The Organization of Islamic Action (Amal)

While the other fundamentalist Shi'ite organizations emerged in Najaf or were based on Najaf-educated cadres, the Organization of Islamic Action (Munazzamat al-Amal al-Islami) emerged in Karbala. The period of its emergence is a matter of controversy. Other groups claim that it was born in the period following Khomeini's ascendancy in Tehran (1979–80), but Amal claims that, in fact, it started political operations in the early 1960s and specifically military ones in 1976. Whatever the case, it is widely believed that its membership is more limited than that of the Da'wa, even though its internal structure is based on the same principle of a closely knit, clandestine party.

Amal was established and is still led by two Karbala-based, blood-related families. One is centered on Ayatollah Hasan al-Shirazi, who fled from Iraq in 1969 and moved to Beirut, where he established a number of Islamic institutions and was assassinated by Iraqi Ba'thist agents in May 1980; and his older brother, Ayatollah Muhammad al-Husseini al-Shirazi, who was formerly more active but who lives at present in Tehran and whose connection to the movement appears increasingly tenuous. The other family is centered on the Shirazis' younger, "turbaned" cousins, Muhammad Taqi and Hadi al-Mudarrisi. Unlike the Da'wa, which keeps a fairly clear separating line between its various branches (e.g., the Iraqi branch consists almost entirely of Iraqis), Amal is multi-national and includes Iranians, Bahrainis, Afghans,

North African Arabs, and Africans from Nigeria, Zaire, and elsewhere. While the Da'wa is still based largely on Iraqis who joined the movement during the 1960s and 1970s, Amal draws the majority of its membership from people who poured into Khomeini's Iran soon after the Shah's downfall. It is based in Tehran, Damascus, and London, with some underground cells inside Iraq. Like the Da'wa, Amal, too, formerly engaged in international terrorism. This activity declined in the late 1980s.

Another organization of some importance is al-Mujahidun, established in 1980 by Abd al-Aziz al-Hakim, Muhammad Baqir's younger brother. This movement acts in full coordination with SAIRI and seems, in fact, to be an extension of it. Members of al-Mujahidun take pride in defining themselves as "suicide squads," and, like SAIRI's military unit, these squads derive almost all of their membership from the Iraqi expatriates and prisoners of war in Iran. According to their own sources, they concentrate on young people, between the ages of ten and twenty-five, because they are as yet "pure souls" and easier to be molded.

In addition to these, there are other, lesser organizations of which very little is known: al-Afwaj al-Islamiyya (The Islamic Battalions), Harakat Tahrir al-Mustad'afin (The Movement of the Liberation of the Oppressed), and Jund al-Imam (The Imam's Soldiers) among others.

Reaction to the Invasion of Kuwait

When Iraq's troops invaded Kuwait, the reaction of the three most important opposition groups, the Da'wa, Amal, and SAIRI, was practically identical. All three movements rigorously denounced the invasion as a crime contradicting the Islamic Shari'a and Islamic principles. Despite their deep resentment of Kuwait's support for Iraq during the Iran-Iraq war, and despite their rejection of the Kuwaiti regime, the spokesmen of the movements made it very clear that any unification of the two countries ought to have been achieved through mutual consent. The Kuwaitis, they argued, are brothers and are an Islamic "people" *(sha'b)* like any other.[4] The movements' press gave full publicity to the atrocities of the Iraqi army and security forces in Kuwait and they called upon the Iraqi people to topple their criminal Ba'thist rulers.

As for the presence of Western troops on Saudi territory, their position became strikingly ambivalent. On the one hand, they called upon the international community to punish Saddam and his regime, and, in so doing, they condoned, albeit implicitly, the presence of foreign troops in the Gulf region which had precisely this idea in mind. Similarly, on occasion the movements' spokesmen blamed Saddam for the presence of the Christian armies in the area and made it clear that they would demand and work toward the evacuation of all foreign forces only after Kuwait was liberated.[5] On one occasion SAIRI's head, Muhammad Baqir al-Hakim, flatly turned down an appeal from one Sunni Muslim, pro-Saddam delegation in Tehran to join forces in fighting the Western troops in the Gulf. Al-Hakim even went so far as to point out that the Muslims of the world must fight Saddam and "refrain from any mistake" as to the side they chose to support. Any such mistake, he pointed out, would endanger "the very existence of the Islamic nation."[6]

Playing to a radical anti-American audience, however, these groups could not resist the temptation of attacking the West as well. They often denounced the presence of Christian armies. They never had any doubt that the Americans used Saddam's invasion as a pretext to occupy the oil-rich area of the Gulf for their own ends. And occasionally, they even demanded the immediate evacuation of these troops, leaving the whole Kuwaiti and Iraqi affair to the Islamic nations to solve. This was, for example, the case with a joint communiqué published by the three Shi'ite fundamentalist movements and several other political groups (Kurdish parties, the Communist Party, ex-Ba'thists, and others). In this communiqué, the opposition movements called for "applying pressure on the [Ba'thist] regime to force it to withdraw from Kuwait unconditionally," and at the same time they pledged "to mobilize all forces for the withdrawal of the foreign armies from the region."[7] "If the Americans will decide to launch a shooting war," said al-Asifi, the Da'wa's spokesman, then the Muslims should "apply pressure" on the U.S. and "drive it out of their land."[8]

This ambivalence toward the West was also reflected in the fundamentalists' repeated complaints that the Western powers chose, and still choose, to ignore the Islamic opposition to Saddam. It finds expression even in the terminology used by the Islamic fundamentalists. Whenever they appeal for Western help, they phrase it as an appeal to the "international community" or to "world public opinion," or to "those who take interest in the future of Iraq."[9] When they feel the need to denounce the West, they call it "imperialist" or "the arrogant haughty forces" *(quwa al-istikbar)*. The movements complain that they were not and are not allowed by the Western powers to work against Saddam's regime, and that the Western media is ignoring them.[10] Despite their open hostility to the West, and in particular to the United States, they did their best throughout the Gulf crisis to make their case before the Western media and influence the Western public through it. One glaring example of this appeal to the West occurred when a central Da'wa activist, the London-based Dr. "Abu Ali," told the American public, in an interview on ABC news in early November 1990, that the opposition expected the West to provide it with "money, arms and information" so that it could assassinate Saddam Hussein. As he explained it, his organization knew Saddam's whereabouts within a radius of one mile. What they needed, he intimated, was information about his whereabouts within a radius of a few yards, and this he expected the West to supply.

Another area where the Shi'ite fundamentalist movements exposed their ambivalence was in regard to the means to liberate Kuwait and, more importantly, to topple Saddam.

In an interview, I was told by a senior Da'wa activist in Europe that the Da'wa supported the embargo against Iraq in the hope that the hardships that it would create would force Saddam to his knees. At the same time, however, the party demanded that the embargo be limited to arms and spare parts but exclude foodstuffs, because the Iraqi people should not suffer on account of Saddam.[11] This kind of partial embargo, coupled with an increase in underground activity, my interviewee felt, would suffice to kill or topple Saddam.

The official position of the Shi'ite opposition groups was that a shooting war was to be avoided because it ran the risk of destroying Iraq's infrastructure and "sending it back to the middle ages." A war threatened also to destroy the Iraqi national entity by splitting it three ways between Sunnis, Shi'ites, and Kurds, and by providing neighboring countries with an excuse to dismember Iraq. Moreover, a war might result in the destruction of the Iraqi army, which is "the property of the Iraqi people" and which the country would need in the future. However, when confronted with the possibility that, in the absence of a food embargo and military action, Saddam might be able to ride the storm and even strengthen his position, my interviewee admitted that some military action might be necessary, as long as it was limited to military targets.[12] Thus, if one penetrates the rhetorical fog, the conclusion must be that the Shi'ite movements were actually in favor of the embargo, which necessitated the presence of allied forces in Saudi Arabia, and even perhaps of military action. But they were concerned lest too much harm befall the Iraqi people and they be held responsible for the embargo or the military action.[13]

All the opposition movements agreed, however, that after the Iraqi evacuation of Kuwait, foreign forces should evacuate the area immediately. Their basic anti-Western stance was evident in their collective communiqué of 14 August 1990, pledging that after the liberation of Iraq from the Ba'thist yoke the new regime would "fulfill its national duty by fighting imperialism and Zionism and their schemes."[14] Indeed, all the fundamentalist Shi'ite movements of Iraq show even more intense hostility toward Israel and Zionism than they show toward the West. In their view, Israel has no right to exist in the heart of the Islamic homeland, and it thus should be eliminated. Occasionally, the Shi'ite fundamentalists even criticized Yasser Arafat for his readiness to recognize Israel in exchange for the establishment of a Palestinian state alongside it. In their mind, the whole of Palestine is an Islamic land and not one square inch of it can be conceded to the Jews. It is noteworthy, however, that the Shi'ite fundamentalists did not engage in any anti-American or anti-allied activities in the Gulf between August 1990 and April 1991.

A very sensitive point for the Shi'ite fundamentalist opposition was the fact that many Islamic movements in the Sunni world adopted Saddam as their hero and saw in him a latter-day Saladin. The Shi'ite fundamentalists were totally exasperated when they realized that some Muslims sympathized with Saddam and his regime. To combat this view, they argued, in long and bitter discussions, that Saddam and his regime were both criminals and atheistic enemies of Islam. Not only did the regime fail to apply the rules of the Shari'a in Iraq and prohibit alcohol drinking in public and sexual corruption; it also murdered thousands of pure, devout Muslims for their belief.[15]

The Gulf Crisis and Change in the Islamic Movements

It was not easy for the Shi'ite oppositional groups to devise a practical program of action. The assassination of Saddam was, by their own admission, a near-impossible task, and by their appeal to the West to provide them with the means to do so, they, in fact, admitted their impotence. Moreover, SAIRI's declaration that it could easily mobilize 50,000 to 100,000 warriors inside Iraq and outside of it had a hollow ring to it.[16]

Between the invasion of Kuwait and the end of the ground war, there were no reports of any significant sabotage or other opposition activity inside Iraq. Following a wave of mass demonstrations in 1979-80, the government was able to identify the party's cadres and destroy them. The opposition groups thus naturally feared that as long as the regime was well-entrenched, even if it was fighting a losing war, any open political agitation inside Iraq would expose their underground organization and lead to its destruction.

Abroad, however, after the invasion of Kuwait the Shi'ite opposition movements began a new relationship with the media in the West. Before the end of the Iran-Iraq war in 1988, opposition leaders had preferred to remain incommunicado. This changed gradually after that time, and dramatically after the invasion of Kuwait. British and American journalists were now virtually overwhelmed by requests for media coverage.

As a result of the Gulf crisis, the various opposition groups, including the Shi'ite fundamentalist ones, augmented their efforts to coordinate their actions and create a political front. In view of the fact that even within the Shi'ite fundamentalist camp there were and still are deep rivalries, the difficulty of these efforts cannot be underestimated. Seventeen opposition groups—including Communists, the main Kurdish parties, pro-Syrian Ba'thists, ex-Ba'thists, independent liberals and others, and all the important Shi'ite fundamentalist organizations—met several times after August 1990 and issued joint communiqués.[17] From the fundamentalists' viewpoint, the most difficult concession was to issue a joint communiqué with the Communist Party, which, in light of its atheism, they regarded as their chief opponent.

But there was another, more important concession in these communiqués—the call for liberal parliamentary democracy. Following an interim period of one to two years, when a constitution would be drafted and all the necessary preparations for elections would take place under a coalition interim government, the Iraqi people would participate in secret and direct elections with freedom of the press and of assembly guaranteed. These principles imply acceptance of the verdict of the majority, even if it is not in harmony with the Shi'ite fundamentalist demand that Iraq become an Islamic republic. In the case of the Da'wa and Amal, this acceptance was made explicit.[18] As confided to the present author by a member of the Da'wa, if the majority votes against the concept of an Islamic Republic, then it would be a mistake to try and impose this principle by force. A rejection of the principle of Islamic rule would be evidence that the Iraqi people are not ready as yet for such rule, and thus the party would need to accept reality and start a long-term educational campaign. Any resort to force would only create another dictatorship like that of Saddam. The Da'wa member even went so far as to criticize Khomeini for imposing Islamic rule on a reluctant Iranian populace. The dual result was that Iran moved toward dictatorship and that the majority of its population in fact did not adopt Islam in a sincere manner.[19] Here, too, however, one finds a great degree of ambivalence in the Arabic-language publications of the Da'wa and even more so of SAIRI. In these publications, rather than suggestions of a liberal democratic future, one often comes across a clear commitment to the establishment of Islamic rule in a liberated Iraq, without any qualification.[20]

The conclusion must be, then, that the Islamic movements, and in particular the Da'wa and Amal, have made some steps toward a more democratic way of thinking. In this regard, it has to be borne in mind that many of their leaders have lived for a decade or more in the West. But one must also conclude that the transition is far from complete, and that their political conduct will greatly depend on circumstances. If they have absolute or near-absolute power, they may be expected to revert to their dogmatic approach of earlier years. If, however, the Islamic movements will have to share power with other opposition groups and with the army, and if the influence of the more radical circles in Iran is limited, their conduct may be expected to be more democratic.

The Shi'ite fundamentalist opposition's approach to the Iraqi army is of interest in this context. Apparently admitting to themselves that their own grassroots support inside of Iraq is insufficient to topple Saddam and secure effective control over the country, the various movements rely on the army to do this work. In all their documents in which the army is mentioned, as well as in the Da'wa activist's interview, they express the hope that the army will save the country from Saddam's and the Ba'th's yoke. In a somewhat naive fashion, they believe that when this happens, the army will be in need of legitimization and will invite the opposition parties to come home and share power. Indeed, according to this vision, the army will be ready to give up political power after a short while and remain a docile arm of the democratically-elected government. It is not clear whether this notion has changed since the army cracked down on the Shi'ite revolt in March 1991.

After the invasion of Kuwait the opposition parties, including the Shi'ite fundamentalists, were active on another front: opposition leaders of all colorings moved back and forth between London, Damascus, Tehran, and Riyadh. The Shi'ite fundamentalists' main connections are with the Ba'thist regime in Syria (mainly the Da'wa and Amal) and with Rafsanjani's government in Tehran (mainly SAIRI). But also noteworthy has been the new, tentative connection, especially by the Da'wa, with Saudi Arabia. Understandably, both sides, the Saudis on the one hand and the fundamentalists on the other, are suspicious of each other, but according to reliable reports a dialogue has started.[21]

The Shi'ite Revolt

Following the Iraqi defeat by allied forces in February 1991, a well-coordinated revolt erupted in at least a dozen towns in the Shi'ite south of Iraq on 2 March. Basra, Najaf, Nasiriyya,

Diwaniyya, Karbala, Samawa, Suq al-Shuyukh, Zubayr, and Kut were at its core. According to eyewitness reports, in Basra alone between four and five thousand people, civilians and army deserters, fought against government troops. Because the city was effectively cut off from the main body of Iraq by American troops, the central government's control over Basra was substantially weakened. This revolt, aided to an extent by small arms, ammunition, and Iraqi expatriates who crossed over from Iran, was an impressive demonstration of Shi'ite power. Yet it is impossible to tell how many of the fighters were members of the activist organizations' underground inside Iraq, how many crossed over, and how many of the revolutionaries were disaffected soldiers and other non-affiliated Shi'ites.[22] The single most important organization that seemed to be behind the fighting was SAIRI, and on 3 March 1991 its leader, Ayatollah al-Hakim, claimed that he was directing the revolt in Basra and elsewhere. However, by late March, the Republican Guard and other government troops had reconquered all the main Shi'ite cities at a horrendous price in human lives and property.

The revolt was based on two assumptions: first, that the Iraqi army in Kuwait and southern Iraq, and especially the Republican Guard, had been severely weakened in the war; and, second, that the United States would not allow Saddam to use attack helicopters against the rebels. Both assumptions proved wrong. Saddam managed to reorganize the Republican Guard at tremendous speed, mainly because it had not been seriously affected by the war. For example, it was left with some 700 operational Soviet-made T-72 tanks at the war's end. In addition, possibly in response to a request from the Saudis, who feared a fundamentalist and pro-Iranian Shi'ite victory in Iraq, the U.S. and British troops did not limit Saddam Hussein's use of attack helicopters.

The Shi'ite rebels who faced the Republican Guard (composed almost entirely of Sunni Arabs) were thus badly out-gunned: they were lightly armed, poorly organized, and received only limited logistical support from Iran. The

Iranians, for their part, were unwilling to be drawn into a new war with Iraq or into a new confrontation with the United States.

Saddam's tactics were also to prove decisive. He concentrated all his forces against the Shi'ite rebels and left the Kurdish north for later. Control of the oil fields in the Iraqi south and the outlet to the Gulf was of much greater importance to his survival than securing the Kurdish mountains. In the south, the Guard quelled the revolt in the various Shi'ite cities one by one, starting with Basra. This tactic of concentrating firepower gave the government another obvious advantage.

In addition to these factors, the revolt may have suffered from a collapse of morale as a result of the statements of a particularly influential religious leader. In late March, Grand Ayatollah Abu'l-Qasim Khoi was forcefully taken to Baghdad to meet Saddam. This unprecedented action was apparently taken in response to rumors that came from Lebanon on 18 March that Khoi had called upon the Shi'ite masses to revolt against the Ba'thist regime and that he may even have established a Shi'ite government. In fact, the Da'wa has recently publicized the communiqués issued by Khoi during the height of the uprising in the south. They seemed based upon a conviction that the Ba'th regime was disintegrating; under these circumstances, the ayatollah apparently deemed it appropriate to depart from his traditionally quietist path and to attempt to direct the anticipated restructuring process in the hope of avoiding anarchy among the Shi'ite groups and in the population at large.

The first communiqué, of 5 March 1991, called upon the Shi'ites to "guard the territory of Islam," to "look after its holy places" while upholding Islamic values in the country, and to guard both the honor and the property of the people and preserve the public institutions of Iraq. The second communiqué, of 7 March 1991, established a "Supreme Committee" under whose leadership the Shi'ites would preserve Iraq's security and stabilize public, religious, and social affairs. The nine names listed as members of the Supreme Committee were ulama congenial to Khoi's view of the postwar process, including Ja'far Bahr al-Ulum, a former student of both Baqir al-Sadr and Muhammad Taqi al-Khoi, possibly one of the ayatollah's sons. The Supreme Committee was not defined as a new government for Iraq, but its clear basis in local Shi'ite authority was sufficiently reminiscent of Khomeini's doctrine of the "rule of the jurist" to alarm Saddam and inspire the "kidnapping" of Khoi.[23]

In a televised interview with Saddam Hussein after his abduction, Khoi denounced the revolt in the south, expressing dismay at the great destruction that had been brought upon the Shi'ite cities as a result of the rebels' action. Since then, he has been reported to be under house arrest in his home town of Najaf.

In his essay for this volume, Said Arjomand mentions that the first reports of Khoi's anti-Ba'thist statements came from Shaikh Muhammad Fadlallah, the putative leader of Hizbullah in Lebanon, who has close connections with the Da'wa Party. Both he, as a politically engaged Shi'ite leader, and the Da'wa had an interest in invoking the authority of the widely respected Khoi against the Ba'thist regime. The fact that Khoi has traditionally refrained from involvement in political activity made his communiqués all the more significant. His quietism had been one of the main differences with Ayatollah Khomeini, his rival for Shi'ite preeminence, and a bone of contention between them when Khomeini was a political refugee in Najaf (1964–78). Although several of the leaders of the Da'wa were Khoi's students, they too have adopted a more activist approach, without, however, expressly criticizing Khoi's quietism.

Despite Khoi's greater activism in March 1991 in order to stave off what he thought would be the likely adverse effects of political disintegration in the south of Iraq, it is unlikely that he has completely abandoned his basically apolitical approach. Even when he expressly denounced the revolt, he doubtless consented to do so in order to save the institutions that he headed and, as he likely saw it, the Shi'ite community in Iraq as a whole. One cannot but compare this conduct with that of Muhammed Baqir al-Sadr who, in April 1980, flatly refused to compromise with the Ba'th regime and was promptly executed.

The decisive defeat of the Shi'ite opposition may serve to encourage more pragmatism in a number of spheres. First, the various groups will need to cultivate relations with countries other than Syria and Iran. Saudi Arabia and the Gulf states are the most promising candidates. Second, since the relations between Islamic and non-Islamic oppositional forces in Iraq thawed in 1990, further cooperation may be expected, even with the Communists. The longer such cooperation takes place, the more established it becomes and one may expect tolerance toward the non-Islamic organizations to grow. In its own turn, this may bring about a more democratic outlook. If, however, the Kurdish opposition reaches a separate agreement with the Ba'th regime, this process may be arrested. Finally, at least in theory, if they realize that they can be helped by the West, the Iraqi Shi'ite fundamentalists may become less hostile. In the case of SAIRI, this process will be substantially hampered, however, as long as Iranian-American relations remain as hostile as they currently are. If and when these relations improve, it will be easier for SAIRI to tone down its hostility toward the United States and perhaps even to seek some degree of cooperation.

Conclusion

There is no doubt that the readiness of the Shi'ite fundamentalist movements to form a united front with non-Islamic organizations and to adopt the principle of liberal democracy is largely the result of the invasion of Kuwait. It may be a step toward a less sectarian, less totalitarian political approach. In this respect, the Da'wa's and Amal's commitment seems more sincere than that of SAIRI's. This may be ascribed in part to their greater independence, as well as to their more democratic internal workings.

But it must be borne in mind that a degree of internal democracy in an elitist party does not automatically guarantee a democratic regime when this party comes to power; in its internal affairs the Ba'th itself was a fairly democratic party during its first years in power (1968–73). The willingness on the part of the Da'wa to talk to the Saudis, whom it regarded as archenemies until August 1990, and its ambivalence about the American presence in the Gulf zone are additional signs of growing pragmatism. At this point, however, all these changes are still reversable. The core of the Shi'ite fundamentalists' worldview remains an absolutist vision, according to which Islam is as much a social and political order as it is a divine message, and thus mosque and state cannot and should not be separated. The first crack in this view, in the form of an explicit acceptance of the rule of the majority, important as it is, will need to be substantially enhanced before the liberalization process becomes difficult to reverse.

Endnotes to Chapter 2

1. See, for example, al-Hakim's speech to his soldiers, *Liwa al-Sadr (Al-Sadr's Standard*, SAIRI's weekly newspaper), 24 February 1991. Al-Hakim even mentioned the need to assure the success of the "Imam's practice" in Iraq— i.e., of Shi'ite supremacy. Also see Shaikh al-Asifi, *al-Jihad al-Duwali (International Jihad)*, 11 December 1989, on the need to implement the "Imami" policy; and "Abu Jihad's" statement in *al-Jihad*, 12 November 1990. For the view that the Islamic opposition deserves to play the leading role because it paid with the most blood, see *al-Jihad*, 19 November 1990. The joint communiqué of the Islamic movements promises to correct the historical wrong of anti-Shi'ite discrimination and give the Shi'ite majority its full rights: *al-Jihad*, 17 September 1990.

2. A *mujtahid* is a high-ranking Shi'ite authority who is authorized to issue a religious legal opinion *(fatwa)*, based on the interpretation of the Qur'an and the traditions *(Sunna)*.

3. An interview with a senior Da'wa activist in Europe, 10 September 1990. The interview was given on condition of anonymity.

4. For example, al-Hakim for all the Islamic-Shi'ite opposition movements, *Liwa al-Sadr*, 11 November 1990.

5. For example, al-Hakim to a Japanese TV station, Ibid., 10 December 1990.

6. Ibid., 7 October 1990, p.1.

7. "Bayan Quwa al-Mu'arada al-'Iraqiyya" ("A Communiqué of the Iraqi Opposition Forces" [in Arabic]), 27 December 1990; and al-Hakim, *Liwa al-Sadr*, 19 August 1990.

8. *Al-Jihad,* 27 August 1990. A leader of Hizbullah from Lebanon defined the American presence in the area as more dangerous than the invasion of Kuwait: *Liwa al-Sadr*, 12 August 1990. "Bayan al-Haraka al-Wataniyya wa'l-Islamiyya al-'Iraqiyya Hawla al-Ijtiyah al-'Askari al-'Iraqi li'l-Kuwait wa Makhatir al-Tadakhkhul al-Ajnabi fi'l-Mintaqa" ("A Communiqué of the Iraqi Patriotic and Islamic Movement on the Iraqi Military Invasion of Kuwait and the Dangers of Foreign Intervention in the Area" [in Arabic]), London, 14 August 1990. "Abu Bilal" said that, in the case of war, the Iraqis should fight both the Allied forces and Saddam: *al-Jihad*, 3 October 1990.

9. For example, Shaikh al-Asifi, *al-Jihad*, 6 August 1990.

10. For example, al-Hakim, *Liwa al-Sadr*, 19 August 1990.

11. See also "Abu Bilal" from the Da'wa, *al-Jihad*, 10 December 1990; and Shaikh al-Asifi, *al-Jihad*, 17 September 1990.

12. Interview. For the need to apply economic pressure, see also a Da'wa communiqué, *al-Jihad*, 6 August 1990. Al-Hakim expressed the fear that war would split Iraq and harm the people: *Liwa al-Sadr*, 28 October 1990; 4 November 1990. "Abu Bilal" spoke of the army being one of Saddam's "hostages" in *al-Jihad*, 10 December 1990.

13. See, for example, an implied support for a limited war, provided it was to be "against Saddam and his regime," and not against the Iraqi people, in SAIRI's view on UN Resolution 678: *Liwa al-Sadr,* 9 December 1990. Also *al-Jihad*, 27 August 1990.

14. "The Communiqué of the Iraqi Patriotic and Islamic Movement."

15. For example, a communiqué by the forces of the Islamic opposition, *Liwa al-Sadr*, 23 September 1990; "Abu Mujahid," a member of the Da'wa's supreme body, *al-Jihad*, 12 November 1990; al-Hakim, *Liwa al-Sadr*, 19 August 1990; and ibid, explaining Islamic support for Saddam by the fact that American presence on the "holy land" of Arabia angered many Muslims.

16. Al-Hakim, *Liwa al-Sadr*, 19 August 1990.

17. The most important of these documents is "Bayan al-Haraka al-Wataniyya wa'l-Islamiyya," signed among others by the Da'wa and SAIRI. See also, "Appeal for Democracy and Human Rights in Iraq" (in English), London, 17 February 1990. Among the signatories were one member of the Da'wa and one independent Shi'ite religious scholar close to the Da'wa. See "A Communiqué of the Iraqi Opposition Forces" (in Arabic), 27 December 1990.

18. Interviews with "Abu Bilal," *al-Jihad*, 3 December 1990 and 10 December 1990; interview with Hojjatulislam Hussein al-Sadr of the Da'wa, *The Guardian*, 15 January 1991. Also see Muhammad Taqi al-Mudarrisi, *An al-'Iraq wa'l-Haraka al-Islamiyya (On Iraq and the Islamic Movement)* (London: al-Safa Press, 1988), pp. 23, 24, 43.

19. Interview.

20. See, for example, a "Communiqué of the Forces of the Iraqi Islamic Opposition" (in Arabic), *al-Jihad*, 17 September 1990.

21. See for example a report in *Le Monde* from Damascus, as reproduced in *HaAretz*, 25 February 1991. See also a report from London in *HaAretz*, 1 March 1991. "Abu Bilal" said that "a few meetings with senior Gulf officials" have born "no fruits so far": *al-Jihad*, 3 December 1990. The BBC World Service interviewed Da'wa's Dr. Munaffaq al-Rubayi in Riyadh on his talks with Saudi officials: 5 April 1991.

22. See, for example, *Newsweek*, 18 March 1991; *Time*, 18 March 1991; Saddam Hussein's speech *Radio Baghdad*, 16 March 1991.

23. The communiqués first appeared in *al-Jihad*, 25 March 1991. After seeing the communiqués and learning their exact dates, I tend to believe that they were authentically from Khoi.

3

A VICTORY FOR THE PRAGMATISTS: THE ISLAMIC FUNDAMENTALIST REACTION IN IRAN

Said Amir Arjomand

In Iran, Iraq's populous non-Arab neighbor, the revolution of 1979 brought the Islamic fundamentalists to power. The Iranian revolution went through the typical cycle of the rule of the moderates (1979–80), take-over by the radicals (1981–83), and finally a "Thermidorian" return to more moderate rule and consolidation of the revolution.[1] After the consolidation of its power, or more precisely from 1985 onward, Iran's revolutionary elite developed a pragmatic approach to foreign policy which required movement toward a rapprochement with the West. This pragmatic approach was resisted by Ayatollah Khomeini, but has prevailed since his death. Throughout the Gulf crisis and war, the pragmatic leadership was successful in preempting the rhetoric of the radical fundamentalists—the faction that has sustained the original, radical ideological attitude. As a result, the radical faction was of relatively little consequence during the crisis.

The victory of the pragmatists within the political elite was the decisive factor in determining the role that Iran played throughout the crisis. Given the fact that the Shi'ite majority in Iraq remains bitterly opposed to Saddam Hussein's Sunni regime in the aftermath of the Gulf war and the failure of the Shi'ite rebellion in southern Iraq, Iran's role in the region will be even more critical for the foreseeable future. In this, however, as during the crisis itself, Iran's political elite will be guided not by the commitment to export the Islamic revolution that determined much of its foreign policy in the early 1980s, when the radical fundamentalists were in power,[2] but by sober calculation of its interests as a regional power—a regional power that has gained enormously from the destruction of Saddam Hussein's might.

The Radicals and the Pragmatists

Under Ayatollah Ruhollah Khomeini's leadership, Islamic militants overthrew the monarchy in Iran in 1979, and gradually gained complete control of government shortly thereafter. The militants who were thus transformed into the new political elite of the Islamic Republic of Iran have been in power for over a decade; and holding the highest offices of the state has changed their outlook, especially concerning foreign policy. After it ousted President Bani-Sadr and took over the state in June 1981, the Islamic fundamentalist revolutionary elite gradually split into a pragmatic and a radical faction.[3] The first group tended to argue for the consolidation of the Islamic regime in one country, namely Iran, while the second stressed the ideological commitment to the Islamic revolution and its spread throughout the Muslim world, especially the Middle East. This was a fluid process in which positions were defined gradually and individuals often changed sides. Nor did a pragmatic approach to foreign policy necessarily go hand in hand with conservatism in socioeconomic policy. The position of the Majlis (Parliament) Speaker and the leading pragmatist, Ali Akbar Hashemi Rafsanjani, on socioeconomic policy and on the need to make Shi'ite jurisprudence more flexible—to give an important example—did not differ significantly from that of the radical fundamentalists.[4] Furthermore, Khomeini was remarkably successful in orchestrating a measure of unity among these factions.

The pragmatic faction tended to predominate with the consolidation of the revolution, and especially after the end of the war with Iraq in 1988, when the pragmatic President, Ayatollah Sayyid Ali Khamanei, prevailed over the radical Prime Minister, Mir Hossein Musavi, who was dismissed. Khomeini, however, prevented the complete ouster of the radicals. The radical fundamentalists, whose greatest asset was access to Khomeini, were easily outmaneuvered after his death, and became outsiders. In contrast to the pragmatic elite in power, these radicals have not modified their original outlook. Their primary goal remains the export of the Islamic revolution with its two corollaries: struggle against U.S. imperialism, and the liberation of Jerusalem. Since 1985 the pragmatists, now the insiders, have seen the ending of Iran's diplomatic isolation as crucial to its national interests. Accordingly, they have been pursuing a policy of rapprochement with the West, including the United States, the most important obstacle to which was Khomeini himself, who sabotaged it more than once.[5]

The Assembly of Experts, popularly elected but composed exclusively of religious scholars (*ulama*), is the body in charge of selecting the "Leader of the Islamic Republic" —as Khomeini's position was defined in the Constitution of 1979. After Khomeini's death in June 1989, the Assembly chose President Khamanei as his successor. Majlis Speaker Rafsanjani became President at the end of July, and the constitution was amended to eliminate the position of Prime Minister in order to concentrate executive power in the President's hands.[6] Despite this impressively swift resolution of the problem of succession to Khomeini, the pragmatist victors were able to exclude the radical fundamentalists from positions of power only gradually and with extreme caution. In fact, as we shall see, the decisive power struggle between the two factions did not take place until the autumn of 1990.

The two factions that I have distinguished can both be properly described as "fundamentalist" in view of their commitment to the creation of an Islamic regime based on the rule of Islamic law. The "radical fundamentalists" are more narrowly defined as those who, in addition to this basic commitment, persist in maintaining the original expansionist Islamic revolutionary outlook, with its anti-Americanism and commitment to the Palestinian cause undiminished. This definition is not entirely *ad hoc*; a strong case can be made that inflexible attitudes and doctrinaire positions have played a vital role in reinforcing and sustaining this basic commitment of politicized Shi'ite fundamentalism since the 1970s.

Who are the radical fundamentalists according to this definition, and what institutional and popular strongholds do they possess? As is the case with the other factions in the Islamic Republic of Iran, the radical fundamentalist faction is dominated by religious scholars. Foremost among these are Hojjatulislams[7] Ali-Akbar Mohtashami, formerly the Interior Minister and Ambassador to Syria; Muhammad Musavi Khoiniha, the former Prosecutor General and the leader of the occupation of the American embassy in Tehran; and Sadiq Khalkhali, the former "blood judge" of the revolutionary tribunals. The most important personalities sympathetic to this faction are Khomeini's son, Ahmad, and the Majlis Speaker, Hojjatulislam Mehdi Karrubi. Like Mohtashami, Karrubi served in missions abroad in the Middle East, and has had extensive contacts with Islamic movements in other countries.

It is difficult to identify an independent popular constituency for the radical fundamentalist faction, but whatever impact they may have is transmitted through the institutional and political framework of the Islamic regime. The most important stronghold of the radical fundamentalists is the Majlis, the Iranian Parliament, whose 260 members are popularly elected every four years. The radicals also have very considerable influence in the Society of Militant Clergy (Jam'iyyat-e Ruhaniyyun-e Mobarez), the political club of the Shi'ite ulama which endorses candidates for elections, and whose function became more important after the abolition of the Islamic Republican Party in 1987.[8] One may venture to assume that some sympathy for the radical fundamentalist position exists among the Revolutionary Guards, though here evidence is very hard to come by. One would also infer that laymen like the former radical Prime Minister Musavi are sympathetic to the radical fundamentalists.

Before the Gulf crisis erupted, the radicals were of course no more sympathetic to Saddam Hussein and his Ba'thist regime than were the pragmatists in power. Eight years of devastating war only deepened the common hatred of both groups for a secular regime that they had already condemned before the onset of hostilities in 1980. The radicals and the pragmatists alike also supported the Shi'ite opposition to Saddam Hussein under the leadership of the Iraqi ulama whom Amatzia Baram discusses in his chapter. But the crisis of 1990–91 forced each faction to weigh its natural hostility to Saddam Hussein against a countervailing tendency, namely, the anti-American and anti-Zionist sentiments that deepened as the war unfolded and as Baghdad was devastated by allied bombing.

The initial reaction of both Iranian factions to the Iraqi invasion of Kuwait in August 1990 was one of serious concern. But before even a month had passed after the invasion, Saddam made a desperate bid for Iranian support against the coalition forces by offering sweeping unilateral concessions to Iran regarding the disputes that had resulted from the Iran-Iraq war. It was only then that Khalkhali, speaking in the Majlis, denounced the Kuwaiti ruling family; that another radical deputy cursed the House of Saud for inviting the infidels into the land of Revelation; and that the Speaker of the Majlis, Karrubi, promised that the Muslim nations would eject the American troops from Saudi Arabia ignominiously.[9] Furthermore, it is interesting to note that the position of Khalkhali and Karrubi differed from that of Khoiniha, who persisted in expressing grave concern over Saddam's expansionism and skepticism over the Americans' ability to stop him.[10] As for the pragmatists in power, they were not greatly moved by the Iraqi overtures. Later disclosures indicated that they communicated the substance of the offers made by Iraq to the Kuwaiti Foreign Minister.[11]

In September 1990, Sayyid Ahmad Khomeini and Karrubi, although subscribing publicly to the official Iranian condemnation of both the Iraqi invasion and the presence of American troops in the region, began to press the government to adopt a more emphatic anti-American position. On 13 September, Ayatollah Khamanei, Khomeini's successor as the Leader of the Islamic Republic, responded to this pressure, perhaps preemptively, by declaring combat against the United States to be a holy war or *jihad*. A few days later 160 Majlis deputies issued a statement in support of Khamanei which demanded the immediate withdrawal of the American (and Iraqi) troops.

Meanwhile, President Rafsanjani and Foreign Minister Ali Akbar Velayati were vigorously engaged in diplomatic activities marked by particularly close contacts with Syria and Turkey. Since the Iraqi invasion of Iran in 1980, a common enmity of Saddam Hussein has brought the governments of Iran and Syria closer together, leading to cordial diplomatic relations and significant economic exchanges between the two nations. Late in September, President Hafiz al-Asad of Syria visited Iran for intensive discussions with Iranian President Rafsanjani. A joint Iranian-Syrian commission was established for the purpose of maintaining constant consultation throughout the crisis.

Al-Asad's visit also marked the onset of a new round in the power struggle between the pragmatic fundamentalists in power and their radical opponents. Rafsanjani and his supporters seized the opportunity offered by the election of the Assembly of Experts to administer a serious defeat to the radicals. The ulama jurists of the Council of Guardians,[12] in their supervisory capacity, rejected the candidacy of Mohtashami, Khalkhali, and other radical fundamentalist religious scholars by failing them at a humiliating examination in Shi'ite jurisprudence. Significantly, the Society of

Militant Clergy was made to endorse a list of candidates that included Ahmad Khomeini, who still basks in the charisma of his late father, but excluded the radicals and their other sympathizers entirely. Ayatollah Khamanei supported the Council of Guardians in this move. The radical fundamentalist Majlis deputies registered their discontent by staying away from the Parliament, and the session on 7 October was cancelled because of the lack of a quorum. The elections did take place, however, on 8 October 1990. On the same day, Israeli security forces in Jerusalem killed twenty-one Palestinian demonstrators on Temple Mount (known to Muslims as al-Haram al-Sharif), near the historic site of Solomon's temple and the current site of al-Aqsa mosque (see Jean-François Legrain's chapter). The pragmatists were perhaps fortunate that the outcome of the power struggle had already been decided before this radicalizing event was reported and absorbed in Tehran.

The Gulf War in the Context of Middle Eastern Politics

Before the Gulf crisis the Islamic revolutionary elite in Iran enjoyed extensive financial, military, and ideological links with other Islamic fundamentalist movements in the region. After the Iraqi invasion of Kuwait, however, these ties with the Shi'ite fundamentalist movements in Iraq and Kuwait produced contradictory effects.

On the one hand, sympathy for the Arab Shi'ites in Iraq was heightened by the Gulf crisis. The Iranian prisoners of war who were repatriated by the Iraqi government in August and September 1990 included a number of religious scholars who had served as Islamic ideological commissars, and their reports of captivity in the Iranian press deepened popular antipathy toward Iraq. Popular interest in the Iraqi Shi'ite cause was also stimulated by the increased visibility of the Supreme Assembly for the Islamic Revolution in Iraq (SAIRI), a kind of Iraqi government-in-exile formed in Tehran in 1982 during the Iran-Iraq war and never disbanded. The activities of this body of Iraqi Shi'ite religious leaders had, understandably, received little publicity during the peace negotiations with Iraq. During President Al-Asad's visit to Tehran, however, the leader of SAIRI, Ayatollah Sayyid Muhammad Baqir al-Hakim, issued a statement to the effect that the formation of an anti-Saddam coalition with Iraqi oppositional elements in Damascus was under consideration.[13]

On the other hand, the Gulf crisis also evoked sympathy in Iran for Shi'ites in Kuwait in their own struggle against the Kuwaiti government. In mid-November 1990, the Kuwaiti Shi'ite fundamentalist leader, Hojjatulislam Sayyid Muhammad Baqir Musavi Mehri, who was released as a result of the Iraqi invasion, spoke in Shiraz of his suffering in Kuwaiti prisons, and the similar plight of 120 other Shi'ite militants there.[14] As far as can be judged, however, these cross-cutting currents and the deepened sympathy of Iranians with their oppressed fellow Shi'ites in Iraq and Kuwait had no discernable impact on Iranian politics. It was otherwise with the Palestinian issue.

As elsewhere in the Islamic world, reports of the October killings in Jerusalem produced in Iran a wave of indignation and sympathy for the Palestinians. Rather than allow Saddam Hussein to exploit this sense of outrage in Iran as he tried to do in the Arab world, the Iranian government made a vigorous show of championing the Palestinian cause independently. Israel, Zionism, and American imperialism were strongly condemned in the press and in statements by Ayatollah Khamanei and the Iranian officials. Early in December 1990, an international conference was convened in Tehran to mark the third anniversary of the *intifada,* referred to as "the Islamic uprising of Palestine." The participants included the leaders of Islamic fundamentalist movements in the West Bank and Tunisia. This deft reaction on the part of Iran's elite invites comparisons with the declaration of jihad by Ayatollah Khamanei and his sustained anti-American rhetoric throughout the crisis. The primary objective of both exercises was in fact to preempt Saddam Hussein in his calculated bid to emerge as a champion of both Islam (through his declaration of holy war against the West) and of the Palestinian cause (through his espousal of "linkage" between the Gulf crisis and the Arab-Israeli conflict).

This studied reaction of Iran's ruling elite during the crisis was part of a policy designed to prevent Saddam Hussein from wresting actual, or even nominal, Islamic revolutionary leadership from Iran. But it also had an important domestic consequence: it took the wind out of the radical fundamentalists' sails. In other words, the rhetoric of the Iranian government in regard to the Gulf crisis and the Palestinian question, in spite of its radical overtones, did not in fact reflect a substantive radicalism in the ruling elite or portend a shift toward the strategies of the non-compromising fundamentalists whom Saddam Hussein hoped to mobilize in his cause. For example, Ayatollah Khamanei's strong anti-American rhetoric did not stand in the way of his endorsement, on 14 November 1990, of the diplomatic efforts of the Iranian President and the Foreign Minister, who had recently concluded a round of negotiations with the President of Turkey, Iraq's other populous non-Arab neighbor. Moreover, at the beginning of December, Iran declared its support for the United Nations Security Council resolutions, and on 4 December, even as the Foreign Minister opened the conference on Palestine, the First Deputy President, Hasan Habibi, declared that Iran was opposed to any concession by the West to Iraq.[15]

Subsequently a round of confrontation between President Rafsanjani and his radical fundamentalist opponents began a few days before the outbreak of the Gulf war. The radical Majlis deputies succeeded, by one vote, in dismissing the Minister of Health, who had the strong support of President Rafsanjani and Ayatollah Khamanei;[16] and, on the eve of the air attacks by the allied forces, Majlis Speaker Karrubi once again denounced the United States. While the Iranian government declared its neutrality in the war, Mohtashami and Khalkhali strongly condemned the United States in the Majlis and argued that Iran should side with Iraq against the United States, the greater evil.[17] But a demonstration organized by the Society of Militant Clergy against the war on 21 January 1991 proved an embarrassing failure, with no more than 3,000 participants.

Majlis Speaker Karrubi was quick to draw the inference that popular support in Iran for the radical fundamentalists was weak or non-existent. The failure of the effort to mobilize the masses demonstrated that hard-line ideological arguments would fall on deaf ears among a population beset by serious economic problems and disaffected by the previous international ventures of the regime. Within three days, Karrubi proposed his own peace initiative. Yet he soon reached an agreement with President Rafsanjani and, deferring to him, abandoned the initiative. All the while, of course, Ayatollah Khamanei continued to perform his rhetorical function with strong anti-American statements matched by verbal attacks upon the Iraqi regime.

In February 1991, President Rafsanjani launched his own peace initiative, drawing in the Soviets and the European Community, while Foreign Minister Velayati conducted a busy round of shuttle diplomacy. Tehran became the major port of call for Middle Eastern, Soviet, and European diplomats; Pakistani volunteers, seeking to cross Iranian territory to fight on the side of Iraq, were denied permission.[18]

In this period of intense official diplomatic activity, there were few, if any, signs of open public activity by the radicals. Three possible exceptions, however, are worth noting. First, it is possible that the radical fundamentalists may have drawn closer to the conservative, traditionalist ulama; they may have particularly had some influence on Grand Ayatollah Muhammad Reza Golpaygani, who issued a statement to the effect that the invasion of Kuwait did not justify the slaughter of the Muslim population of Iraq by American bombs.[19] Second, the Islamic Jihad, the Lebanese organization which has had close ties with Mohtashami, claimed responsibility for throwing small explosive devices into the Italian and other embassies in Tehran on 20 February 1991.[20] Third, the launching of the ground offensive on 24 February, after the American rejection of the Soviet peace initiative, caused apprehension among the radicals, as among other groups, and the Deputy Speaker of the Majlis denounced the war as a war of the United States and Britain, "the old hyena," against Islam.[21] However, these incidents were relatively minor and it is reasonable to conclude that the radical fundamentalists, recognizing their lack of popular support as well as the entrenched position of President Rafsanjani, chose to maintain a low profile.

The radical fundamentalist reaction in Iran to the U.S. military presence in Saudi Arabia and to the Gulf war is, then, best described as a deviation from the consistently maintained official Iranian position of neutrality in the Gulf war promoted by the pragmatists. Rhetoric apart, the reaction of the radicals consisted of the demand that the Iranian government tilt toward Iraq as an expression of Islamic solidarity against imperialism and Zionism. Of course the Iranian radicals knew better than to accept Saddam's overnight claim to embody Islamic faith against Western infidelity. Their central argument did not therefore depend on Saddam's integrity or lack thereof. Rather, they insisted that the war would be an instrument for furthering the designs of Zionism and imperialism.

During the war, the radical fundamentalist faction failed to mobilize public opinion in war-weary Iran, and did not have any appreciable impact on Iranian foreign policy. The adroitness of the Iranian political elite contributed significantly to this failure. The pragmatic ruling elite effectively neutralized the radical fundamentalists by anticipating and muting the rhetorical "linkage" between the Iraqi annexation of Kuwait and the Palestinian question. This shrewd strategy eclipsed whatever possibility the radical faction may have had of building popular support after the tragedy in Jerusalem in

October; its success is one reason for the difference between the fundamentalist reaction in Iran and the fundamentalist reaction in the rest of the Islamic world.[22]

The Aftermath of the War

Immediately after the crushing defeat of the Iraqi army by the ground forces of the United States and its allies at the end of February, the chairman of the Supreme Assembly for the Islamic Revolution in Iraq, Muhammad Baqir al-Hakim, began to urge a Shi'ite uprising against Saddam Hussein. This was done with the evident support of President Rafsanjani, who effectively put Iranian broadcasting facilities at the disposal of the rebellious Iraqi Shi'ites. Meanwhile, in close coordination with Syria, the Iranian government supported a broad coalition of forces that included the Kurds and secular Iraqi oppositional groups. On 8 March, however, Rafsanjani indicated his dissatisfaction with the ongoing diplomatic maneuvers by calling for the resignation of Saddam Hussein.

This call indicated a hardening of Iran's position, and came in the wake of the Damascus agreement of 6 March 1991 among eight Arab states, which excluded Iran. Deputy President Habibi and Foreign Minister Velayati were already in Damascus for talks with the Syrian President, and to protest Iran's exclusion from the agreement. Iran had been carefully cultivating economic and political ties with the Gulf states, and Rafsanjani had considered his diplomatic efforts hampered by not having diplomatic relations with Saudi Arabia. The Syrians undertook to convey Iran's concerns to other Arab countries, while negotiations to resume diplomatic relations with Saudi Arabia soon began through Oman's mediation. Iran's embassy in Riyadh was reopened on the last day of March. In April, President Rafsanjani announced that the Saudi government had agreed to increase the quota for Iranian pilgrims to Mecca from 45,000 to 100,000, and to permit them to hold rallies while on pilgrimage.[23] The Saudi Foreign Minister, Prince Saud al-Faisal, visited Tehran in June 1991, the first visit by a senior Saudi official to Iran since the revolution.[24]

Meanwhile, the "policy of preemption" continued after the war, signaling the Iranian leadership's desire to maintain its primacy over Islamic movements even as it pursued pragmatic political goals. One example is particularly instructive. The serious predicament of the Shi'ite population in the wake of the postwar uprisings in Hilla, Najaf, and Karbala induced the aged, traditionalist and remarkably apolitical Shi'ite leader resident in Iraq, Grand Ayatollah Abu'l-Qasim Khoi, to issue an edict appointing a Shi'ite shadow cabinet for Iraq.[25] This decree was made public on 18 March by the Lebanese Shi'ite leader, Shaikh Muhammad Fadlallah.[26] On the same day, Ayatollah Khamanei expressed the hope that "an Islamic and truly popular government based on the wishes of the innocent people of Iraq" would come to power. The coincidence is significant. Khoi, the highest Shi'ite religious leader (*marja' al-taqlid*) in Iraq,[27] had been Khomeini's chief rival; pictures of Khoi were burned during the Iranian revolution. In postwar propaganda the Iranian pragmatic ruling elite did not want to be outdone by Khoi any more than by Saddam's declaration of holy war in August 1990, or by the Iranian radical fundamentalists throughout the crisis. Ayatollah Khamanei's statement, however, did not affect Iranian policy: President Rafsanjani would categorically deny that Iran provided troops or military assistance to the Shi'ite rebels in Iraq. He said that the Iraqis could do their own work.[28]

The collapse of the Kurdish opposition to Saddam and the massive flight of the Kurdish population toward Turkey and Iran did, however, require some response. The Iranian government could not show indifference to the plight of the hundreds of thousands of Kurdish refugees, especially in the light of the broad international sympathy for their cause. Iranian officials accused the United States of giving mixed signals to the Iraqi rebels and failing to assist them;[29] and in the Friday sermon on 5 April 1991, Ayatollah Khamanei urged the Iraqi dissidents to continue their rebellion until the end, forewarning them of the most stern oppression if they failed to do so. Nevertheless, Iran accepted American and allied assistance in dealing with the Kurdish refugee problems. It negotiated with the United States through Swiss diplomatic channels, accepted German supplies and military personnel on its own territory, and declared its air space open to international relief missions.[30]

Indeed, in all but one of the elements of Iran's postwar policy, the fundamentalists had no reason to challenge the pragmatic ruling elite. There was no significant difference of emphasis between the two concerning the Kurds, or regarding close ties with Syria. The one major matter of contention was the question of relations with Saudi Arabia. The radical fundamentalists, following Khomeini, considered the Saudi rulers unfit for the custodianship of Islam's holy places,[31] and ferociously attacked them for inviting American troops to the central land of Islam. The postwar resumption of relations with Saudi Arabia can therefore be considered a significant victory for the pragmatic political elite, and a clear indication of the continuing weakness of the radical fundamentalist faction.

Conclusion

During the Gulf crisis, national interests rather than revolutionary zeal formed the basis for Iran's foreign policy decisions. A range of options was open to the Iranian government after the war, including military support for SAIRI; the arming of the Iraqi prisoners of war who had refused to return, and the newly arriving Kurdish refugees; and the use of the Iraqi military planes that landed in Iran during the war. The exercise of any of these options would not have necessarily signaled a concession to the radical fundamentalist faction in the Majlis. National interests did not, for example, exclude the possibility of military support for the Iraqi Shi'ite fundamentalists, who have been Iran's special clients. But, because the radical faction spent its political capital during the crisis arguing that Iran should help Saddam Hussein, such support, to be effective, would have had to come from the pragmatic elite.

In the months following the end of the war, the radicals found it difficult to reclaim the rhetoric of revolutionary Islam from the propagandists of the governing elite. Indeed, the pragmatists' control of Iranian foreign policy and fundamentalist rhetoric alike was clearly demonstrated in the Iranian response to events in Algeria in June 1991 (see Hugh Roberts' chapter). The confrontations there between the Islamists, especially the Islamic Salvation Front (FIS), and the Algerian army elicited a comment from Iranian Foreign Minister Velayati which aptly expressed the pragmatists' nuanced position regarding the spread of Islamic fundamentalism. "As a Muslim nation, we wish that Islam rules in [Algeria]," Velayati said, " . . . but this does not mean interference in that country's internal affairs."[32]   Ayatollah Khamenei, playing once again the role of Iran's official spokesman for fundamentalist Islam, predicted that "the Muslims will triumph."[33]

A most complex set of international factors is at work to determine whether or not Iran has a say in the new postwar order in the Middle East, as Secretary of State Baker has suggested it would.[34] Foremost among these are the postwar policies of the United States, Saudi Arabia, and Syria. If Iran's influence in the postwar order is perceived as slight or negligible, the radical fundamentalist faction could conceivably revive its earlier effort to characterize the pragmatists' foreign policy as a total failure. But the Gulf crisis left the radical, not the pragmatic, fundamentalists in a weaker position within the ruling elite of Iran.

Endnotes to Chapter 3

1. The work most often cited in this connection is Crane Brinton's *The Anatomy of Revolution* (New York: Vintage Books, 1938). An earlier analysis of this pattern can, however, be found in Lyford P. Edwards, *The Natural History of Revolution* (Chicago: University of Chicago Press, 1927). For a general analysis of the Islamic revolution, see Said Amir Arjomand, *The Turban for the Crown, The Islamic Revolution in Iran* (New York: Oxford University Press, 1988). For a detailed account of the rule of the moderates under provisional Prime Minister Mehdi Bazargan and President Abd al-Hasan Bani-Sadr, see Shaul Bakhash, *The Reign of the Ayatollahs* (New York: Basic Books, 1984).

2. For an account of Iran's foreign policy in this period, see Robin Wright, *Sacred Rage: The Wrath of Militant Islam* (New York: Simon and Schuster, 1988).

3. For the development of these political alignments within Iran's clerical elite, see Shahrough Akhavi, "Clerical Politics in Iran Since 1979," in Nikki R. Keddie and Eric Hooglund, eds., *The Iranian Revolution and the Islamic Republic* (New York: Syracuse University Press, 1986), pp. 57-73; and Eric Hooglund, "Elite Factionalism in the Islamic Republic of Iran," *The Middle East Journal* 41 (2) (1987): 181–201.

4. See Shaul Bakhash, "Islam and Social Justice in Iran," in Martin Kramer, ed., *Shi'ism, Resistance and Revolution* (Boulder, Colo.: Westview Press, 1987).

5. The last occasion was the Rushdie affair.

6. According to the Constitution of 1979, the official position of Khomeini as the supreme Shi'ite Jurist *(faqih)* was that of the Leader of the Islamic Republic. On the position of the Leader of the Islamic Republic, the elimination of the position of Prime Minister and other constitutional amendments of July 1989, see Silvia Tellenbach, "Zur Änderung der Verfassung der Islamischen Republik Iran vom. 28. Juli 1989," *Orient*, 31 January 1990, pp. 45-66; and Said Amir Arjomand, "Constitution of the Islamic Republic," forthcoming in *Encyclopedia Iranica*.

7. The term means "proof of Islam," and gained currency as an honorific title for Shi'ite ulama in the nineteenth century. See S.A. Arjomand, *The Shadow of God and the Hidden Imam: Religion, Political Order, and Societal Change in Shi'ite Iran from the Beginning to 1890* (Chicago: University of Chicago Press, 1984), pp. 238, 246. It underwent a process of gradual depreciation, and is currently used for a religious leader who ranks below Ayatollah. The latter term means "the sign of God," and is currently used to designate a member of the ulama who is authoritative in Shi'ite jurisprudence. The highest echelon of this category consists of the Grand Ayatollahs, who are considered the "Sources of Imitation" *(maraji' al-taqlid)* by their Shi'ite followers. (See footnote 27.)

8. For a general description of ulama-controlled organizations and institutions in the Islamic Republic of Iran, see *The Turban for the Crown*, chapter 8.

9. Majlis session of 21 October 1990.

10. Interview in *Ettela'at*, 20 October 1990.

11. *International Herald Tribune*, 21 March 1991.

12. The Council of Guardians is in effect an appointed upper house with the power of veto over the Majlis legislation, and of supervision of elections. It consists of six plenipotentiary ulama members, appointed by the Leader of the Islamic Republic, and six lay members with greatly restricted powers. For further details, see my forthcoming "Constitution of the Islamic Republic."

13. *Kayhan*, 23 September 1990.

14. Ibid., 19 November 1990.

15. Ibid., 4 December 1990.

16. Ibid., 14 January 1991.

17. Ibid., 20 January 1991.

18. *International Herald Tribune*, 4 February 1991.

19. *Badische Zeitung*, 4 February 1991.

20. *International Herald Tribune*, 21 February 1991.

21. Ibid., 25 February 1991.

22. Notwithstanding the differences that follow from the division between the Arabs and the non-Arab Muslims.

23. *International Herald Tribune*, 22 April 1991.

24. *The Independent*, 7 June 1991.

25. Grand Ayatollah Khoi was abducted a few days later by Saddam's men, and forced to appear on Iraqi television to express his gratitude for the restoration of order. *International Herald Tribune*, 25 March 1991.

26. *Badische Zeitung*, 19 March 91.

27. As was pointed out in footnote 7, the Shi'ite hierarchy is dominated by a handful of Grand Ayatollahs who are considered the *maraji' al-taqlid* (sources of imitation; singular *marja' al-taqlid*). This traditional institution of Shi'ite religious leadership was consolidated in the nineteenth century. See Abbas Amanat, "In Between the Madrasa and the Marketplace: The Designation of Clerical Leadership in Modern Shi'ism," in S.A. Arjomand, ed., *Authority and Political Culture in Shi'ism* (Albany: State University of New York Press, 1988), pp. 98-132. Although this traditional institution has survived the Islamic revolution in Iran, the authority of the *maraji' al-taqlid* is increasingly threatened in that country as it detracts from that of the Leader of the Islamic Republic. See my "Ideological Revolution in Shi'ism," in *Authority and Political Cultures in Shi'ism*, pp. 196-98.

28. *International Herald Tribune*, 29 March 1991.

29. Ibid., 2 April 1991.

30. *Badische Zeitung*, 25 April 1991.

31. Diplomatic relations had been broken off in 1987, following the death of over 400 Iranian pilgrims in clashes with Saudi security forces in Mecca in July.

32. Interview with Velayati, as broadcast on "Voice of the Islamic Republic of Iran," Tehran, 29 June 1991, reported in BBC *Summary of World Broadcasts* ME/1113/A/7, 2 July 1991.

33. "Algeria Says Two Opposition Chiefs Face Trial on Conspiracy Charge," *The New York Times*, 2 July 1991.

34. *International Herald Tribune*, 7 February 1991. At this writing the ques-

tion of Iran's influence upon the fate of American hostages held in Lebanon, and how it might use this influence, is paramount in the quest for normalized relations between Iran and the United States, as is the question of Iranian assets frozen by the United States government.

4

A DEFINING MOMENT: PALESTINIAN ISLAMIC FUNDAMENTALISM

Jean-François Legrain

The Gulf war precipitated a crisis, or moment of decision, for Hamas, the Islamic resistance movement of the West Bank and Gaza Strip. Often termed a "fundamentalist" movement because of its "zeal" in pursuing an Islamic sociopolitical agenda built in part upon a principled refusal to negotiate with the Israelis and a dedication to the elimination of the Zionist state altogether, Hamas and its confrontational stance was enjoying a new-found political credibility among Palestinians in 1990 even as the Gulf crisis unfolded. The militant attitude taken toward Israelis had lifted Hamas to an unprecedented level of popularity as efforts of the Palestine Liberation Organization (PLO) to achieve a negotiated settlement through diplomatic channels entered its third frustrating year and as violence escalated on the West Bank and Gaza.

But the radical, uncompromising fundamentalism for which Hamas was known and increasingly admired would be put to the test as the movement quickly found itself in an ideological dilemma: should it follow the emotional lead of the Palestinian populace in support of Saddam Hussein, their self-styled liberator and fearless enemy of the Zionist state, or should the movement look to its future and to its immediate financial and organizational needs by distancing itself from the oppressor of its benefactor Kuwait?

The fact that the PLO, its rival for hegemony in the Palestinian resistance movement, chose the former course, was one important element in the calculations of the Islamic movement's leadership. Any crisis involves both opportunity and danger. By quietly choosing to restrain its natural enthusiasm for any anti-Western agent, and by anticipating that the Iraqi "liberator of Palestine" would fail, Hamas appears to have turned the crisis into an opportunity for expansion and to have proved itself, in this instance at least, to be more adept at reading the signs of the times than its nationalist rival. The long-term outcome is yet to be seen, but in the short-term Hamas may well have reaped financial and political benefits for its deft reactions to the crisis.

The Emergence of the Palestinian Islamic Movement

During the first ten years of the Israeli occupation of the West Bank and Gaza Strip (1967–76), Islam rarely constituted the primary justification for the liberation struggle of the Palestinians.[1] This, rather, was maintained in the name of Arab or Palestinian nationalism. The "official" Islam of the West Bank was an integral part of Jordanian authority; in Gaza, it existed under the auspices of the Israeli military administration. In both cases the Islamic leadership was content to preside solely over religious matters.

At the end of the 1970s, however, a new type of Islamic activism appeared. Claiming the authority of the Muslim Brotherhood tradition and linked with its Egyptian and Jordanian branches, though financially supported by Kuwait and Saudi Arabia, this movement had as its primary preoccupation the re-Islamization of society. This quest for re-Islamization was characterized by vigorous preaching in the mosques, but also by attacks on unveiled women and the destruction of bars and cinemas. Anti-Israeli radicalism was the theme of its discourse: the liberation of Palestine is fundamentally a religious question which concerns the entire Islamic community; the protection of Islam in the face of repeated attacks by the West is, in fact, the main challenge of this century; since Israel constitutes the spearhead of this aggression, the Western menace can only be eliminated through the destruction of the "Jewish entity."

For the next decade—the ten years preceding the *intifada*—the Muslim Brotherhood refrained from confronting the occupying power and confined its political activity to the struggle against the Palestinian Communist Party. Fatah, the main wing of the PLO, and Jordan were happy to encourage this Islamist attack on the "left," and Israel too had an interest in encouraging any divisions among the Palestinians. Although this decision not to engage in direct resistance to the Israelis cost them political legitimacy among many Palestinians, the Brothers did manage to establish a large social welfare network in the Gaza Strip. There Shaikh Ahmad Yasin emerged as a charismatic and influential leader. His Islamic Assembly (al-Mutjamma' al-Islami) infiltrated the majority of mosques and came to control the Islamic University among both administrators and students (regularly winning 65 to 75 percent of the vote). But on the West Bank, in spite of the spread of religious associations, the Brothers failed to establish a network or to find themselves a viable leader. The majority of mosques escaped their control, and their only strongholds were in the universities where they obtained roughly 40 percent of the votes in student elections.[2]

It was only with the appearance of a second movement, rivaling the Muslim Brotherhood in the field of Islamic activism but fundamentally different in political behavior, that Islam became integral to the politics of the occupied territories. In the process, the Muslim Brotherhood itself was radically transformed. This second Islamist movement appeared publicly in 1983 and made *jihad* against Israel in all its forms, including armed struggle, the central religious duty. The generic name of "Islamic Jihad" was applied to the various groups embracing this principle, each with a different structure and "guide" at the helm. Principal among the leaders were Fathi Shqaqi, a pharmacist from Rafah, who was particularly concerned with the military side of things, and Abd al-Aziz Uda, a lecturer at the Islamic University and spiritual leader of the movement.

The small groups that make up this movement are united by a common ideology influenced by the thought of the Muslim Brother intellectual, Sayyid Qutb (executed by the Egyptian regime in 1966); by the assassins of Egyptian president Anwar Sadat; and, although these groups are Sunni Muslim and resolutely Palestinian, by the Islamic revolution in Iran. As a general rule, activists come either from the ranks of the Muslim Brotherhood, whose political conduct they criticized; or from the religious wing of Fatah. The Israeli army attributes the formation of the Brigades of Islamic Jihad (Saraya al-Jihad al-Islami) to this wing of Fatah, and, in 1986–87, through a series of anti-Israeli guerrilla operations,[3] they played an important role in inciting the intifada.

Almost spontaneous at the beginning, the uprising very quickly became organized through local and regional committees. In the case of PLO partisans, these committees reported to the Unified National Leadership of the Uprising (UNLU, al-Qiyada al-Wataniyya al-Muwahhida li'l-Intifada); and, in the case of the Muslim Brotherhood, they reported to the Movement of Islamic Resistance or, as commonly known in the Arabic acronym, Hamas (Harakat al-Muqawama al-Islamiyya). The small groups that made up Jihad remained outside of these command structures.[4]

Established at the beginning of January 1988, the UNLU immediately took charge of decisions concerning the appropriateness and timing of general strikes, demonstrations, and other forms of civil disobedience. This was done by the regular publication of numbered communiqués. Its political program reaffirmed the principle that the PLO is the sole representative of the Palestinian people and demanded the holding of an international conference under United Nations auspices for the creation of an independent state.

Among the non-PLO groups, Jihad became the victim of Israeli repression.[5] Virtually destroyed two or three months after the start of the uprising, it reemerged only at the end of 1988 in the form of periodic communiqués, a symbolic monthly strike, and the organization of a number of commando operations launched mainly from outside of the West Bank and Gaza. While the Jihad group of Shqaqi and Uda has been reestablished in south Lebanon,[6] another group has developed in Amman and is influenced by the person and ideas of Shaikh As'ad Bayyud al-Tamimi.[7] Yet another faction, developing in the summer of 1990, has coalesced around Ibrahim Sarbil in Amman. With its top command thus outlawed and in exile, "Islamic Jihad" has not been able to reconstitute an effective organization in the occupied territories.

By way of contrast, Hamas has operated within the occupied territories from the early days of the uprising. Led by Shaikh Ahmad Yasin and Dr. Abd al-Aziz al-Rantisi,[8] a teacher at the Islamic University of Gaza, Hamas initially attracted Muslim Brothers on an individual basis only. In February 1988, however, the Brotherhood formally adopted Hamas as its militant arm.

In making the liberation of Palestine in its entirety— "from the (Jordan) river to the sea"—its new priority, the Brotherhood was brought into line with Jihad (without, however, the merger of their organizations). By taking part publicly in the struggle against Israel, the Brotherhood could now hope to gain the political legitimacy for which it had waited so long but which had been denied it because of its political quietism. Although at first willing to submit to the timetable of the nationalist and largely secular UNLU, tension set in. In light of Hamas' enhanced position and the PLO's relatively weakened one on the political chessboard, there was soon mutual consultation, but little substantial agreement, between the two main groups.

The Gulf Crisis and
the Dilemma of Hamas

The position that Hamas took on the Gulf crisis must be seen in the context of its competition with the PLO for political ascendancy in the occupied territories. One could characterize Hamas' position as one of embarrassment: its leadership was caught between public opinion favorable to Saddam Hussein, on the one hand, and its financial dependence on the Gulf states, on the other.

There were many indications of this tension. Several *imams* were expelled from their mosques by Palestinian mobs for preaching against the Iraqi invasion of Kuwait, while the command of Hamas took two weeks to publish its position on the question. Communiqué 61, although dated 3 August 1990, ignored the invasion of Kuwait the day before. During the first two weeks of the crisis, Hamas did nothing more than reproduce two Jordanian communiqués—the declaration of the Jordanian Muslim Brotherhood of 5 August and the speech by one of its deputy leaders, Sulaiman Mansur, on 8 August. Only after 13 August did Hamas publish its own pronouncements, and only three of these treated the Gulf question in detail.[9] Moreover, between 3 August 1990 and 9 January 1991 (Communiqués 61 to 68), Hamas called for 19 days of general strike, but only two of these were devoted to condemnation of events in the Gulf. It advocated 37 particular demonstrations, yet not one had the Gulf War as its theme. As Palestinians increasingly demonstrated their support for Saddam on the streets, the leaders of Hamas returned the theme of mobilization against Israel to pride of place in their communiqués.[10] They also called for unity with the PLO.

Hamas adopted basically the same framework of analysis in responding to the Gulf crisis that it employs in addressing the Israeli-Palestinian question: this is another episode in the fight between good and evil, a new "crusade" by the West, "a hateful Christian plot against our religion, our civilization and our land" which aims to put an end to the blessed movement of Islamic expansion.[11] The United States "commands all the forces hostile to Islam and the Muslims," and George Bush is "the chief of the false gods," "the leader of the forces of evil."[12] Although present in a minor way, anti-imperialist themes were not ignored: in communiqué 64, for example, Hamas charges that "America has exploited the entry of Iraqi forces into Kuwait and has used it [as an excuse] to occupy the region directly, whereas before it had occupied [the region] and had controlled its riches through the intermediary of its collaborators in the region."

This ontological-theological framework of analysis allows for little mention of the participation of Arab and Muslim troops in the anti-Iraqi coalition. Insofar as it is mentioned at all, Arab governments are depicted as having imposed on their people a decision which is contrary to religion, but which is regrettably consistent with their policy of undermining Islam "as a total way of life." The consequence can only be "decadence, back-sliding, and the breaking up of the *umma* [Islamic community]."[13]

Hamas also rejected the coalition's argument that it was defending international law: "Where were these states on the day when the Jews absorbed the land of Palestine, Sinai, and the Golan Heights, on the day when they invaded southern Lebanon?"[14] Moreover, the Security Council constitutes "world dictatorship in its most hideous form."[15] There the right of veto is exercised by Great Britain, which, through the Balfour Declaration, had "planted this cancerous body [Israel] on our land," and by America, "strategic ally of the sons of vipers."[16] The American forces "have exchanged their old colonial clothes to put on a new costume of support for international will in defense of right, justice, and legitimacy, but we are under no illusion: it is in fact a matter of preparing for the invasion of Iraq's territory and of facilitating the invasion of Jordan by Israel."[17]

Hamas endorsed the twin core principles that it is necessary "to resolve Arab differences within the Arab family," and that it is equally necessary to refrain from using force, which can only lead to "the shedding of blood. . . between sons of the same umma and the opening of the door to hostile forces and states." [18] Once stipulated, however, these principles were eclipsed by an almost exclusive preoccupation with the question of a foreign presence in the region. Indeed, the Hamas command steered between total obfuscation of the Iraqi invasion itself and detailed reference to the plight of Kuwait.

In the declaration of 5 August, the Muslim Brotherhood made reference to "the entry *(dukhul)* of Iraqi forces into Kuwait." The expression, used again later, can appear lenient,[19] but Iraq's entry is nonetheless condemned in the name of the principle that Arabs should not spill Arab blood. Yet this unfavorable mention disappeared entirely from the declaration of Sulaiman Mansur of the Jordanian Muslim Brotherhood, reproduced by Hamas. For Mansur, the crisis was "the most brutal of aggressions led by the Christian and Zionist coalition full of hate toward our umma."

The communiqué of 13 August took the same line and highlighted the demands of the movement: "the withdrawal of American forces from Arab territory, which they have profaned, and the leaving of Arab affairs to the Arabs themselves." It demanded that "Iraq and Kuwait, brothers like all the Arab states, should work to resolve their problems between themselves," but it was not precise about the nature of the problem or an eventual Iraqi withdrawal.

Communiqué 63, on the other hand, elaborated upon the question of Kuwait, from the humanitarian as well as the political angle. "We here in Palestine, in the depth of torment, we feel better than anyone the bitterness of the loss of our homeland, the suffering of exodus and diaspora. . . . Our faithful Palestinian people do not forget the attitudes of goodwill and generosity taken by their brother Kuwaiti people toward the Palestinian people throughout their ordeal." However, Hamas was quick to add: "We are sure that our Iraqi brothers will grant to their Kuwaiti brothers the safety and protection of their persons, finances, belongings, and liberties." This expectation that Iraq would treat the Kuwaitis justly was expressed, no doubt, for the benefit of Hamas' Gulf state benefactors—a placatory statement made all the more necessary by the obvious absence of compassion for the Kuwaitis on the Palestinian streets.

The political position detailed in the remainder of the tract seemed to ally Hamas more closely with the Gulf states and thus threatened to distance Hamas further from the Palestinians on the streets and from the Iraqi regime. For Hamas was, in fact, introducing new, balancing, demands. Now the demand for the withdrawal of foreign troops was accompanied by a demand for "the retreat of Iraqi troops from Kuwait," as well as for the "constitution of an Arab or Islamic [peace-keeping] force in hotly contested frontier regions." Hamas also called for:

> the people of Kuwait to have the right to determine the future of their country. Disputes [must] be settled within an Arab or Islamic framework, which would successfully carry out a study of Iraq's claims, whether it be a matter of referring to the drawing of frontiers or to the cancelling of debts from the war with Iran.

Communiqué 64 went on to reaffirm that the "Kuwaiti people should be able to exercise their right to self-determination and to selecting the regime of their choice."

Hamas, therefore, did not fully endorse Iraq's position, even if certain Iraqi claims were favorably regarded, nor did it completely align itself with Kuwait. The question of Palestine was always at the heart of the matter: "Our fight in the Gulf against the Crusade is our fight in Palestine against Zionism."[20] Thus, although continuing to hope for the destruction of Israel as a prerequisite of Palestine's liberation, Hamas did not appear to believe that Saddam Hussein would be the instrument of either. In its communiqué of 22 January 1991, for example, it acknowledged, "We rejoiced to see Arab weapons strike the bunkers of the Zionist enclave in the heart of Tel Aviv and elsewhere. The Jews will drink the same cup which they have forced our people to drink everyday." Yet it had called on Iraq to "strike the heart of Tel Aviv" only if Iraq had become the victim of "Western, crusader-like aggression."[21]

These attitudes lead one to conclude that the Hamas command inside the occupied territories never considered a victory for Saddam Hussein a real possibility, but, rather, had its eye consistently on the postwar situation. There was always a need to be seen as not running against Palestinian public opinion; and, at the same time, it could not precipitate a cut-off of Gulf finances on which it was partly dependent. This latter concern was all the more important because Hamas' rival, the PLO, was bound to be weakened by its alignment with Iraq and the resultant loss of *its* Gulf revenues. While it is difficult to be precise about this financial linkage, certain estimates place the total amount of recent direct Kuwaiti financial aid to institutions in the occupied territories at approximately $100 million annually. At the Arab summit in Baghdad in 1990, Kuwait announced that it had paid $27 million to the PLO and $60 million to Hamas in the previous year. Over the past ten years, Kuwait, Saudi Arabia, and the United Arab Emirates have probably given $10 billion to the PLO.

Hamas' rather pragmatic attitude in the Gulf crisis was both a reaction to this financial history and a gamble on the future. Looking to the future is one indication that a movement is becoming increasingly organized and institutionalized; in the case of Hamas, forward thinking during the Gulf crisis was a sign, and a result, of the movement's enhanced legitimacy in the political life of the occupied territories due to its role in the recent history of the intifada. In perceiving the Gulf crisis as an opportunity to challenge the PLO for control of the Palestinian resistance movement, the leadership of Hamas seemed to be building on this momentum.

The Palestinian Future:
Between the PLO and Hamas

At the end of the first year of the intifada in 1987, the nationalist camp seemed to be the victor. Basing himself on the claims of the UNLU to be directing the uprising, Yasser Arafat had succeeded in making his line prevail at a crucial meeting of the Palestine National Council: the proclamation of the State of Palestine on 15 November 1988 had been enthusiastically welcomed by the majority of Palestinians (even by those opposed to the policy of diplomacy rather than military struggle), while the acceptance of Security Council Resolutions 242 and 338 opened the way to a dialogue with the United States. The PLO, officially playing the American card for a diplomatic settlement, thus gave priority to the political need for a sharing of the land between two states— Israel and a truncated Palestine—over the emotional attachment of all Palestinians to an undivided Palestine. In the West Bank and Gaza Strip, it was understood that the uprising would continue with the same methods which had proved their effectiveness during the first year—that is, civil disobedience, rather than a policy of outright destruction of the enemy.

Hamas, which dominated the Islamic camp after the virtual eradication of Islamic Jihad, constituted henceforth the only organization opposing any negotiated solution and upholding the demand for the liberation of the whole of Palestine by armed struggle. After a thousand days of rebellion and in spite of undeniable gains, especially the break with the idea of a "normalized occupation," the nationalist, PLO camp found itself at a diplomatic and political impasse. Whereas the dynamism of the uprising was showing signs of flagging in the face of the immovability of both Israel and the international community, many people hoped for more radical methods. Serious, bloody events would provide Hamas with the opportunity to try to transform itself into the undisputed leader of the intifada.

In 1990, two years after the crucial meeting of the Palestine National Council in Algiers, the PLO approach had not succeeded. Not only was the state of Palestine still a quasifiction, but even the most favorable political interpretation of the uprising, which argued that at the least it would stimulate a new climate of negotiations, had been sabotaged. Israel refused to subscribe to the "Baker plan,"[22] and earlier both the Mubarak and Shamir plans had been stillborn.[23] The United States put an end to its dialogue with the PLO in June 1990, and, for its part, the United Nations showed itself to be incapable of enforcing its resolutions on the Palestinian question.

Parallel with these political setbacks, the situation in the occupied territories continued to deteriorate. A list compiled on 30 September 1990 showed 861 dead and 101,550 wounded since the beginning of the intifada. On 20 December 1990 the Israeli army acknowledged that, at one time or another, it had arrested around 70,000 Palestinians—that is, one-twentieth of the population. Furthermore, 65 people had been deported from the territories.

Economically, the situation at the time of the Gulf crisis was catastrophic, and it remains so. Per capita income is thought to have fallen by at least 35 percent since the beginning of the uprising and the possibilities of work in Israel grow fewer by the day. The number of holders of green identity cards, which forbid the holder to enter Israel, is, in fact, constantly increasing: before October 1990, some 3,400 inhabitants of the West Bank and 5,000 Palestinians from the Gaza Strip had been issued them; at the beginning of December 1990 security sources announced that at least 2,400 more would receive them in the West Bank alone.

At the same time, Israel's hold on the occupied territories tightened, particularly on Jerusalem, with the creation of new colonies outside and within the city and with the accelerated program of Jewish home-building in the old city. The massive immigration of 160,000 Soviet Jews in 1990 led to a deepening of the Palestinians' fear of being swallowed up. In addition, the supporters of the policy of "transferring" the Palestinian population to the east bank of the Jordan saw General Rehavam Zeevi, one of their spokesmen, enter the Israeli government at the height of the Gulf war.

Alongside these external threats, internal tensions increased in 1990. The struggle against presumed "collaborators" intensified. According to Israeli army figures, 176 "collaborators" were executed by Palestinian groups in 1990, compared with 139 in 1989 and 16 in 1988.[24] Agreement has not been reached among the different Palestinian commands as to how to deal with those suspected of working closely with the Zionist authorities. Moreover, clashes have occurred between nationalists and Islamists on the one hand, and among various nationalist groups on the other. The tension in the Democratic Front for the Liberation of Palestine (DFLP) outside of the occupied territories was echoed within the territories.[25] By the end of 1990 the top leaders of the Abd Rabbu wing were dismissed from their positions, only to be replaced by partisans of Nayef Hawatmeh.[26] The greatest tension occurred between the Popular Front for the Liberation of Palestine (PFLP), which urged a radicalization of the methods of the intifada, and the other parties of the Unified National Leadership—a disagreement which led, in the spring of 1990, to a temporary alliance between the PFLP and the Islamists against planned municipal elections.[27]

Because of this infighting, the intifada might have lost its impetus entirely. But two events of exceptional gravity relaunched it and allowed Hamas to attempt to present itself as the natural leader of the intifada. First, on 20 May 1990, at Rishon Lezion (south of Tel Aviv), an Israeli killed seven Palestinian workers in cold blood and wounded about ten others. The repression of the demonstrations during the hours that followed resulted in seven more deaths and more than 500 wounded. Second, on 8 October, in the very heart of Jerusalem, on the esplanade of al-Haram al-Sharif—where the al-Aqsa mosque and Dome of the Rock are located and near the spot Jews believe Solomon's temple once stood clashes resulted in 21 Palestinian deaths and nearly 150 wounded. During the weeks that followed, curfews kept one million people in their homes while Israel refused to accept a United Nations investigative commission.

Immediately after the events at al-Aqsa, what very quickly became called "the war of the knives" began, with Jerusalem most often the theater. The Hamas command argued that "the massacre at al-Aqsa showed that our fight with Zionism is a fight between Islam and Judaism,"[28] but nonetheless kept legitimate targets restricted to soldiers and settlers. Simultaneously Hamas called for "the intensification of operations of jihad in the interior and overseas."[29] Several Israelis were stabbed, and the Israeli authorities resolved to move against Hamas. Four of its leaders were deported to Lebanon on 8 January 1991, and several hundred arrests were made in the ranks.

Hamas sought to elevate this "war of the knives" to the status of a new intifada strategy. However, the adherents of the PLO (with the exception of the PFLP) showed some hesitation as to whether they should support these activities, as a segment of Palestinian public opinion demanded, or condemn them, as world public opinion urged. What is clear is that the PLO was markedly on the defensive in the contest with Hamas for the Palestinian soul.

In the spring of 1990, Hamas made a number of demands on the PLO leadership, not the least of which was that there be a full return to "the military option" and that Hamas be given representation on the Palestine National Council commensurate with its strength on the ground. It estimated that it commanded the loyalty of forty to fifty percent of the population.[30] Needless to say, the PLO refused these demands and mounted a counter-attack. An editorial in the 8 July 1990 issue of *Filastin al-Thawra (Revolutionary Palestine)*, the journal of Fatah, accused Hamas of being the plaything of Israel and the United States and of intending to replace the PLO itself as leader of the Palestinian movement.[31] Clashes between Hamas and Fatah, previously confined to the prisons, now occurred throughout the territories—in July 1990 at Rafah and in Gaza; in September, in Tulkarm, Burayj, and Jabalya camps and in Jenine. Refusing to alter its policy, Hamas again appeared to be the victor. On 19 September 1990, a reconciliation of sorts was agreed, whereby Fatah and Hamas undertook to coordinate orders to their followers and to set up committees in the prisons.[32] Yet in June 1991 new clashes erupted in Nablus and Gaza. A fundamentalist shot a PLO member in Nablus and then attacked him again on the operating table of the Anglican hospital. In Gaza, tension rose over Hamas' insistence that all women, including schoolgirls, wear the headscarf, or *hijab*. Slogans appeared on the walls which proclaimed, "Hamas considers the unveiled to be collaborators of a kind."[33]

In general, the contours of the larger picture remained the same after the Gulf war ended and Saddam Hussein was defeated. Hamas managed not to alienate popular support, while at the same time it refused to align itself with the Iraqi position. Combined with the increasing adoption of more radical methods of struggle against the occupation and the continuing failure of all efforts to resolve the Palestinian question, this skillfully calibrated Gulf policy brought Hamas new bases of support. In the weeks immediately after the war, it became clear that the PLO leadership was also in disarray. Weakened internationally because of its support of Saddam and deprived of its Gulf revenue, the PLO seemed paralyzed by new internal rivalries in its leadership and thus is unable to formalize a new policy. Indeed, the PLO's choice seemed stark: to stand aside before this pressure, or to resume its former, radical strategies. In either case Islamic fundamentalism, as represented by Hamas, would claim the political spoils that go to the victor.

Endnotes to Chapter 4

1. For detailed bibliographic references, see Jean-François Legrain, "The Islamic Movement and the Intifada," in Jamal Nassar and Roger Heacock, eds., *Intifada: Palestine at the Crossroads* (New York: Praeger, 1990), pp. 175–90.

2. Jean-François Legrain, "Les élections étudiantes en Cisjordanie, 1978–1987" ("The Student Elections on the West Bank, 1978-1987"), *Egypte-Monde Arabe* 4(4)(1990). On the West Bank, the Muslim Brotherhood's lists greatly over-represent men and slightly under-represent the refugee camps. This contrasts with Fatah, which is especially rural and refugee-based, and the Popular Front for the Liberation of Palestine (PFLP), which is urban and refugee-based. Moreover, the Muslim Brotherhood is over-represented in the north and the south, unlike the Marxist groups which are concentrated in the center, but identical with Fatah. In Gaza, Brotherhood lists under-represent the camps (the opposite of the PFLP and Fatah) and over-represent the north (the opposite of Fatah).

3. Made up solely of a few commando-cells (some on the West Bank) and small groups from the Islamic University of Gaza but without any real network, the Jihad gained its best university score in Gaza as soon as it entered the contest (January 1983), receiving almost 20 percent of the votes. Like the Muslim Brotherhood on the West Bank, the Jihad afterwards experienced a strong setback and did not begin its climb upward again until just before the uprising. Its candidates, almost exclusively men, accentuate the tendencies already observed in the Muslim Brotherhood—a slight over-representation of non-refugees and strong representation of the Gaza region.

4. Zeev Schiff and Ehud Yaari, *Intifada: The Palestinian Uprising—Israel's Third Front* (New York: Simon and Schuster, 1990); Jean-François Legrain and Pierre Chenard, *Les voix du soulèvement palestinien: Edition critique et traduction française des communiqués du Commandement National Unifié et du Mouvement de la Résistance Islamique 1987-1988. (Voices of the Palestinian Uprising: Critical Edition and French Translation of the Communiqués of the Unified National Command and of the Movement of Islamic Resistance)* (Cairo: Centre d'études et de documentation economique, juridique et sociale [CEDEJ], 1991).

5. Its leaders were deported from the occupied territories at the beginning of 1988.

6. Its mouthpiece is *Islam wa Filastin (Islam and Palestine)*, published in France but based in the United States and Cyprus.

7. This movement has fabricated a past for itself, which seems not to be based on fact: for example, its claims to having made attacks against Israeli buses near Ismailia on 9 February 1990, and near Eilat on 25 November 1990, have been challenged by security sources.

8. In the occupied territories Hamas has published its own, thirty-six page version of its history, *Fi'l-Dhikra al-Thaniyya li'l-Intilaqa; Hamas, Ishraqat Amal fi Sama' Filastin (On the Occasion of the Second Anniversary of the Uprising, Hamas Sparkles with Hope in the Sky of Palestine)*, 9 December 1989. See also *Filastin al-Muslima (Muslim Palestine)*, unofficial organ of the movement published in Great Britain.

9. Communiqué 67 of 13 August 1990, Communiqué 63 of 29 August 1990, and Communiqué 64 of 26 September 1990.

10. For instance, Communiqués 65, of 11 October 1990, and 66 of 31 October 1990, are almost entirely concerned with the events in Jerusalem on 8 October near al-Aqsa mosque and the Temple Mount. Communiqué 68 of 17 December 1990, is entirely concentrated on the repression directed against Hamas. It is not until 22 January 1991, that a communiqué concerning the war was issued.

11. Communiqué 64 of 26 September 1990.

12. Communiqué of 22 January 1991.

13. Declaration of 5 August 1991, of the Jordanian Muslim Brotherhood.

14. Communiqué 63 of 29 August 1990.

15. Communiqué 66 of 31 October 1990.

16. Ibid.

17. Communiqué 62 of 13 August 1990.

18. Declaration of 5 August 1990.

19. Unlike *Filastin al-Muslima* which, several times, speaks of Iraqi "aggression" *(ghazu)*.

20. Communiqué 63.

21. Communiqué 62.

22. On 10 October 1989, the American State Department, using the Israeli plan of 14 May 1989 as a basis, announced propositions in 5 points. The main provision was for a meeting in Cairo between Palestinian and Israeli delegations, but preparatory dialogue broke down over the presence of Palestinians from outside the occupied territories.

23. The Mubarak plan specified that all the Palestinians in the occupied territories (including the residents of Jerusalem) should be able to take part in elections—a necessary step toward the adoption of a definitive settlement of the Palestinian question. The Shamir plan, urged by the United States, proposed the election of an "intermediary to lead the negotiations toward an interim period of autonomy" in the course of which "negotiations with a view to reaching a permanent settlement would be undertaken" to achieve peace "between Israel and Jordan." The plan opposed the establishment of a "supplementary Palestinian state in the Gaza Strip and in the territories situated between Israel and Jordan," and it excluded the PLO from the negotiations. In July 1990, Yitzhak Shamir excluded the inhabitants of Jerusalem from the process, refused to prohibit further construction of Israeli settlements, and insisted on the end of the uprising before elections could take place.

24. *The Jerusalem Post*, 1 January 1991.

25. Paul Lalor, "DFLP Differences Reflect the Debate Within the PLO," *Middle East International* (27 April 1990): 17–19.

26. Replaced were the heads of the women's union and of the association of trade-unionists.

27. Conflict occurred between Fatah and the Democratic Front for the Liberation of Palestine (DFLP) in Askar camp at the end of June 1990, and between the DFLP and the Palestine Communist Party at Idhna at the beginning of July 1990. For information on the municipal elections, see Joel Greenberg,

"Marxists and Moslem Fundamentalists in Areas Join Move against Fatah," *The Jerusalem Post*, 2 April 1990.

28. Communiqué 66.

29. Communiqué 67, also see unnumbered special communiqué of 16 December 1990.

30. Memorandum of 6 April 1990, to Shaikh Abd al-Hamid al-Sa'ih, president of the Palestine National Council. This body has around 550 members (among whom are 186 representatives of the occupied territories who are forbidden to participate by Israel). Only 5 Islamists have a place on the Council at present: Abd al-Rahman al-Hawrani and Abdullah Abu Izza, who also belong to the Central Council of the PLO; Amin Agha, Ahmad Salim Najm, and Jamal Hasan Ayish.

31. This editorial received a reply in *al-Sabil* (*The Way*), reproduced in *Filastin al-Muslima*, September 1990, pp. 14–15.

32. The text is reproduced in *Filastin al-Muslima,* October 1990, p. 4.

33. *The Independent*, 5 June 1991.

5

A TEMPORARY ALLIANCE WITH THE CROWN: THE ISLAMIC RESPONSE IN JORDAN

Beverley Milton-Edwards

With the outbreak of the Gulf war, Jordan's politicians found themselves in a difficult predicament. The country, which has a population of 3.5 million (of which 50 percent are Palestinians), declared itself neutral. Yet there was an increasing isolation from the West combined with a move toward Iraq as the government found itself captive to public opinion. The path that Jordan took was partly dependent on the ability of the largest political faction to respond to the crisis and to formulate an effective policy toward it.

This faction, which enjoys both popular support and political legitimacy through its representatives in the elected legislature, is, for the sake of convenience, broadly called "the Islamic Movement." It consists mainly of the Muslim Brotherhood, but also of a number of smaller Islamic parties. All are inspired by the traditionally critical attitude of Islamic reform ideology, which rejects Western interference in the Muslim world. Politically dependent on King Hussein, the Movement—especially the Brotherhood—was caught in a dilemma. Popular outrage would not tolerate anything less than the Movement's outspoken denunciation of the anti-Saddam coalition, but it could not be seen to be outdistancing the King who hoped to act as a mediator in the dispute. As the situation deteriorated and even the King seemed to conclude that all hope of a peaceful resolution of the conflict had evaporated, the Movement threw caution to the wind and became a decisive player.

Although the King was still the center of the political system, Islamic activists were able to use the system to telling effect. As members of Parliament and, from January to June 1991, of the Cabinet, they magnified their voices and, in the process, assured their popularity while simultaneously increasing the pressure on the King. The control of their own institutions—mosques, schools, and social welfare centers—enhanced their ability both to respond to the currents of popular disquiet and to shape and direct it. The Movement had a good war. But, having encouraged popular dissatisfaction without contributing to a solution of Jordan's manifest economic and political difficulties, and in being identified with the regime to some extent, its postwar prospects are less certain.

The Islamic Movement

According to Shaikh Abd al-Rahman al-Khalifa, the leader of the Jordanian Muslim Brotherhood, the Brotherhood was founded in Jordan in 1934. "King Abdullah extended his favor to it" [1] and thus a long relationship between the monarchy and Islamic activists began. Even when, in 1957, King Hussein proscribed all political parties, the Muslim Brotherhood was allowed to continue its political activities. It has contested elections and always held seats in Parliament.

The relationship between the Muslim Brotherhood and the monarchy has been the linchpin of the group's political longevity. Nevertheless, the relation between the two has been characterized by peaks and valleys and Muslim Brother support for the monarchy has not been unwavering. As early as 1956 the Muslim Brotherhood organized protests and a general strike against the King's policy of allowing a British presence in the country. The relations during this period were summed up by Dr. Yusuf al-Azm, formerly Minister for Social Development. "Sometimes the relations between us and the government were very good; when they were nearer Islam and justice we supported them, but the further they moved away from Islam the less we supported them."[2] In 1980, the King's use of the Brotherhood in pursuit of foreign policy objectives emphasized the expedient nature of the relationship. In a continuing dispute with President Al-Asad of Syria, the King allegedly allowed the Jordanian Muslim Brotherhood to establish para-military bases near the Syrian border to facilitate the Brotherhood's training of its Syrian counterparts. *The New York Times* reported that President Al-Asad accused the Brotherhood of "plotting to overthrow his government . . . and [that] Syria and Jordan apparently came close to war over, among other things, the question of the Muslim Brotherhood's activities."[3]

Through his support during this period, the King empowered the Muslim Brotherhood and this, in turn, increased its political confidence. Members began to criticize top-heavy distribution of political power in the system and press for the application of the *Shari'a* or Islamic law. The direct attack on the King's political legitimacy did not go unnoticed in the royal court and forced a change of attitude therein. The Muslim Brotherhood now presented a cogent threat to the monarchy and steps were taken accordingly to limit its power.

In 1985, the King took the unprecedented step of publicly attacking the Muslim Brotherhood. In a climate of improved relations with Syria, the King blamed "Islamic elements" for the crisis of 1980. He declared:

> . . . the truth was revealed to me. . . some of those who had something to do with what had taken place in Syria in terms of bloody acts were among us and had sought shelter in the houses of a minority which had deviated from the truth . . . [and] dressed up in our religion.[4]

The King ended his address to the nation by stating:

> I should warn this misguided handful of people, which abused our confidence, that there is no place among us for the treacherous, the wicked, the conspirator, of those who receive orders from enemies and coveters, or for the corrupt who try to harm our commitments and pledges to those near or far.[5]

After this denunciation there followed a period of less-than-friendly relations between the King and the Muslim Brotherhood. The Jordanian secret service (the Mukhabarat) moved against the Muslim Brotherhood and arrested a number of them. The group's most prominent figures were singled out. Abdullah al-Akayila, recently Minister of Education, was forced to resign his post as a parliamentary deputy in 1988 following his outspoken criticism of the Mukhabarat's campaign against the Muslim Brotherhood. Al-Akayila tried to return to his teaching post at the University of Jordan, but the Ministry of the Interior refused his application because he had criticized their actions.[6] "We were deprived from our jobs, hundreds were dismissed, and some even had their passports taken away."[7]

By the late 1980s, however, there was another upswing in relations. According to Dr. al-Akayila, "the collapse stopped. The King promised to end the pressure and hardships." This move appeared to signal that, after his initial muscle-flexing, the King preferred a policy of trying to coopt the Brotherhood, and the Islamic Movement generally, into the political system.

In April 1989, the King announced that the first elections for twenty-two years would be held in the following November. Undoubtedly, King Hussein's hand was forced on this issue. An International Monetary Fund rescue package for Jordan's ailing economy had forced the government to cut subsidies over a wide range of basic commodities and the populace at large was faced for the first time with the consequences of decades of economic mismanagement. Genuine hardship and popular outrage at the levels of court corruption led to the outbreak of five days of serious disturbances in the south of the country. The disturbances, particularly in Ma'an, involved Bedouin groups normally regarded as staunch allies of the King. The south is also regarded as a Muslim Brotherhood stronghold; the parliamentary representative for the Ma'an district is the Brotherhood stalwart, Dr. Yusuf al-Azm. The riots alerted King Hussein that the time had come to take drastic measures concerning the political future of the country, which was being crippled by serious economic problems. The solution that he chose was unexpected and unusual, especially given the fact that the rioters' anger had not been directed at the King. Nonetheless, he decided to initiate a process of democratization in Jordan.

The campaign for the elections was remarkable because of the unprecedented freedom enjoyed by candidates in articulating and promoting their policies before the Jordanian public. The streets of Amman were literally covered in election banners, and leaflets published by the various groups were strewn throughout the capital. The Muslim Brotherhood and other Islamic activists greeted the opportunity for elections with characteristic zeal and enthusiasm. The election slogan of the Brotherhood at the large rallies they organized throughout the country was "Islam is the Solution." Unlike other candidates campaigning for seats in Parliament, the Muslim Brotherhood had the advantage of over twenty years of relative freedom of political association and perceived the elections as a unique opportunity to capitalize on the constituency of support it had built over the years.

In the election of 8 November 1989, the Islamic Movement won thirty-four out of the eighty seats in Parliament. Twenty-two of those seats were won by the Muslim Brotherhood and the remaining twelve by Islamic independents.[8] Following the election victory these independents formed a parliamentary coalition and became known as the "Islamic bloc." The bloc included such figures as Laith Shbailat and Yaqub Kush, who formed a tactical alliance called the House of Qur'an (Dar al-Qur'an) Party, and Jamal Saraieh, an Islamic independent representing the district of Karak. To add to their strength in Parliament, they joined the Muslim

Brotherhood to form the "Islamic Movement."

Thus King Hussein's policy of coopting the Islamic activists threatened to be counterproductive, and fears were raised about the future stability of the regime. The King, like many of his subjects, was genuinely surprised at the Islamic victory. The low voter turnout (60 percent) was blamed for the low secular vote. After the elections, the King declared that he would not let the country be divided along religious lines. His views were shared with others in the newly-elected House of Representatives. His influence was apparent in the Cabinet appointments announced on 8 December 1989. On the day that the appointments were announced, Islamist parliamentarians were to be found engaged in rigorous lobbying efforts in the corridors of the House of Representatives in an effort to secure posts in the new Cabinet. However, Prime Minister Mudar Badran was determined not to grant their wishes at that point. Despite the broad efforts of the Islamists, therefore, they were unsuccessful, and their challenge was temporarily resisted. Yet, according to one Reuters journalist, "the fundamentalists" remained "deeply loyal to the King."[9]

The outbreak of the Gulf crisis deepened the level of political cooperation between the Islamic fundamentalists and the King. Historic changes were afoot, yet the impetus for change on both sides lay in an overwhelming concern to respond to popular pressure. Initially critical of Iraq's invasion of Kuwait, the Muslim Brotherhood changed its views with the stationing of Western forces in Saudi Arabia, the site of Islam's two most holy shrines. As a result, the Islamic Movement entered into its first coalition with the nationalists and secularists (the National Front) and organized anti-American rallies and demonstrations from mosques after Friday prayers. Islamic Movement figures inveighed against the American government and called on the King to support Iraq.

In response to the way in which the Islamic Movement harnessed popular opinion and maintained its political strength in Parliament, the government announced a new Cabinet, on 1 January 1991, in which the Islamic Movement was represented for the first time. This historic step reflected the need of the King and his supporters to coopt the powerful Islamic Movement by bringing it into the highest echelon of the political system. In the months preceding the Cabinet appointments, the Movement had been split on whether or not to accept posts in the Cabinet. In the period leading up to the outbreak of the war, it did indeed support the King's attempts to act as a peace broker between the American and Iraqi governments. At this point the Islamic Movement had entered a new phase, whereby the old relations and ideas of the Muslim Brotherhood, including criticism of the Ba'th regime and a history of support for Saudi Arabia and the Gulf states, were sacrificed to the groundswell of Jordanian popular opinion. In particular, the relationship between Saudi Arabia and the Muslim Brotherhood was irrevocably strained. In the past it was alleged that the Saudi government had funded Muslim Brother activities in Jordan,[10] and there have always been strong links between the Brotherhood in Saudi Arabia and in Jordan.

It should be noted finally that in addition to the mainstream Islamic Movement, there are two more radical Islamic groups that operate on the fringe of political activity in Jordan. One is Islamic Jihad-al-Bait al-Muqaddas ("The Holy House"—i.e., Jerusalem), which is based in Amman and led by Shaikh As'ad al-Tamimi. Shaikh al-Tamimi's uncompromising stance toward the presence of the Western alliance in the Gulf was apparent on 21 January 1991 when he called upon his supporters to launch suicide attacks against Western interests. The Shaikh declared, "We will not spare any target that our hands can reach. Based on our previous coordination with Baghdad, Saddam's speech gave us the green light to hit."[11] As Jean-François Legrain also notes in his contribution to this volume, although this is a Palestinian Islamist group, it is distinct from other Palestinian Jihad cells led by Dr. Fathi al-Shqaqi and Shaikh Abd al-Aziz Uda.

The second radical group operating in Jordan is the Islamic Liberation Party (Hizb al-Tahrir al-Islami), founded in 1952 in the West Bank by Shaikh Taki al-Din al-Nabahani. The main thrust of its ideology is that the Islamic state can only be established after the current political order has been crushed by means of a *coup d'état* or limited armed intervention. The party was denied a license by the Jordanian authorities to work as a political organization. It has worked underground, its activities are considered to be illegal, and it has a small number of supporters. Its spokesman, Ata Abu Rushtah, was arrested during the Gulf crisis, on 24 January 1991, but later released by the Jordanian authorities.

Parliament and Government
Respond to War

The 1952 constitution of the Hashimite Kingdom describes the country as a constitutional monarchy. Parliament is in the form of a bicameral system, with an appointed Senate and an elected House of Representatives. In reality many legal and executive powers rest firmly in the hands of the monarch. Nevertheless, since the general election of 1989 it has become apparent that the King is taking steps toward democratization, and this has been reflected in the relatively unhindered role played by the House of Representatives since then.

The initial response of the Islamic Movement, as parliamentary representatives, to the onset of hostilities in the Gulf was summed up in a statement issued by Parliament on 18 January, declaring that, "We salute Iraq's refusal to go along with American demands and ask it to play its historic role in resisting the great Satan who is threatening every Arab country and belief." The influence of the Islamic Movement representatives on the wording of the statement was discernible: "God will decree victory for the Iraqi people and humiliation for all enemies of God and humanity. Tell those infidels they will be overcome and cast into the furnace of hell."[12] The antipathy of the Islamic Movement toward the West, especially the United States, has been a long-standing feature, but it was exacerbated now by the deployment of Western forces in the arena of conflict.

The primary reaction, then, reflected the popular sentiment of outrage. However, political leaders were only too aware of their need to respond to external pressure and influences and thus were careful to maintain their "neutral" status throughout the war. Islamic Movement members who were parliamentarians and Cabinet ministers during this crucial period also desired to work through acceptable channels of political behavior. For example, in his role as Speaker of Parliament, Dr. Abd al-Latif Arabiyyat (a Muslim Brother), sent a cable of protest to the French government about its participation in the Western alliance. The Islamic Movement also sent a delegation to meet the Turkish Ambassador in Jordan. In their meeting, the Muslim M.P.s "expressed their regret at, and denunciation of, the Turkish government's position on the Gulf war."[13]

As the weeks of the war passed, however, the reaction of the Movement to events came under increasing public pressure. Popular resentment increased against the American role in the war in the wake of U.S. air attacks on Jordanian truck convoys travelling Iraqi roads. The Muslim Brotherhood and Islamic bloc M.P.s, along with others, urged the King to side openly with Iraq in the war. They also called on the government to be circumspect in relations with America, and to penalize those Arab countries supporting the Western coalition. Relations with the United States were, in fact, at an all-time low, and the King's speeches, notably one on 6 February 1991, became more pro-Iraqi in tone and earned a strong rebuke from President Bush. The American aid program to Jordan came under review in Washington, and Congressional sentiment turned decisively against Jordan. On 22 March Congress passed a bill that would have cut off approximately $113 million in aid for the fiscal years of 1990 and 1991, but the threat of a Presidential veto effectively gave

Jordan a reprieve. On 19 June the United States House of Representatives again voted to cut off military aid to Jordan in response to King Hussein's support of Saddam Hussein during the war, but left the implementation of the cut-off to President Bush's discretion.

Although the relationship with the United States had thus turned sour, there was no break in diplomatic relations with any of the Western alliance nations.

Response from the Streets

The relatively restrained reaction of the Islamic Movement's parliamentarians and governmental figures can be contrasted with the reaction of their supporters in the streets. There the rank and file of the movement voiced vociferous support for Iraq against the great "Satan," America. For example, they drew attention by marching to the American Embassy in Amman in the first three days of the war to express these views.

Just five days before the outbreak of the war, a Muslim Brother delegate, attending the Islamic conference convened in Baghdad in order to rally Muslim support for Iraq, declared that *jihad* was near. He urged Muslims "wherever they are to be ready to destroy American interests in case of aggression against Iraq."[14] Such rhetoric was soon heard on the streets of the Jordanian capital. Shaikh Abd al-Munim Abu Zant, one of the Muslim Brotherhood's more outspoken figures who won the second largest number of votes in the 1989 elections, preached against the American role in the crisis and connected the conflict, in characteristic Brotherhood manner, to the machinations of anti-Islamic forces against a beleaguered and betrayed Muslim world. Reflecting one of the principal tenets of Brotherhood ideology, Shaikh Abu Zant was quoted as declaring, "This battle is not between Iraq and America but between Islam and the Crusaders. . . . It is not between Saddam and Bush but between the infidel leaders and the Prophet of Islam."[15]

Abu Zant's attack on America's position typified the manner in which the Muslim Brotherhood perceived the Gulf crisis and how it sought to depict it to the Jordanian public. For the Muslim Brotherhood leaders, the American government was the source of all ills in the Middle East. Abu Zant declared, "Why is Iraq the focus? Because the Zionists and American enemies don't wish to see the Arabs or Muslims possess any power that can stand against Israel. . . . The Saudis have lost their credentials as Muslims by allowing foreign forces to come to our Holy Land, which only God can protect! They have brought the Americans, and what the Americans have brought to the Holy Land is V.D. and AIDS."[16] On the occasion of the first Friday prayers following the outbreak of war, it was reported that Islamic Movement supporters had organized anti-Western marches and demonstrations at which American, British, French, and Israeli flags were set on fire. Although harassment of individual nationals was discouraged, there were reports that foreigners had been assaulted and that a British bank and the French cultural center had been attacked by Islamic fundamentalists.

Fired by popular support, the Muslim Brotherhood issued a statement on 6 February, declaring support for Iraq in the face of the Western alliance. Condemning the United States and its interference in the political systems of the region, the statement ended on a rhetorical note. It "called on the Muslims in all parts of the world to confront the aggressor infidels, join the battle of destiny, and support their brothers in Iraq to purge the holy land of Palestine and Najd and Hijaz [i.e., Saudi Arabia] from the Zionists and imperialists."[17]

Islamic rhetoric in reaction to the war also emanated from the fringes of the Islamic activist trend in Jordan. When the Gulf war began, both the Islamic Jihad-al-Bait al-Muqaddas, and the Islamic Liberation Party issued calls for a jihad against all those supporting or involved in the Western alliance against Iraq. In an interview broadcast by Baghdad Radio, Shaikh al-Tamimi, leader of the Islamic Jihad-al-Bait al-Muqaddas, declared his full support for Saddam Hussein's war aims and stated: "This is a battle between faith and atheism. . . the side of faith is led by Saddam. . . those who fight beside America today are doomed, for they have betrayed their nation and faith."[18]

Yet the reaction and organizational skills of the mainstream Islamic Movement were not undermined by these smaller fundamentalist groups. From its established position in the social and religious fabric of Jordanian society, it was able to marshal Islamic support for Iraq. As *imams* in mosques, Muslim Brothers responded to the feelings of ordinary Jordanians on the events of the war, and encouraged them to find an expression for those feelings. The Movement declared that the conflict should be seen from an Islamic perspective. For the Muslim Brotherhood, "Islam is the solution," and it would argue that, with the outbreak of the war, popular Jordanian opinion supported that view.

Mobilizing the Masses Around Islamic War Issues

Fortunately for the Islamic Movement, the primary institutional and organizational channels of the Kingdom were open to them to build upon this reaction. Before the "era of democratization," heralded by the general elections of November 1989, the channels available to them were severely restricted, and they were non-existent for other political factions that had not enjoyed decades of the King's benign patronage. It would thus be useful to examine, first, how the Islamic Movement used such institutional channels as the Parliament, Cabinet, and office of the King to mobilize the people; and, second, how it utilized its own organizational structures.

Coalition of Interests

The war engendered an historic coalition of interests in the Jordanian political system. The King and his supporters, who still ultimately control the institutions of the political system,[19] allowed the Islamic Movement a considerable amount of freedom to mobilize Jordanian support. This is seen in the Cabinet changes of January 1991. With these appointments, seven of the twenty-five Ministers were from the Islamic Movement. They included Muslim Brotherhood notables Dr. Yusuf al-Azm, Dr. Abdullah al-Akayila, and Adnan al-Jaljuli. It might appear at first glance that the King's supporters neutralized the power of the Islamic Movement through the type of appointment that was given. However, rather than the portfolios of Foreign Affairs, Defense, Information, and State (which in the Western democratic models are considered the most powerful positions), the Islamic Movement itself requested the appointments to the Ministries of Education, Religious Affairs, and Social Development. In the first Cabinet appointments in December 1989, the Islamic Movement had declared that its participation in the government and support for it was conditional on these kinds of appointments.

Like their Haredi counterparts in Israel, the Islamic Movement in Jordan desired these types of ministries knowing that they would give it a high domestic profile and that it could concentrate on using its positions (and the budgets that come with them) to encourage grassroots support. The fact that the Islamic Movement held these particular positions during the Gulf crisis and that there is no principle of collective responsibility in the Jordanian cabinet system also gave it another advantage: it precluded political responsibility for any deterioration of foreign and other political relations falling on its shoulders. Instead, it was able to use its power, particularly in the Ministry of Religious Affairs, to mobilize Jordanians around Islamic issues that the war brought to light. For example, the Minister of Religious Affairs, an

Islamic bloc member, called on Jordanians to boycott the 1991 *hajj* to Mecca and Medina if American troops were still deployed on Saudi Arabian soil. There was also no doubt that as long as the Islamic Movement controlled Religious Affairs, there would be no effort to stop mosques being used throughout the Kingdom as a rallying-point for individual displays of political rhetoric on the war.

In Parliament, according to former Health Minister Adnan al-Jaljuli, a Muslim Brother, M.P.s had "worked in mobilizing [the] masses and directing public opinion against allied attacks."[20] Islamic Movement M.P.s even received the Iraqi Ambassador, who brought messages from Saddam Hussein exhorting them to continue their support for jihad.[21] Already a majority in Parliament, the Islamic Movement was effectively reinforced in the Gulf war by the paucity, even lack, of dissenting voices against Iraq. The formation of the "National Front" illustrated political unity across all parliamentary factions. Nevertheless, parliamentary opportunities were limited. Despite the "era of democratization," parliamentarians and government members were still dependent, for the main part, on the role the monarchy undertook during the crisis.

Prayers and Politics: The Muslim Alternative

The Islamic Movement's own organizational framework, however, was not dependent on these factors and provided an essential opportunity for it either to reflect or to command the opinions of its supporters. The structure of the Muslim Brotherhood, which consists of the leader (in this case the administrative and spiritual role is combined), Consultative Assembly (Majlis al-Shura), and charitable branch (called the Islamic Center Society), provides a solid institutional base. It is worth noting that individuals elected as deputies to the Jordanian Parliament and who are Ministers in the government, such as Arabiyyat and al-Azm, also occupy important positions in the structure of the Islamic Movement.

As President Saddam Hussein tried to put an Islamic gloss on his war aims, including adding the slogan "Allahu Akbar" ("God is Greatest") to the Iraqi flag, the Islamic Movement in Jordan through its organizational structures sought to combine this perspective with its own time-honored anti-American ideology. The Movement has always drawn supporters because of its Islamic activist anti-Western rhetoric—a theme consistently popular with the Movement's constituency. The leader of the Muslim Brotherhood, Shaikh al-Khalifa, has declared in the past that "the United States works against Islam in general, and against the Muslim Brotherhood in particular, because our task is to awaken these people."[22] Following the outbreak of the war, the Brotherhood, along with the rest of the Islamic Movement in Jordan, intensified its efforts in the task of "awakening people" and mobilizing them in support of fundamentalist aims.

According to Adnan al-Jaljuli, the Brothers "organized rallies and demonstrations to express their anger; they have also organized seminars, public lectures, and Friday speeches to develop public awareness and muster the populace against Allied attacks." The offices of the Brotherhood, the Islamic hospital in Amman, and other centers were all used as venues for the meetings. These places also served as a rallying point for members who played a part in organizing the marches. The Muslim Brotherhood also attempted to unite Jordanians in an effort to provide practical help to the Iraqis. According to al-Jaljuli, the Brotherhood "established special organizations to collect medical supplies, food stuff, and financial donations."[23]

The leadership of the Muslim Brotherhood also played its part in building on the reaction to the war. The members of the Majlis al-Shura, the Consultative Assembly, including Shaikh al-Khalifa, organized, along with others in the Islamic Movement, a delegation which met with leaders in Jordan, Saudi Arabia, Iraq, Kuwait, and Iran in an attempt to seek an Arab-Muslim solution to the conflict and to stop Western "interference" in the area.

In addition to its own structures the Islamic Movement in Jordan was able to utilize the mosque to rally public support further. The mosque has long played a vital part in its organization, providing its members with a forum to express their political opinions. Throughout Jordan certain mosques are known to attract supporters of particular preachers from the Islamic Movement. The occasion of Friday prayers offered an opportunity for Muslim leaders from the House of Qur'an Party, Islamic Jihad, the Islamic Liberation Party, and the Muslim Brotherhood to voice their party line on the war and to encourage others to support them. A recurrent theme was that the stationing of Western forces in the "sacred area" of Saudi Arabia was "an act of military occupation to protect Western interests and exploit the wealth of our people in the region."[24] The increasing numbers of rallies and marches occurring after Friday prayers testified to the success and potency of exploiting the issue of American involvement in these terms.

The Postwar Order:
The Islamic Perspective

The postwar period remains a troubled one for Jordan and its monarch. Dependent upon the Americans for vital economic and military assistance, King Hussein must attempt to repair his poor relations with the United States without disavowing earlier statements of sympathy for Saddam Hussein. Urged by the United States to take a decisive stand in favor of a peace conference with Israel, he can afford to alienate neither Washington nor the people on his own streets. Many Islamists are vehemently opposed to any negotiations with Israel and are particularly resentful of what appears to be heavy-handed American pressure. In addition, the relationship with the Gulf monarchies—once natural allies—continues to be difficult. The Kuwaitis have not forgotten the popularity that Saddam acquired in Jordan, and they are especially bitter about the pro-Iraqi sentiment that the Islamic groups had displayed. Singling out the Muslim Brotherhood speaker of Parliament, one Kuwaiti commentary thundered:

> Where is Islam in all this, Mr. Arabiyyat? Where is Islam regarding the oppression, suppression, rape, pillage and destruction endured by the Kuwaitis throughout the months of occupation? Where are the eternal values of Islam that call for resisting and confronting injustice against mankind . . . by words, deeds, and faith?[25]

To complicate matters further, the Kuwaiti martial law court named Jordanians—mostly Palestinians with Jordanian citizenship—as collaborators with Saddam's regime and sentenced them to life imprisonment or death. On 19 June demonstrations against Kuwait broke out in Amman, and some feared a mass exodus of Palestinians from Kuwait to Jordan.[26]

Against this charged background, there is no absence of opinion on what form the postwar internal and regional order should take. Like other political actors in the Gulf crisis, the Islamic Movement in Jordan has expressed its own ideas. The prominent feature of its plans is the overwhelming desire to manufacture an exclusively Arab Muslim solution. It wants to increase levels of Arab Muslim cooperation and, more importantly, exclude the West from playing any part in determining the future of the Middle East. The Brotherhood in particular has expressed the hope that Iran, Iraq, and the other Gulf states will tackle the issues of the region without depending on the West. Governments "should indulge seriously in a comprehensive plan to achieve a wider range of economic, social, and political integration. Muslims and Arabs should unite to share effectively in building a new international order [which would be] free from American hegemony, [and be] more just and equitable."[27]

Regarding the future of Jordan, the Islamic Movement does not have immediate plans to demand the imposition of an Islamic state, but it wishes to reform society along Islamic lines. The Muslim Brotherhood's control of the Ministries of Education, Religious Affairs, Health, and Social Development from January to June 1991 provided it with an ideal opportunity to gain a high domestic profile and consolidate its power over grassroots supporters. Yet, at the same time, the Brotherhood's desire to control the social order and impose its will on Jordanian life sparked a heated debate in Jordan's secular community after a series of Brotherhood rulings affecting the segregation of the sexes in the workplace, banning fathers from watching daughters in school sports, and ordering prayers (in which America is attacked) in state schools. Similar outcries were noted earlier when male hairdressers were prohibited from working in women's salons.[28]

The controversy, however, was ultimately about a much more important issue than these. The basic issue underlying both episodes was the nature of democratic life in Jordan and the relationship between the majority and the minority. Although it is not clear whether the Islamic Movement represents the majority in Jordan, it is continuing to increase its presence and power in all sectors of society. In June 1991 it won control over the executive board of yet another of Jordan's Professional Associations. Election results at the Pharmacists' Association confirmed that the Islamists had won seven out of nine seats on the executive committee. Many secular minded Jordanians, particularly in the middle classes, have felt imposed upon by the Islamists, and the debate over the rules of the game that is behind such tension remains basically unresolved as Jordan travels down the road of democratization.

Partly in response to such ferment, on 9 June 1991 King Hussein approved a new National Charter which allows a multiparty system, provides for greater rights for women, and enhances the freedom of the press. It appears to be a calculated attempt to increase the popularity of the monarchy while circumscribing the power of the Islamists. The charter does enshrine the principle of Islamic law by declaring that the Shari'a would be the source of all law in the country. But when the King said, "There is no single party that can claim to possess the truth,"[29] the Muslim Brotherhood could not have been far from his mind or the implications of his initiative any less clear for the Islamic Movement in general.

Indeed, on 17 June the Movement suffered at least a temporary setback when King Hussein, without public notice, dismissed the Cabinet he had appointed in January, including Prime Minister Mudar Badran, who had brought the Muslim Brotherhood into the government. The King asked Foreign Minister Tahir al-Masri, a Palestinian who favors a negotiated settlement with Israel, to serve as Prime Minister and to form a new administration. On 18 June the Muslim Brotherhood's leader al-Khalifa said, "We will not participate in any government that will negotiate with Israel or with its American partner."[30] Al-Masri's Cabinet does not include the major Islamic Movement figures that had joined the government in January 1991.[31]

Despite this development the Islamic message remains a broadly popular one, and it will be remembered that the sense of national unity and purpose that was created during the crisis led to the increased popularity of the King and the "loyal opposition" as well. Yet the fact remains that both supported the losing side in the war. There can be no doubt that Jordan's support of Iraq led to serious economic and political problems for the country in its relations with its Gulf neighbors and former Western supporters. If these relations are not repaired and economic conditions continue to deteriorate, domestic attention may no longer be distracted by external events. In such a situation, political leaders of all colors may become the natural scapegoat.

Endnotes to Chapter 5

1. A. H. Abidi, *Jordan: A Political Study, 1948-1957* (London: Asia Publishing House, 1965), p.147.
2. Interview with Dr. Yusuf al-Azm, Amman, 20 June 1989.
3. B. Gupte, "A Look into the Muslim Brotherhood: Antipathy for Syria, Praise for Jordan," *The New York Times*, 7 December 1980.
4. "King Husyan's letter to Prime Minister on Anti-Syrian Group" (Excerpts from 10 November letter, read on Jordanian television), in BBC, *Summary of World Broadcasts* (hereafter *SWB*), ME/8106/A/2, 12 November 1985.
5. Ibid.
6. Interview with Dr. Abdullah al-Akayila, 22 June 1989.
7. Ibid.
8. *Al-Dustur (The Constitution)*, 11 November 1989.
9. J. Rice, "A Challenge, But No Threat," *The Jerusalem Post*, 15 November 1989.
10. It is rumored that Saudi Arabia funded the Brotherhood and supported its role during the Ma'an riots in Jordan in 1989.
11. "Jordan based Islamic group warns of suidcide attacks on allied interests," *SWB* ME/0977/A/14, 23 January 1991.
12. "Pro-Iraq passions build in Jordan," *Middle East Mirror*, 21 January 1991.
13. SWB, ME/0982/A/8, 29 January 1991.
14. "Delegates at Baghad Islamic Conference Warn of Attacks against U.S. Interests," Ibid., ME/0968/A/4, 12 January 1991.
15. Milton Viorst, "A Reporter at Large: The House of Hashem," in *The New Yorker*, 7 January 1991, p 32.
16. Ibid.
17. Ibid., ME/0990/A/5, 7 February 1991.
18. "Islamic Leader says Saddam Sent by God to help Palestinians and Rule Iraq" (Baghdad Radio excerpts from interview with Shaikh As'ad al-Tamimi), Ibid., ME/0995/A/7, 13 February 1991.
19. The King has the power to dissolve Parliament and call elections whenever he chooses to do so. While the House of Representatives is elected, the Senate's members are appointed by the King. None of these is from the Islamic Movement.
20. Interview with Adnan al-Jaljuli, then–Minister of Health, Amman, 27 February 1991.
21. *SWB*, ME/0997/A/12, 15 February 1991.
22. Interview with Shaikh Abd al-Rahman al-Khalifa in *al-Watan al-Arabi (The Arab Nation)*, 9 June 1989, p. 23.
23. Interview with al-Jaljuli.
24. Ibid.
25. KUNA (Kuwait News Agency) commentary of 6 June 1991, in *SWB*, ME/1093/A/4, 8 June 1991.
26. *The Guardian*, 20 June 1991. The death sentences were commuted to life imprisonment on 26 June 1991. See *The New York Times*, 27 June 1991.

27. Interview with al-Jaljuli. For King Hussein's view of the postwar world order, see his speech of 22 May 1991 to the Royal War College in *SWB*, ME/1080/A/10–13, 24 May 1991. In addition to calling generally for a settlement of the Arab-Israeli conflict consistent with Palestinian aspirations and for greater reliance on international organizations, he appealed to his "Arab brothers to work together to open a new chapter away from the tendencies of the pre-Islamic age [*jahiliyya*]."

28. See *The Wall Street Journal*, 7 May 1990.

29. See *The Chicago Tribune*, 10 June 1991. For the text of King Hussein's speech opening the National Conference on the National Charter, 9 June 1991, see *SWB* ME/1095/A/5–7, 11 June 1991.

30. "Jordanian King Moves to Isolate Islamic Militants," *The New York Times*, 19 June 1991.

31. For the text of the royal decree on 19 June appointing the new Cabinet under al-Masri, see *SWB*, ME/1104/A/1, 21 June 1991.

6

AN UNCERTAIN RESPONSE: THE ISLAMIC MOVEMENT IN EGYPT

Gehad Auda

When the Gulf crisis was set in motion by the Iraqi invasion of Kuwait on 2 August 1990, the Islamic movement was thrown for the first time since its revival during the 1970s into a protracted situation of international crisis. This situation provided an opportunity for Islamic groups to seize the day by influencing significant segments of the Arab masses. However, in the case of Egypt, the opportunity backfired and the Islamists seemed to be headed for a setback.

The purpose of this chapter is to explain the positions adopted by the Islamic movement in Egypt on the Gulf crisis and war. The explanation is based on an analysis of the impact of both domestic and international variables and how these variables shaped the reaction of the Egyptian Islamic movement to the Gulf crisis. In short, I argue that the attempted "internationalization" of Egyptian fundamentalists in response to the Gulf crisis undermined its cumulative domestic gains achieved under President Hosni Mubarak and interrupted the process of consolidating the different streams of the movement in Egypt. Iraq's use of Islamic discourse to justify its actions and the outbreak of full-scale war represented a challenge to both the moderates and the radicals among Egyptian Islamic fundamentalists. This challenge was compounded by the rifts in the Islamic movement in the Arab and Muslim worlds at large over how to understand the crisis, respond to the war, and design strategies for the future.

In Egypt and the Arab world, there are two competing views of the impact of the crisis in the Gulf upon the broader Islamic movement. The first argues that the crisis offered the Islamic movement opportunities to mobilize and consolidate its base of support in a manner that has brought specific groups close to the assumption of political power. This view, influenced by Leninist ideas, points to a number of radical factors that have emerged from the Gulf crisis and that have created a revolutionary situation: Iraqi Islamic propaganda, mass mobilization throughout the Arab world behind Islamic slogans, a general sense of governmental ineffectiveness, a pervasive identity crisis, and the success of the Islamic movement in projecting itself as the most likely alternative able to regain Arab Muslims' control over their destiny.

The second view, elaborated upon in this chapter, holds that the manner in which the Islamic movement in Egypt dealt with the crisis induced deep ideological and behavioral uncertainty in its ranks. In this sense, the crisis exacerbated an already complex situation whereby the simple dichotomy between "moderates" and "radicals" was no longer sufficient to describe the Islamic groups' response to the government. The confusion that the Gulf war created may well be detrimental to the growth and cohesion of the Islamic movement and its ability to mobilize popular support and seek power.

A Career Profile of the Islamic Movement: Changing Norms of Radicalism[1]

The current wave of the Islamic movement as an opposition social movement is the second such wave in the modern history of Egypt. The first wave was initiated by Hasan al-Banna in 1928 with the establishment of the Society of the Muslim Brotherhood (Jam'iyyat al-Ikhwan al-Muslimin).[2] During the 1930s and 1940s, through the skill of its leadership, mass mobilization, and the periodic resort to violence, the Brotherhood grew into a major social movement impacting upon the political-cultural discourse of the society. It mainly attracted its rank and file from urban middle class professionals and university students and graduates.

The Brotherhood clashed many times with the authorities before and after the 1952 revolution. Three of these confrontations were detrimental to its future: the first in 1949, when the government engineered the assassination of al-Banna; the second in 1954, when its leadership was implicated in an assassination attempt on Gamal Abdul Nasser, the Egyptian leader; the third when it was accused, in 1965, of running an underground organization dedicated to violent political change.

Each clash left the Brotherhood in more ideological and organizational disarray. The first clash induced factional rifts and splits, particularly between its military faction and its more pragmatic faction. This split continued to affect the Brotherhood's decision-making structure after 1952 and allowed the military faction to make its attempt on the life of Nasser.[3] The second clash resulted in the trial of the Brotherhood's high command. Six leaders were executed, several thousands of its members were imprisoned, and thousands more fled to Saudi Arabia, the Gulf states, Europe, and the United States.

The events of 1965, which included the arrest of Sayyid Qutb, the great Brotherhood ideologue,[4] produced far-reaching changes. First, there was a growing tendency among some members, particularly the young, to advocate all-out violence as the means for socio-political change, rather than the selective and limited violence that had formerly been used. Second, Brotherhood leaders and members were increasingly inclined to see the society in terms of a stark division between what is Islamic and what is un-Islamic. This attitude contradicted the traditional Brotherhood approach of conceptualizing the society as Islamic to a greater or lesser degree. Third, the organizational and financial autonomy of the Brotherhood began to erode. Now, ideological sources from

Pakistan—principally, the writings of Abul-Ala Maududi—came to shape the views and conduct of some Brotherhood members, while the influence of al-Banna's ideas declined. Moreover, finances were linked, for the first time in the history of the Brotherhood, to sources outside Egypt. Fourth, the membership profile changed, with more socially marginalized young people drawn in. These young members were selected not because of their potential professional future as had been the standard practice previously, but because of their inclination to withdraw from society and attack it.

The 1970s were to inspire the growth of other movements such as the Jam'iyyat al-Takfir wa'l-Hijra (Society of Excommunication and Emigration). More radical in outlook, they were influenced by the evolution in Brotherhood thinking, the military defeat of the 1967 war, the crisis in political legitimacy with Anwar Sadat's rise to power in 1971, and his manipulation of the Islamic movement for his own political purposes. These new groups contested the Brotherhood's right to champion the Islamic cause and came to regard themselves as the only true Muslims.

After many of its members were released from prison in the early 1970s, the Brotherhood attempted to regain its primacy by adopting radical postures on selected external issues such as the Arab-Israeli conflict and the Soviet invasion of Afghanistan; and by projecting itself as the group best suited to interpret Islam and advance implementation of the *Shari'a* (Islamic law). Not surprisingly, this strategy led to hostile relations with the radicals even as it limited the Brotherhood's affinity with the state, particularly over international Islamic issues.

Sadat's designs for full manipulation of the Islamic currents proved in practice to be unrealistic. By the end of the 1970s both radicals and moderates of the Islamic movement were once again imprisoned. Sadat was assassinated in 1981 by an Islamist officer with lower middle class origins and an affiliation with a radical organization, Tanzim al-Jihad (The Jihad Organization). Under Sadat's successor,

Hosni Mubarak, the Islamic movement was affected by the regime's policy of democratic accommodation and increased tolerance of diverse political perspectives, its dismantling of the Jihad Organization, the Iran-Iraq war, and the hoped-for return of Egypt to the Arab fold. In particular, the Muslim Brotherhood attempted to control the professional and university student associations at the decision-making levels. It also formally allied itself with legal political parties and participated in the elections of 1984 and 1987.

As a result of these political and international developments, the concerns of the Islamic groups expanded beyond the question of the Islamic legitimacy of the Egyptian regime, which had been the overriding challenge of the 1970s. Now the concern included the threats against the Islamic world coming from both inside and outside of it. On such international issues the Brotherhood held to its more radical stand.[5] It rejected the idea of an international peace conference on the Arab-Israeli conflict and criticized peace overtures by the Palestine Liberation Organization in the 1980s. The Brotherhood continued to support the Islamic resistance in Afghanistan financially and with medical and social assistance to Afghan refugees. The radical Islamic groups in Egypt even sent their own members to fight in the resistance. After a period of hesitation over the revolution in Iran, the Brotherhood resolved to support (Sunni) Iraq in its war against (Shi'ite) Iran. Moreover, it celebrated the implementation of the Shari'a in Sudan but quarreled with the Sudanese Islamic movement (basically a Muslim Brotherhood movement) because of its relative independence of the Egyptian Brotherhood.

As for the radical Islamic current, it expanded to include a legal political party, the Labor Party.[6] Intending to channel Islamic activism into a loyal opposition party, President Sadat had in fact been one of the founders of the party in 1978. At first the party espoused a nationalistic socialist ideology under the name of the Socialist Labor Party. From the very beginning the party understood and defined nationalism in

Islamic rather than secular terms. However, the Islamic dimension did not dominate party ideology until 1985, when the word "Socialist" was dropped from the party name. Apparently the change in ideological emphasis was prompted by the need to regain popularity among voters who had moved into the Islamic current and had voted the "Socialist" Labor Party out of Parliament (People's Assembly, Majlis al-Sha'b) entirely in the 1984 elections. In 1987 the renamed Labor Party (Hizb al-'Amal) formed a coalition with the Muslim Brotherhood that came to be known as the Islamic Alliance. The Alliance promptly won sixty seats and became the leader of the opposition in Parliament.

The Labor Party is based in the professional segments of the middle class and seeks to lead and influence the intellectual circles of Egyptian society. It does not enjoy a wide base of support among the lower classes in urban centers but is popular among university students and urban professionals. It has brought the concerns about Egypt's relations with the larger Islamic world and the West to the top of the Islamic political agenda.

With regard to the Jihad Organization, identified in the early 1980s with the assassination of Sadat and with the notion that the ruler is "the infidel" rather than the society as a whole, a number of Jihadist Jama'at or "Associations" emerged during the period 1985–90 as the leading champion of the use of agitation and violence against the state. Nevertheless, some of these associations, particularly in Upper Egypt, forged an alliance of convenience with local authorities. The government has moved from a position of outright confrontation with these groups to one of cooptation and isolation in order to control their more violent elements.

On the eve of the Gulf crisis, the Islamic movement in Egypt was struggling with the question of how the challenges of rapid international change could be integrated with a fundamentalist Islamic agenda. Three competing views on the most desirable relationship between Islam and international change divided the movement.[7] The first view held that the self-conscious internationalization of the Egyptian Islamic movement would open more opportunities for Islamic activists to influence the direction of change, particularly on the Arab regional level. Proponents of this view advanced the need for regional cooperation among Islamic movements in the Arab world. The second view saw internationalism as placing additional constraints upon the Islamic movement. Proponents of this view preferred to restrict their radicalism to the domestic or regional level of operations. The third view saw the changes in the international scene as determined by a Western Christian conspiracy against the Islamic world. This conspiracy theory demanded an extreme response of Muslims: they had either to confront Western domination vigorously or resign themselves to it totally.

Interpretations of the Gulf Crisis

The Labor Party

Since it adopted Islam as an ideology for political and national renewal during the parliamentary elections of 1987, the Labor Party has been active in detailing its vision according to an Islamic framework and mobilizing public opinion behind it. It has especially emphasized the role that Islam should play in international leadership and, specifically, in promoting regional cooperation and conflict resolution. The contention is that Islam as a cultural system, and individual Islamic countries, have sufficient normative and material capabilities to influence the world and shape its destiny. The party's position on the Gulf crisis, as articulated in articles by Abd al-Hussein, the editor of its newspaper, *Al-Sha'b (The People),* and statements by Ibrahim Shukri, its chairman, reflected this general framework.[8]

The party opposed, but did not condemn, the Iraqi invasion of Kuwait, because it believed that any crisis among

115

Islamic countries should be solved through Islamic mediation. From this perspective, condemnation would not have helped mediation to succeed. In addition, it believed that Iraq had legitimate cause to complain about Kuwait. It did not hide its belief that Kuwait was an effective instrument in larger Western schemes designed to thwart Arab Muslim efforts to regain control of their resources, particularly oil. In this sense it distinguished between legitimate Iraqi grievances against Kuwait and the illegitimate invasion of Kuwait as a way to redress those grievances.

Before the war began on 17 January 1991, however, the party was inclined to encourage Iraq to go to war against the United States, and, once it began, the party differentiated between the Iraqi war efforts, which were legitimate, and American war efforts, which were illegitimate. This stand was consistent with the party's view of the United States as the major obstacle to not only the liberation of the Third World, but also and more importantly the establishment of an Islamic state that would unify the Arab Muslim people. From this perspective, the party condemned the international alliance on the grounds that it aimed to destroy or undermine the strategic potential of the military in Muslim Arab nations in order to establish an American-Israeli hegemony in the region. Standing against the alliance and with Iraq was thus to strike a blow for Arab Muslim dignity and to enhance the potential for a new Arab Muslim identity and self-reliance to emerge.

Following from this position, the Labor Party criticized the official Egyptian military participation in the alliance against Iraq. The Egyptian government had revealed its dependence on the United States and the utter irrationality of its foreign and security policies. It had been misled by the Americans, whose real aim was to destroy Iraq. In allowing itself to be manipulated by the United States, the government damaged Egyptian interests in the Arab world. National security was threatened by Israel, not Iraq, and therefore standing against Iraq contributed to the strength of Egypt's enemy. Furthermore, Egypt made its stand without taking into consideration the large number of Egyptians working in Iraq, or ensuring American approval of the Egyptian demand for the de-nuclearization of Israel as a trade-off for limitations in Iraqi military potential. Nor did the Egyptian government link the Egyptian military contribution to a greater role for Egypt in the postwar period.

The Soviet Union had been no better than the United States in the crisis, according to the Labor Party. The war in fact proved that the Soviet Union was in a tacit alliance with the Americans. The party newspaper severely criticized the role of the Soviets in the negotiations with Iraq before the ground offensive began on 25 February 1991. Describing this role as sinister, it charged that the Soviets had portrayed Iraq as a defeated country and thus caused a decline in the morale of the Iraqi military. It linked Soviet involvement in this crisis with what is believed among many Arab historians of the Arab-Israeli conflict to have been the Soviet role in deceiving Nasser in 1967.

The party described the international alliance as crusaders against the values of Islam and Arabism, and referred to many American strategic decision-makers and the new Soviet Foreign Minister as Jews. It also used inflammatory language against the United States and spoke of Iraq in laudatory terms. The party ridiculed the official Egyptian efforts in supporting the alliance, and explained the passive support of the Egyptian public for efforts to stop the war as a result of the false consciousness created by official propaganda. Finally, the United States and Europe had waged war on Iraq—and before that, encouraged war between Iran and Iraq—in order to prevent Islam from emerging as an effective international force. Iraqi resistance to the allied military assault was depicted as a major stimulus to Islamic rebirth in the region.

The impact of this rhetoric upon the Egyptian public was, however, muted by the fact that the party did not choose to risk violating martial law in Egypt, which makes any public action by parties pending upon the approval of the Ministry of the Interior. Thus the suggestive and aggressive terminology appeared only in the party newspaper and during meetings inside party headquarters.

The Muslim Brotherhood

The Brotherhood was the first among the Egyptian political forces and parties to condemn the Iraqi invasion of Kuwait. Hours after the invasion, it called upon Iraq to withdraw its forces. However, this initial position evolved with the development of the crisis and was reflected in the statements of the General Guide, Muhammad Hamid Abul Nasser, and two leading Brotherhood figures, Ma'mun al-Hudaibi and Mustafa Mashhur. Once Iraq began to rely heavily on Islamic propaganda and Saddam began to project himself as a reborn Muslim, they came to see the invasion as an expression of hostility between two Islamic forces. They continued to condemn the invasion and ask for Iraqi withdrawal, however now within the context of settling the conflict of interests between Iraq and Kuwait. When Egypt and the Gulf states called on friendly foreign military forces to help counter the Iraqi threat to Saudi territorial integrity and to liberate Kuwait, the Brotherhood saw this as an expression of the feuds among the leaders of the Arab world and the beginning of a major threat to the integrity of the Islamic *umma* (pan-Islamic community).

With the heavy American military presence in the Gulf, the Brotherhood began to voice fears that it would only benefit Israel, the historic enemy of the Arabs and Muslims, and revive the legacy of the Crusades. It demanded that the principles of international legitimacy be applied to Israel, as they were applied in the Gulf. After the outbreak of the war, it called for a ceasefire because the war only served America's interests in preserving its control over oil. It called for the withdrawal of the Egyptian military forces from the Gulf because of the change in the goals that these forces were sent to fulfill. Whereas Egyptians had been commissioned to defend Saudi Arabia, the war in the Gulf now meant the destruction of Iraq. The Egyptian government should also put an end to its propaganda campaign against Iraq and offer anti-war forces the chance to explain their views in the media.

Starting from a position of condemnation of the Iraqi invasion of Kuwait, the Brotherhood ended with virtual support for the governing regime in Baghdad. The growing involvement of the United States accounted for this change. Indeed, the Brotherhood has long viewed the United States with suspicion, arguing that it has consolidated its influence over world affairs as its control of the United Nations Security Council clearly demonstrates. What is more, the United States and Zionism could not have been successful in penetrating the Islamic world and subjecting it to their will without the help of authoritarian regimes in the Arab world. Struggling against American imperialism and Zionism thus means struggling against these political regimes as well.

The massive air bombardment of Iraq and the preparation for the ground offensive led the Brotherhood to join other Muslim groups in their second declaration from Pakistan on 17 February 1991, in which the war was depicted as an assault against Islam and its civilization. The Brotherhood approved the declaration's description of the Western-led coalition as an alliance of infidels led by the United States and Zionism, and linked resistance to this war with the Islamic resistance in Palestine, Afghanistan, and Kashmir. The declaration called for transcending existing borders because they are part and parcel of the colonial legacy and against the interest of the Islamic umma and stressed the need for an immediate unification of Islamic groups and peoples. Finally, it urged the Muslim people to struggle for their rights to political participation.

The Islamic Jama'at

The basic view of the majority of the Jama'at on the Gulf crisis was twofold: first, the Gulf crisis was a manifestation of a larger Western conspiracy to control the Islamic countries and humiliate Muslims; and second, Saddam Hussein was part of this conspiracy because of his aggression not only against Kuwait, but also against the Islamic movement in his country and the Islamic revolution in Iran. Based on this perspective, the crisis and the war were a conflict among conspirators within a larger Western conspiracy. As for Kuwait, the Jama'at viewed it as part of the Western scheme and an infidel country because it did not apply the Shari'a.

Within this general perspective, the Jama'at differed among themselves in emphasis. For example, Abbud al-Latif Hasan al-Zumur, the imprisoned military leader of the Jihad Organization, was quoted as warning that one of the American objectives of the war was to reshape the Arab-Islamic mind to accommodate Western supremacy in the region and to accept humiliation.[9] Umar Abd al-Rahman, the head of the Islamic Jihad Jama'a, was quoted from his self-imposed exile in the United States as saying that a Muslim killed in a war that was not fought for the word of God could not be considered a Muslim martyr.[10] It should be noted, however, that neither al-Zumur nor Abd Rahman called for jihad on behalf of Iraq. We further notice this neglect in a statement made by Ahmad al-Mahalawi,[11] a radical preacher, who has always railed against the continuing Western hegemony over the Arab world. He advanced the proposition that the Gulf crisis should be seen as part of a long chain of crises in the region which has enabled the West to consolidate its hegemony. In order to overthrow this hegemony, the whole Arab-Islamic environment should be changed and a new generation of believers created.

A minority of the Jama'at, such as the one in Bani-Suef in Upper Egypt, saw the Gulf crisis in a different light.[12] They viewed the conflict as between, on the one hand, the United

States, representing the great Satan, and its followers in the Arab Muslim world, including Saudi Arabia; and, on the other, Islam. They thus called for a jihad on behalf of Iraq.

Islamic Political Action During the Crisis

Of course ideological stands are not the only determining factor in the making of Islamic political actions. The political dynamics of the society, rules of the game, and state policies are also critical and constraining variables. The particular dilemma of the Islamic movements in acting in response to the Gulf crisis emanated from two sources. The first was their limited political experience in influencing international events. Since the foundation of the Muslim Brotherhood over sixty years ago, the various streams of the Islamic movement have accumulated significant experience in influencing government behavior on domestic issues through numerous means, including protests, propaganda, financial manipulation of bank deposits, and violence. But the Gulf crisis presented an international rather than a domestic opportunity, at least in the understanding of the Islamic fundamentalists. And, despite a broadening of the horizons of the Islamic movement in the 1980s, the fundamentalists had not acquired sufficient international experience or influence. In fact, they were still attempting to carve a niche in Arab politics when the Gulf crisis erupted. How, then, could existing channels of fundamentalist influence be appropriated in pursuit of a goal for which they were not developed? This was the first basic challenge for the Islamic activists.

The second source of the Islamic movement's dilemma in Egypt during the Gulf crisis was the need to operate within the parameters of Egyptian politics itself. Given the continuing hegemony of the Egyptian government, the domestic successes of the Islamic movement, such as they were, had been predicated upon the rules of the game of "liberalized" Egyptian politics. The Islamic groups had become "normalized" to a considerable extent by virtue of their participation in the structures of domestic politics. This participation in quasi-democratic structures depended upon an implicit social contract between the Islamic groups and the government that required of both parties a degree of accommodation.

Yet the Gulf crisis jeopardized the foundations of this "policy of accommodation" by rekindling internationalist ambitions among Islamic political leaders. The ambition to champion the cause of the pan-Islamic movement involved the Egyptian fundamentalists in a dynamic process that threatened their domestic status. The processes of normalization and accommodation were based, for example, upon the acceptance of the principle that foreign policy issues belong properly in the realm of national security and thus come under the jurisdiction and sovereignty of the state. Accordingly, the state prohibits political parties from interfering in foreign policy matters. Yet internationalization required of the Islamic movement, especially the Muslim Brotherhood, a violation of the principle of non-interference in foreign policy including, among other things, a prominent stance in opposition to Egyptian participation in the allied coalition.

The dilemma of the Islamic groups in Egypt in a time of international crisis was therefore acute. Gaining an advantage by playing by the rules of domestic politics would cast doubts on their leadership of the Islamic umma (which is not contained by nation-state boundaries). But pursuing the path of bold leadership of the umma would transform their hard-won domestic role by violating the social contract according to which they have been allowed to operate. To make matters worse, a half-hearted commitment to both sets of rules at the same time would mean the loss of influence in the domestic and international arenas alike. The Gulf crisis thus put the Islamic groups, at least in the short term, in a "no-win" situation to the Islamic movement. The political responses of the Labor Party and the Muslim Brotherhood reflected the tenuousness of this position.

The Labor Party

The strategy of the Labor Party for advancing its vision consists of mobilizational techniques (the attempt to reach out to different groups and strata in the society with specific emphasis upon recruitment of intellectuals and middle-class professionals); oppositional actions (the effort to be seen as the focal point of opposition against the government); and, consensus-building actions (the effort to find common ground with the different forces within Egypt and ensure that its Islamic vision is not antagonistic to either Copts or secular modernists). Consensus-building is the strategy with direct international implications, as it seeks to mediate, particularly at the popular level, between Egypt and Libya, Egypt and Sudan, and Iraq and Iran.

In the Gulf crisis, the Labor Party followed this three-part strategy. It made it clear that it sought to mediate the Iraq-Kuwait conflict, by which it meant efforts to induce Iraq to withdraw its forces from Kuwait. However, the party found in this an opportunity to enhance its status among the Islamic groups and movements in the Muslim world.

The first mediation efforts were made in cooperation with the Muslim Brotherhood. Muslim Brothers were members of a 13-man delegation representing Islamic movements across the Islamic world, which travelled in September 1990 to Jordan, Saudi Arabia, Iraq, and Iran. Although these efforts did not produce the hoped-for result of Iraqi withdrawal, the party continued its efforts in cooperation with representatives of other Islamic movements. Another visit to Jordan, Yemen, Iran, Iraq, and Syria was initiated in December 1990. During these visits and subsequent ones, the party advocated the avoidance of war, Iraqi withdrawal linked to a settlement of the conflicting interests of Iraq and Kuwait, the right of Kuwaitis to manage their own domestic affairs, and resistance to American attempts to impose hegemony on the Arab world.

123

During those mediation efforts, Labor Party leaders failed to meet the Egyptian government, which apparently refused to see them. They had hoped to meet the Egyptian leadership in order to induce pressure on Saudi Arabia. This failure indicated political difficulties with the Egyptian regime and seemed to affect adversely their mediating efforts as well as their influence in the Egyptian political arena. For example, the party leadership was not invited to a meeting between the President and opposition leaders on the eve of the war.[13]

The Labor Party, in cooperation with all the major opposition parties except the leftist party, had boycotted the parliamentary elections of November 1990. The reasons for the boycott were not related to the Gulf crisis, but, in its propaganda campaign against the elections, the party linked the boycott to its stand against foreign forces in the Gulf.[14] In January 1990, it succeeded in building a front among political parties and forces that opposed the war. This front included the Left, but excluded the Wafd Party which supported the international alliance. The front chose Ibrahim Shukri, the Labor Party leader, as its official spokesman, and, in its first statement, it outlined the following tasks: putting an end to the American aggression; rejecting the participation of the Egyptian military forces in any offensive activities against Iraq; inviting citizens to sign petitions asking the Egyptian authorities to stop the American aggression and withdraw Egyptian military forces from Saudi Arabia; and forming a delegation headed by Ibrahim Shukri himself to visit foreign and Arab embassies in Cairo to express objections to the war.

The party's anti-war efforts were checked by the authorities with the arrest of the assistant to the General Secretary of the party, Magdi Ahmad Hussein, when he engaged in anti-war propaganda in a mosque. He was charged with inciting the people against the government, and, in exchange for his freedom, the party leadership had to promise tacitly that it would restrict its public activities among the masses. It opted to penetrate the Journalists'

Association by nominating the same man to a seat on the Association's Board. Before the Association elections of March 1991, the party ran a campaign based on its propaganda against the war, but Hussein failed to win enough votes.

The Muslim Brotherhood

The Brotherhood has conducted two major types of action since it adopted a policy of normalization with the state. The first has been the efforts of professionals in its membership to control their Association Governing Boards. The second has been working compliance with the rules of the political game in order to enhance its image as a moderate political force and its role as a power broker, particularly in parliamentary elections. Although the Brotherhood has been very cautious in taking stands against the government, it has had to balance its domestic constraints with those emanating from competition with Brotherhood-type forces in other Arab countries. The main competitor of the Egyptian Brotherhood has been the Sudanese Islamic movement, the National Islamic Front. These constraints have been further compounded by the radicalism of the Labor Party, the Brotherhood's partner in the Islamic alliance in Egypt. In the Gulf crisis, the balance of constraints was complicated even further by the involvement of Saudi Arabia and the Gulf emirates, its traditional regional patrons.

After condemning the invasion, the Brotherhood sought to mediate the crisis. As mentioned above, it participated in the effort that the Labor Party launched, but it was hesitant in the early stage of the crisis to use its institutional network of influence in the anti-war campaign. It did not let its cooperation with other political groups, whether in the alliance against the parliamentary elections of November 1990 or against the war, sway this decision.

Only with the massive destruction of Iraq as a result of the air war did the Brotherhood begin to exploit its institutional influence over the university student and professional associations. A week after the beginning of the war, the Brotherhood members of the Board of the Journalists' Association called for a sit-in for five hours to object to American aggression, demand the withdrawal of Egyptian military forces from the Gulf, and protest against the arrest of Magdi Ahmad Hussein. The sit-in did not attract a large audience, but was adequate to demonstrate Brotherhood influence, particularly since the Journalists' Association had not been one of its strongholds. In February, the Brotherhood was largely responsible for three major anti-war protests involving professionals and students: a major meeting at Cairo University Professors' Club; a popular gathering in the Medical Doctors' Association; and large student demonstrations in Cairo and Mansoura Universities.[15]

Conclusion: Two Types of Uncertainty

The Gulf crisis presented a great challenge to the Islamic movement in Egypt. This challenge was the first direct confrontation with the West since the fall of the Ottoman empire. Thereafter, most of the confrontations of the Islamic movements, except in Algeria before independence, and minor clashes with Israel in 1948 and during the *intifada,* were with national regimes accused of being proxies for the West. The Iran-Iraq war indicated dissension in the Islamic umma but did not involve direct confrontation with the West. Iraq's Islamic propaganda and the Saudis' request for Western military protection against Iraq thus made the confrontation of 1990–91 both unique and complex.

The specific nature of the crisis and its evolution into war bred two types of uncertainty in the Islamic movement in Egypt. The first uncertainty was over definition. This was the product of the use of Islamic terminology to justify the positions of both Iraq on one side, and Saudi Arabia and its Arab Muslim allies on the other. Because the Islamic movement has been transformed into a transnational actor and has acquired a degree of instrumentality in the foreign policies of the Arab Muslim states, there is now no clear and exact meaning for such terms as jihad and *kuffar* (unbelievers). These two major terms suggest specific connotations in the realm of domestic politics; in the international arena, however, they lose these specifications without acquiring uncontested and exact new meanings. They can be used to justify an action and its opposing action.

This uncertainty was clearly present in the response of the Labor Party and the Muslim Brotherhood. Both called for jihad, yet their positions differed. The Labor Party was more inclined to launch it against the Arab parties involved in the international alliance, including Saudi Arabia, whereas the Brotherhood was careful not to push the term too far so as to include Saudi Arabia or to instigate concrete actions against the forces of the alliance. The Brotherhood's changing position over time indicated the weakness of its theoretical bases for judgment. A posture of selective radicalism on the issues of the crisis and the war made it appear that the Brotherhood's overall frame of reference was rather vague and shallow. The no-position posture of the majority of the Jama'at also reflected a breakdown in consensus among the Islamic groups and a consequent diffidence in the absence of this consensus.

The second uncertainty was over strategy. The Gulf crisis introduced new doubts into the plans of the Islamic groups for establishing Islamic law and Islamic government at home. From the Islamists' perspective, strategies of moderation and normalization, which had enabled them during the last ten years under Mubarak to enhance their appeal among the public and consolidate their base of power among professionals, limited their ability to translate their radical stands on the war—a foreign policy issue—into concrete domestic actions against the government. The Brotherhood in particular was beset by doubts. It feared that the spill-over of its radical stand on the war into domestic politics might give the government the opportunity to act against it and reduce its margin of freedom. And yet it was also concerned that if it did not oppose the government on the war, it would destroy any chance of leading the Islamic movement in the Arab world and at home. Further hesitation ensued as a result of the general public's support of the war effort to compel Iraq to withdraw from Kuwait. The Islamists could not pursue an aggressive, radical, systematic anti-war mobilization program at home in this climate lest its appeal among the public be endangered. These multiple and contradictory considerations left the Brotherhood without a coherent over-all strategy.

These two uncertainties served to paralyze the Brotherhood and the Labor Party in the aftermath of the war; they did not, for example, adopt a coherent or clear stand regarding the Kurdish and Shi'ite revolts against the Iraqi government in March and April. Their general support for Iraq during the war had crippled their ability to mobilize support for the Kurdish revolt or to condemn Iraqi oppression. Further, their support of Iraq against Iran during the Iran-Iraq war, and their tacit condemnation of Iran for failing to assist Iraq against the United States, made it difficult for them to perceive the Shi'ite revolt in southern Iraq as an Islamic revolt worthy of international Islamic support.

The Gulf crisis may well ultimately prove fatal to the international aspirations of the current Islamic wave in Egypt. In the short term, at least, the Islamic alternative for the Arab world seems to have lost its momentum as a result of the crisis. By demonstrating its inability to act as an international force, the Islamic movement may have doomed itself to act in the future only as a limited local force. On the other hand, if major mishaps occur in the region at the hands of the West, and/or if the Egyptian government changes its general pro-Western policies under the pressures of domestic economic and political constraints, the Islamic groups in Egypt could regain a significant measure of the mobilizational capabilities that were diminished as a result of the Gulf crisis.

Endnotes to Chapter 6

1. For a full account of the Islamic movement after 1952 within the context of the development of the political system, see Gehad Auda, "The Normalization of the Islamic Movement in Egypt," in Martin E. Marty and R. Scott Appleby, eds., *Accounting for Fundamentalisms: The Dynamic Character of Movements* (Chicago: University of Chicago Press, forthcoming).

2. For a history of the Muslim Brotherhood, see Richard P. Mitchell, *The Society of the Muslim Brothers* (London: Oxford University Press, 1969). For another account written by a member of the Muslim Brotherhood see Muhamad Abd al-Halim, *Al-Ikhwan al-Muslimun (The Muslim Brothers)*, 3 vols. (Alexandria, 1979).

3. For an account of the first clash between the government and the Muslim Brotherhood in 1948, see Tariq al-Bishri, *Al-Haraka al-Siyasiyya fi Misr, 1945–1952 (The Political Movement in Egypt, 1945–1952)*, second edition, (Cairo: Dar al-Shuruq, 1983). For the assassination of Hasan al-Banna by the government, see an account based on the British archives: Muhsin Muhammad, *Min Qatal Hasan al-Banna? (Who Killed Hasan al-Banna?)* (Cairo, 1987). For the 1954 attempt on Nasser's life see: Abd al-Azim Ramadan, *Al-Ikhwan al-Muslimun wa'l-Tanzim al-Khass (The Muslim Brotherhood and the Special Apparatus)* (Cairo, 1978).

4. For an analysis of Qutb's intellectual contribution to the Islamic fundamentalist understanding of the world, see Leonard Binder, *Islamic Liberalism* (Chicago: The University of Chicago Press, 1988), pp. 170–205. Also see Emmanuel Sivan, *Radical Islam: Medieval Theology and Modern Politics* (New Haven: Yale University Press, 1985), pp. 16–117.

5. See the Brotherhood's monthly *al-Da'wa (The Call)*, issues of December 1977 to April 1981. On the Muslim Brotherhood's understanding of Islamic da'wa from an international perspective, see Anwar al-Gendi, *Tariq al-Da'wa al-Islamiyya (The Road of Islamic Da'wa)* (Cairo, 1987).

6. The Arabic name of this party is Hizb al-'Amal which can be translated either as "Action Party" or "Labor Party." Following previous English translations the editor of this volume has translated it as "Labor Party."

7. For the Muslim Brotherhood and 1987 elections see Saad Eddin Ibrahim, "Egypt's Islamic Activism in the 1980s," *Third World Quarterly* 10 (2) (April 1988): 644–49.

8. See *al-Sha'b (The People)*, 6 August 1990 to 26 February 1991.

9. Ibid., 19 February 1991.

10. Ibid., 26 February 1991.

11. Ibid., 15 January 1991.

12. For more radical groups and their stand on the war see *Ruz al-Yusuf*, 25 February 1991. The report named the radical Islamic group in Bani-Suef which advocated the stand against the government on the war issue and threatened the peace and order as a Jihadist group affiliated with the Islamic Jihad Jama'a. It explained its radicalism on the issue of war in terms of the local rifts among Islamic groups in Bani-Suef and the absence of Umar Abd al-Rahman in his self-imposed exile in the United States.

13. The meeting was in the evening of 16 January 1991 and was attended by every party leader in Egypt except those of the Left, because he was out of the country visiting Libya, and the Labor Party, who was not invited.

14. On the 1990 parliamentary elections, see Gehad Auda, "Egypt's Uneasy Party Politics," *Journal of Democracy* 2 (2) (Spring 1991): 70–78. Also see the reasons for the Muslim Brotherhood's boycott of the elections, which did not include opposition to the government position on the war, as stated by Esam al-Erian, a leading young member of the Brothers in *Akhar Sa'a (Another Hour)*, 24 October 1990. Also see the statement by the General Guide of the Brothers rejecting the results of the elections on grounds not related to the Gulf crisis in *Liwa' al-Islam (The Standard of Islam)*, 17 January 1991.

15. See an account of the demonstration in *Sawt al-Sha'b (Voice of the People)*, 2 March 1991.

7

A TRIAL OF STRENGTH: ALGERIAN ISLAMISM

Hugh Roberts

The Gulf crisis complicated Algerian politics, radicalized Algerian public opinion, and united, at least for the duration, the Algerian nation. By doing all of these things, it also forced a significant development of the Islamic movement in Algeria and indirectly encouraged the government of Prime Minister Mouloud Hamrouche to overreach itself.

The crisis complicated the political situation by disrupting the pre-existing timetable for the protracted transition to democracy in Algeria, obliging the authorities to postpone the long-awaited elections for the National Popular Assembly. These were originally expected to take place before the end of 1990, then scheduled for the first quarter of 1991, then postponed once again with the onset of the war. While waiting for these elections, Algeria had to continue to make do with a government which lacked democratic legitimacy and so real authority. The capacity of the Hamrouche government to promote economic reforms (beyond the superficial business of introducing new legislation) or even simply to maintain order was severely limited, and the economic and social crisis in the country deepened.

The Gulf crisis also transformed the terms of political debate in the country. Before the crisis, public debate was entirely concentrated on internal matters and was structured by four major political rivalries. First, a new political force, popular Islamism, was represented principally but not ex-

131

clusively by the Islamic Salvation Front (Front Islamique du Salut, FIS), which triumphed in the local and regional elections on 12 June 1990. The Islamists set themselves against the old nationalist elite represented by the ruling party, the National Liberation Front (Front de Liberation National, FLN), which ran a poor second in the June elections. Second, popular Islamism also pitted itself against the other opposition parties, which included modernist, liberal-democratic, social democratic, Marxist and in some cases secularist parties. This particular rivalry was focused on such matters as segregation of the sexes, the kind of appropriate dress, and, more generally, the place of religion in public life. A third rivalry existed between supporters of radical economic reform, who called for the privatization of the public sector and the opening of the economy to foreign investment, and defenders of the public sector and critics of excessively rapid or far-reaching economic liberalization. This conflict has particularly pitted President Chadli, former Prime Minister Hamrouche, and their supporters against the "old guard" of the FLN. Fourth, supporters of a rigorously Arab-Muslim conception of the national culture, who advocate rapid Arabization at the expense of the French language as part of a continuing program of "cultural de-colonization," were pitted against those forces who have a vested interest in continuing close ties with France. These included the modernist intelligentsia and the largest Berber-speaking population, the Kabyles.

After 2 August 1990, the Gulf crisis transcended all of these political divisions, at least temporarily, by distracting Algerian public opinion from domestic preoccupations, by mobilizing nationalist, anti-Western (and especially anti-French) sentiments, and by triggering a vigorous reflex of solidarity with a fellow Arab state. It thereby resurrected attitudes which underlay the original national revolution in Algeria and which had appeared before 2 August to have been definitively superseded with the decline of the FLN and the simultaneous advent of popular Islamism on the one hand

and political pluralism on the other. In doing so, it radicalized the international outlook of the younger generation and helped bridge the gap that had opened between those Algerians who remembered or took part in the national revolution and those born since independence—a generation gap which had been grist to the Islamists' mill and potentially fatal to the FLN.

These consequences of the Gulf crisis owed little to the activities of the Algerian Islamist movement. It is not the case that popular feeling in Algeria over the Gulf crisis was whipped up by the Islamists. Rather, this feeling was a largely spontaneous reaction to the evolution of the crisis itself, and obliged the Islamists to modify their positions very considerably in order to stay in touch with their popular constituency.

Islamist Organizations in Algeria

The Algerian Islamist movement grew vertiginously after the liberalization of the country's constitution in February 1989 following the traumatic riots of October 1988. Before that date, the movement was fluid and nebulous in form and, while capable of mobilizing thousands of supporters on occasions during the 1980s, it had been largely confined to the fringe of Algerian public life.[1]

With the introduction of political pluralism, however, the Islamist movement began to expand its popular constituency and to set much of the agenda of public debate. After February 1989 the movement crystallized into a number of distinct organizations, including both political parties and Islamic associations with religious and sociocultural rather than political objectives. Prior to the Algerian crisis of May–June 1991 (see below), the main Islamist parties were the FIS, the Movement for an Islamic Society, known by its Arabic initials as HAMAS, and the Movement of the Islamic Renaissance (Mouvement de la Nahda Islamique, MNI).

To these may be added the League of the Islamic Call (Rabitat al-Da'wa al-Islamiyya) and a number of smaller parties espousing Islamist positions. Very little solid information is at present available about these smaller groups, however, and their current significance does not warrant further consideration of them in the restricted compass of this chapter. Much better known, and more significant, is the party led by former President Ahmad Ben Bella, the Movement for Democracy in Algeria (Mouvement pour la Démocratie en Algérie, MDA), founded in 1984. But the MDA, while stressing its commitment to Islamic values, has strongly criticized the Islamist movement for its tendency to intolerance and other excesses,[2] and it is not properly described as an Islamic fundamentalist party.

The FIS

The FIS (al-Jabha al-Islamiyya li-Inqadh) is the largest and most influential Islamist party at this writing. Founded in 1989 and legalized in September of that year, it quickly emerged as a major force capable of mobilizing large numbers of supporters and possessing an impressive nationwide organization and appeal.[3] In June 1990, it took control of the Popular Assemblies in 32 of Algeria's 48 *wilayat* (provinces) and in 853 out of the 1,539 communes, winning a landslide majority in virtually all the major cities in particular.

Although official statistics were somewhat confused, the FIS was generally agreed to have received at least 54 percent of the vote on a 65 percent poll, giving it some 33.73 percent of the total electorate.[4] This was nearly twice the share of the FLN (17.49 percent), which came second with 6 provinces and 487 communes.[5] However, these figures may be a misleading guide since neither Ben Bella's MDA nor the other major Islamist movements active in 1991 contested the June 1990 elections. Should National Assembly elections be held in 1991 with the FIS fielding candidates, other Islamic parties will likely attract some voters who supported the FIS in 1990.

The FIS has supported the government's policy of liberalizing the economy but, like Hamas, the MNI, and Rabita, it is first and foremost a fundamentalist movement in that it seeks to reconstitute the Algerian polity on the basis of Islamic law (the *Shari'a)* and the Islamic notion of consultation *(shura)* in place of Western conceptions of pluralism and representative democracy. It has differed from the other movements in three main respects.

First, it has placed more emphasis on the capture of political power as the prerequisite of the reform of society on Islamic lines. It thus may be considered more "revolutionary" than its rivals, although it has so far been willing to operate within the framework of the 1989 constitution while reserving the right to state its principled objections to this constitution as un-Islamic. Second, it has been by far the most populist of the Islamist movements in its political style and strategy; and its discourse remains, at this writing, correspondingly strikingly shallow or "thin" in intellectual and doctrinal content. Finally, its populism and doctrinal eclecticism, while endowing it with a greater mobilizational power than other groups possess, have obliged it to accommodate a far greater degree of social and political heterogeneity within its ranks, and to articulate this diversity through a curiously bi-cephalous leadership.

At the top of the FIS is a Consultative Council (Majlis al-Shura), whose membership is veiled in secrecy. But it probably includes Hachemi Sahnouni, an *imam* in Algiers, and Ben Azzouz Zebda, editor of the FIS's newspaper, *Al-Munqidh (The Savior).*[6] More is known of the group's two main leaders, Professor Abassi Madani (born 1931) and Shaikh Ali Belhadj (born 1954). Madani[7] was a founder-member of the FLN in 1954 and spent most of the war in prison. He became a university teacher after Independence and subsequently obtained a doctorate from the Institute of Education at the University of London in the mid-1970s. Married to an Englishwoman, he personifies in all other respects the middle class, middle-aged, and pragmatic element within the FIS, and seeks to present a reassuringly flexible and reasonable image of the movement. Shaikh Ali Belhadj (born 1954), the imam of the al-Sunna mosque in the popular quarter of Bab el-Oued in Algiers, personifies the younger generation of the FIS, with a powerful appeal to deprived and frustrated urban youth; while Madani is conciliatory, Belhadj tends to be inflammatory and intransigent. It is doubtful, however, that the contrast between Madani and Belhadj reflects a fundamental disagreement instead of a manageable diversity within the FIS; rather, it appears that its leaders have deliberately played on multiple registers in order to accommodate several audiences, and are consciously sustaining an intelligent double-act.

HAMAS

The Movement for an Islamic Society, whose transliterated Arabic initials (Al-Haraka li-Mujtama' Islami) read HAMAS, is an evolution of a previously non-political Islamic association, Al-Irshad wa'l-Islah (Guidance and Reform) founded by Shaikh Mahfoud Nahnah. The new Hamas is a direct allusion to the principal Islamic movement involved in the *intifada* (uprising) in Gaza and the West Bank, which Jean-François Legrain discusses in his contribution to this volume. In outlook, Hamas can be situated in the tradition of the Muslim Brotherhood in the Middle East, but on the left wing of its spectrum.

Hamas was founded in December 1990 and is expected eventually to function as a political party. It may appeal to the more moderate and educated elements of the FIS's constituency. It is likely to adhere to the evolutionary perspective of its predecessor, Al-Irshad wa'l-Islah, which tended to emphasize the need to reform society through Islamic missionary activity before it would be possible to reform the state on Islamic lines. This view stands in direct contrast to the FIS's strategic perspective. Shaikh Nahnah has also expressed a more principled acceptance of the rules of the pluralist political game, in contrast to the FIS's purely tactical acceptance of these.

These differences did not prevent Nahnah from calling on his followers to vote for "Islamists" in the June 1990 elections, and so by implication for the FIS, but they probably explain the decision to found a rival party. This decision came two months after a major meeting on 20 September 1990, held at Nahnah's invitation and attended by over 300 local Islamic associations and several minor parties, which sought to unify the Islamic movement. This move was denounced as divisive by the FIS, which did not attend.

It is difficult to gauge the strength of Hamas at this stage. It has had a strong following in Blida, a large town some 30 miles south of Algiers where Shaikh Nahnah himself is based, it has held well-attended meetings in southern Algeria,[8] and it is reported to have expanded its audience throughout much of the Algérois (central Algeria). It is also reported to have a nationwide network of offices. Little information is available as yet concerning the Hamas leadership, other than that Shaikh Nahnah's deputy is Muhammad Bouslimani.

The MNI

The Movement of the Islamic Renaissance (Mouvement de la Nahda Islamique), led by Shaikh Abdullah Djaballah, also received legal approval in December 1990, although Shaikh Djaballah, who is in his 40s and a lawyer by training, claims that it has existed clandestinely since 1974. Like Hamas, the MNI is close in spirit and outlook to the Muslim Brotherhood, although not organizationally linked to it (any more than Hamas in Algeria appears to be). Unlike the FIS and Hamas, however, the MNI came out strongly against the government's liberal economic reforms, defending the public sector against further measures of privatization. It has therefore appeared to be trying to carve out a place for itself on the left wing of the Islamist movement. This could prove to be one of the FIS's unprotected flanks, given its prior support for economic liberalism.

The MNI does not yet appear to have much of a popular constituency, but is reported to have a substantial following among intellectuals, particularly in Constantine, the cultural capital of eastern Algeria, where Shaikh Djaballah is based, and to be far more coherent intellectually than the FIS. Shaikh Djaballah called for people to vote for the FIS in June 1990, but the MNI was expected to contest the National Assembly elections.

The Islamist Movement and the Gulf Crisis

Saddam Hussein's attempt to play the Islamic card, by declaring Iraq's resistance of the American-led coalition to be a *jihad* (holy struggle), was widely dismissed as bogus by Western commentators, in view of the secular doctrine of the Ba'th Party and its record of repressing Islamic movements in Iraq. Yet the same commentators credited to the influence of Islamic fundamentalist movements the fact that throughout the Maghreb, public opinion was massively pro-Iraqi, and Saddam Hussein himself became a popular hero. The implication is that these movements willingly acted as the conveyors of a spurious call to jihad, and that their popular audiences responded to this agitation in a wholly automatic and undiscriminating manner. This is a fundamental misunderstanding of what happened in the Maghreb in general and in Algeria in particular.

The Islamist movement has always been hostile to Ba'thism. Ba'thism has been the most developed expression of the secular pan-Arab idea transcending religious and social divisions in the Mashreq (the Arab East). In the Maghreb, unlike the Mashreq, Islam historically has been able to play a unifying role because of the absence of a serious Sunni-Shi'ite schism in North Africa and the virtually complete absence of indigenous Christians. It has been the main force transcending class divisions, the ethnic and linguistic differences between Arabs and Berbers, and the more recent cultural dichotomy between francisant and arabisant elements. Because of its unifying potential, Islam, in the puritanical and scripturalist version given it by the Islamic reform movement from the 1920s onwards,[9] has also been able to express the superseding of tribal parochialism in the new national community, as well as the cultural-nationalist refusal of French colonialism's assimilationist ambitions.

As a consequence of these, the opposition between pan-Arabism and pan-Islamism, so familiar to the Mashreq, has never been at home in the Maghreb, where pan-Arab sentiments have never had the connotations of secularism which they have had in Baghdad or Damascus. Pan-Islamic sentiments have, in the main, lacked the conservative, anti-popular, and pro-Western association which have characterized them in Riyadh and Islamabad. Thus the secularism intrinsic to Ba'thism has had little appeal to Algerians. In so far as a secularist tendency has emerged in Algeria, it has expressed the outlook of the liberal middle class intelligentsia whose political models are taken from the West, and who have been moving beyond, if not emphatically rejecting, both the pan-Arab and the social-revolutionary dimensions of the Algerian national revolution. Hence they have no use whatever for the Ba'thist version of these things.

The Algerian Islamist movement has taken its cue from the various brands of Islamic radicalism which have developed in the Mashreq and which have above all been in opposition to secular nationalist regimes. It has therefore adopted wholesale the prejudices of these movements against Ba'thist secularism, while also expressing the hostility to state socialism of many sectors of the Algerian public. Moreover, the Islamist movement in Algeria, and the FIS in particular, have had ties with Saudi Arabia and other Gulf monarchies, and have received substantial financial support from them. Notwithstanding temporary accommodations with Ba'thists, these monarchies have always considered Ba'thism to be their enemy in view of its explicitly antimonarchical and enthusiastically secularist perspectives.

For these reasons, Algerian Islamism has been consistently at odds in its political vision, worldview, and specific doctrines to Mashreqi Ba'thism. Neither ideology nor established self-interest inclined the FIS or the other Islamist movements to take Baghdad's side; quite the contrary. If they did so, this was in response to the evolution of Algerian public opinion as the crisis in the Gulf deepened.

Algeria was the first Arab state to condemn the invasion of Kuwait and, in doing so, the government was almost certainly in line with public opinion. But this position proved untenable once "Operation Desert Shield" began on 7 August. From that point on, the issue of Iraq's aggression against a fellow Arab state was overshadowed by the issue of the massive Western military presence on Arab soil, and the way in which the military deployment had preempted a possible Arab solution to the crisis. This development quickly placed the Islamist movement in an awkward position.

The FIS initially took a balanced, if not ambiguous, stand. Having condemned the Iraqi invasion early on, Madani stated at a meeting on 17 August that there was no reason for frontiers to exist between Muslim countries,[10] while Belhadj expressed a "plague on both your houses" attitude, referring sarcastically to the Iraqi leader as "Haddam" ("destroyed") and "Khaddam" ("manservant") before denouncing the Kuwaitis for having amassed colossal fortunes "against God's will."[11] He also suggested that the Holy Places, Mecca and Medina, belonged to all Muslims and that their management should be entrusted to the *ulama* (doctors of religious law)[12]—a not so veiled attack on the Saudi royal family.

The FIS maintained this attitude for several weeks. At a press conference in Algiers on 13 September 1990, Madani announced that the FIS was engaged in an effort at mediation and declared himself in favor of an Arab solution.[13] He and Ali Belhadj then went to the Gulf, visiting Baghdad twice and Jeddah three times in the hope of using their close links with the Saudis to good effect. This effort was unsuccessful, but the FIS initially persisted in its impartial posture, articulating the restiveness of its popular constituency without breaking the Saudi connection.

This balancing act first began to be undermined by Ben Bella's outflanking maneuver on his return to Algeria on 27 September 1990. He had also visited Baghdad and had no compunction about taking a vigorously pro-Iraqi position on the traditional basis of pan-Arab solidarity and hostility to Western imperialism.[14] This position initially appeared to be seriously out of touch with Algerian public opinion, but events were to show that Ben Bella was simply ahead of it.

Thereafter, as popular feelings grew in the countdown to war, the FIS was obliged to move steadily toward a pro-Iraqi position in order to stay abreast of its own popular support. It did this via an intermediate position, which stopped short of backing Baghdad but made the Western military presence the central issue. The FIS was certainly disinclined to accept Saddam's pretensions to be leading a jihad, and discouraged its supporters from elevating Saddam into a hero.[15] But once the war began, the FIS emerged as the most vociferous and militant supporter of Iraq, notably at the huge demonstration in Algiers on 18 January which reportedly mobilized some 400,000 people and in which virtually all Algerian political parties took part. Whereas most demonstrators marched to slogans and under banners calling for peace, the FIS marched to explicitly pro-Iraqi slogans, and called on the government to set up training camps for volunteers wishing to go to Iraq to fight. It is almost certain that it did so in order to retain its grip on mass Algerian opinion, which was at boiling point by this stage.[16] It hoped simultaneously to increase the stakes and to outflank the other parties in both its rhetoric and the pressure that it was putting on the Algerian government.

The latter's response came in President Chadli's hard-hitting speech to the National Assembly on 23 January 1991 in which he denounced "blackmail and demagogy through anarchistic agitation."[17] Such rhetoric prompted the FIS to mount a further show of strength in a demonstration on 31 January, which mobilized some 60,000 supporters (some sources speak of 100,000), with the other parties staying away. In addition to calling for "victory to Islam and the Muslims" in the war,[18] a partial endorsement of Baghdad's call for jihad, the demonstrators also made clear the internal political issue at stake by calling for a date to be fixed for the National Assembly elections.[19]

The other Islamist parties took a much lower profile on the Gulf than the FIS. This is mainly because they lacked the massive mobilizational power of the FIS and, not having contested the elections of June 1990, they did not yet possess a large popular constituency that they needed to defend. It may also have reflected a somewhat more moderate attitude to the crisis, however, at least in the case of Hamas. Shaikh Nahnah, like the FIS's Madani, strongly denounced the Western military presence in the Gulf, but he equally strongly denounced the Iraqi invasion of Kuwait. He tended to put the two on a par, whereas for the FIS, as for public opinion in general, the Iraqi invasion, while deplorable conduct for an Arab state, was wholly overshadowed by the Western intervention. Nahnah thus appears to have been more cautious than the FIS in respect of the long-term implications of the position he took. He was perhaps less opportunistic, and therefore bolder, in the short-run, in that he apparently made less of a concession to pan-Arab sentiment. Like the FIS, he also reportedly discouraged the popular tendency to lionize Saddam Hussein.

On the major points at issue, however, all the Islamist tendencies were broadly at one with each other and with public opinion, condemning the invasion of Kuwait, but at least as strongly, if not more strongly, condemning the West's military presence in the Gulf. They insisted on the necessity and possibility of a peaceful Arab solution and passionately opposed the allies' decision to launch the war against Iraq and the way in which they conducted it. On all of these points, they were at one with the Algerian government. Thus, all the major forces in Algerian politics, whether Islamist or not, felt the need to remain abreast of the massive movement of public opinion which took place, and to articulate it.

That this movement owed little to specifically Islamist agitation is clear from the terms in which Algerian opinion viewed Saddam Hussein. Despite discouragement from the Islamist movements, public opinion saw him as a hero. Throughout Algeria, the term that was used to refer to Saddam was *fahl*,[20] which literally means the male of any large animal, a stallion for example, and by extension an outstanding personality. The connotations are those of enormous virility, masculine power.

It can be said that Algerian public opinion reacted to the Gulf crisis in essentially two ideological registers: the register of pan-Arab solidarity and anti-imperialism, and the older, and arguably more powerful, register of the traditional code of honor. Saddam was lionized for standing his ground in defiance of America, and for keeping his word (a crucial characteristic of a man of honor in the Algerian tradition) that he would attack Israel. Neither of these registers was that of Islam, let alone radical Islamism. Indeed, the Islamist movement tended to be opposed to both of them, and sought to supersede them. But, because of the close identification of "Arab" with "Muslim" in Algeria (where the idea of Christian Arabs is still all but inconceivable to ordinary people), there has been no sharp distinction between pan-Arab solidarity and pan-Muslim solidarity, and this made it possible for the Islamist movement to take the lead in articulating popular feelings in the vocabulary of Muslim solidarity and self-respect. This exercise was made all the easier for the FIS to undertake because of the disarray of the FLN.

The way in which Algerian public opinion reacted to the Gulf crisis therefore forced the Islamist movement to choose between, on the one hand, important elements of its own doctrinal outlook (hostility to secularism and to Arab socialism) and its connections with the Gulf monarchies, and, on the other, its popular base.[21] This choice was starkest in the case of the FIS, because of the size of the popular following that it had achieved in the June elections and the vested interest that it had acquired in preserving this. It was only natural that FIS would go furthest in expressing the militancy of popular support for Iraq.

It is most improbable that the purpose of the FIS was to destabilize the Algerian state in this maneuver. Rather, as was the case with the other parties and organizations in competition with the FIS, including the Chadli regime, its purpose was to exploit the shift in opinion, which otherwise would not have found institutional means of political expression. It now seems this cost the FIS its former close links with Saudi Arabia, although some uncertainty persists on this score. But what is clear is the extent to which the FIS was willing to put its Algerian constituency before its international links, and its popular character before its Islamist doctrines.

In short, the crisis appears to have marked a major stage in the "Algerianization" of the FIS, and to confirm its doctrinal shallowness but also its populist militancy and political flexibility. It also appears to have emphasized the extent to which, in all of these respects, the FIS is able to claim to be the successor of the old wartime FLN, of which, as we have already noted, Professor Madani was a founder-member.

The Aftermath of the Gulf Crisis

In electoral terms, however, the FIS appeared to be somewhat weakened by the Gulf crisis. Having gone so far out on a limb in its support for Iraq, it suffered from the failure of the Iraqi army to resist the allies' ground offensive more effectively. There is no doubt that Algerian public opinion expected and hoped that Iraq would be able to make a serious fight of it, and was profoundly depressed by the scale and rapidity of the rout that occurred.[22] For the short-term at least, this under-

mined popular confidence in the judgment of both the FIS and
Ahmad Ben Bella's MDA and suggested that the other Islamist parties and especially President Chadli had shown
greater wisdom in their approach to the crisis. By contrast,
the FIS had appeared opportunistic and impulsive.

The apparent weakening of the FIS and the corresponding
recovery of the FLN's electoral prospects[23] seemed to have
produced an excess of self-confidence in President Chadli's
entourage and especially in his Prime Minister, Mouloud
Hamrouche. This new mood of self-confidence was expressed
not only in the decision to name an early date for the National
Assembly elections, which were to be held in two rounds on
27 June and 18 July, but also in a range of measures designed
to hamper if not provoke the FIS. These measures included in
particular a new electoral law designed to minimize the FIS's
representation in the new legislature. They proved mis-
guided and highly controversial.

The new law, which was approved by the National Assembly on 1 April, provided for two rounds of voting, with only
the two parties winning the most votes in the first round
being allowed to contest the second in each constituency. This
provision would have favored the FLN across the country, but
would have favored the FIS only where its support was safe
from inroads from the other Islamist movements or the MDA.
Moreover, in raising the number of constituencies from 295
to 542, the new law would have given much greater weight
than before to the rural districts of Algeria.[24] Since the
successes of the FIS in June 1990 were above all in the towns,
and the FLN's vote had held up well in its rural bases, this
was bound to deny the FIS the share of Assembly seats to
which it felt entitled.

The government also acted to inhibit the FIS in other
ways. A decree enacted by the Ministry of Religious Affairs
in early April banned the use of mosques for party political
purposes.[25] This degree was aimed at the FIS in particular,
since for the last two years it had made the mosques the
organizational center of its political presence. In addition,

attempts by FIS militants to impose their own puritanical views by disrupting concerts of popular music during the holy month of Ramadan were indiscriminately blamed on the FIS and strongly denounced by the authorities. This appeared to be part of a concerted drive by the Chadli regime to counteract the influence of the FIS, to which it had shown greater indulgence in the past.[26]

These developments placed the FIS in a real dilemma. Should it accept the humiliation that would come with bowing to new rules which unquestionably loaded the dice against it, and thus allow itself to be denied fair representation within the new Assembly? Or should the FIS boycott the elections altogether and expose itself to the charge of refusing to play the democratic game? After some hesitation and internal debate, the FIS opted for the audacious strategy of confrontation with the authorities as the only way to break out of the trap that they had set for it.

On 23 May its leaders called for a general strike of indefinite duration to begin on 25 May. This call was not widely heeded, except for the public services under the FIS's own control in local and regional government, and was pronounced a flop by government spokesmen and media commentators. But this judgment overlooked the possibility that the purpose of the strike was merely to raise the political temperature and set the scene for the mobilization of the FIS's real strength, the unemployed youth of the towns. From 26 May onwards the FIS took to the streets and squares of Algiers in force as a part of a campaign of peaceful mass protest. On 27 May, for example, a FIS march in Algiers mobilized 100,000 people. The campaign remained peaceful and only later developed into civil disobedience. At first the authorities made no attempt to intervene, although army units had taken up stand-by positions on the edge of Algiers as early as 2 May. But when riot police were ordered to clear the streets on 2 June, clashes began which developed into fierce fighting on 3 June and lasted for the next twenty-four hours. Army units were called in and a number of people were killed. On 5

June, President Chadli declared a state of siege, postponed the National Assembly elections indefinitely, dismissed Mouloud Hamrouche and his government, and set about striking a new bargain with Abassi Madani and his party.

On Friday, 7 June, Madani and Ali Belhadj told their followers at the al-Sunna mosque that they were calling off the strike and the wider campaign of protest because they had won a promise of both legislative and presidential elections before the end of the year. The following day, the new Prime Minister, Sid Ahmad Ghozali, confirmed in a televised address that legislative elections would be held by the end of 1991, but he was notably vague about the presidential election. He suggested only that it would be held as soon as possible thereafter, yet the implication was that it would be well before the end of President Chadli's current term in December 1993. He also spoke of ensuring that the elections would be "clean and fair," an implicit promise to revise the electoral law which was subsequently confirmed informally by government sources. It was also emphasized that Ghozali would consult Algeria's political parties about the government he was to form, and that this would be "non-party" in character—that is, a government of technocrats and independent personalities dissociated from the FLN, with a purely caretaker role pending the legislative elections and no partisan interest in their outcome.

These developments appeared at first to amount to a major victory for the FIS.[27] It had stood its ground, refused to accept humiliation or a rigged election, and carried its main point.[28] But this resistance by the FIS appears to have strengthened the hand of those elements within the army that had wanted to cut it down to size all along. The FIS's apparent victory furnished these elements within the army with two vital rationales.

First, the fall of Hamrouche had precipitated a crisis within the FLN because it had dashed the hopes of Hamrouche and the young reformers associated with him that an "FLN-Nouveau" might successfully challenge the FIS by running on a platform of economic liberalism and a tacitly Western conception of modernism. The fall of Hamrouche also induced Chadli to resign his position as President of the FLN,[29] and to announce that he would not seek a fourth term as President of the Republic.[30] These developments meant that in the short run the FLN was in no shape to contest the legislative elections with any prospect of winning, and that it needed time to find and agree on a presidential candidate. In the meantime, it clearly had a vested interest in a crackdown on the FIS.

Second, the FIS's apparent victory was interpreted by elements within the army as an intolerable affront to the authority of the state. Army leaders insisted that the concessions to the FIS be balanced by a thoroughgoing suppression of the violent fringe of the Islamist movement and an uncompromising reassertion of the authority of the nation-state. As a result, tension between the government and the FIS quickly revived. At first the FIS leaders did not appear to challenge the army's move against the violent fringe groups and maintained a conciliatory attitude.[31] But on 25 June the army ordered the removal of Islamic slogans from town halls under the FIS's control and replaced them with the FLN's official motto, "By the People and For the People," on 25 June. When the army moved in force into Bab El-Oued and other districts to impose this change, pitched battles broke out and a fresh trial of strength began. This confrontation, which cost an additional twelve lives, culminated in the arrest of Abassi Madani and Ali Belhadj on 30 June.

The ground for this surprising turn of events had been prepared since mid-June. On 12 June, a French national, Didier Roger Guyan, was arrested in Oran in possession of explosives and fire arms. A few days later, Guyan made a televised statement implicating Ali Belhadj in these subversive activities. On 21 June, Belhadj seemed to confirm the allegation by reportedly calling on his supporters to stockpile arms. On 26 June, three members of the FIS's Consultative Council, the Majlis al-Shura, were given access to Algerian television by the authorities and launched a major attack on Abassi Madani.[32] These incidents seemed designed to isolate and stigmatize the FIS's two principal leaders by boosting other factions within the FIS. In an address to the Ibn Badis mosque in the Kouba quarter of Algiers on 29 June, Madani said that he was not intimidated by this and was prepared to stand his ground.[33] The authorities responded by taking him and Belhadj into custody and announced that they would stand trial on charges of "armed conspiracy against the security of the state."[34] Over the next two days more than 700 FIS militants were arrested, bringing the number of arrests since the beginning of June to some 2,500.[35]

The military authorities had evidently decided to use the state of siege to settle accounts with the FIS. The fate of the FIS is not clear at this writing. If the FIS is preserved in some form, a new leadership may develop around Madani's critics on the Majlis al-Shura and be encouraged to function legally and to contest the legislative elections whenever these are held. An emasculated FIS of this type, deprived of the charismatic leadership of Madani and Belhadj (whose future at this writing seems to be imprisonment or exile), would have difficulty appealing to the urban youth. Accordingly, it would not likely pose a major threat to the FLN in the elections. If the FIS does not survive the current crisis, a political reorganization of the Algerian Islamist movement may take place under a new name. Presumably the moderate faction of the FIS would participate in this new party.

In either case, the crackdown on the FIS and the decision to take Madani and Belhadj out of the game shattered the Islamists' naive hope of an easy victory and the establishment of their ideal of an Islamic Republic. The crackdown also undermined the fragile faith of Algeria's urban youth in the possibility of representation for their grievances and redress for their frustrations within the political system of the nation-state. A good deal of scattered unrest and violence seemed likely for the summer of 1991 but the state seemed strong enough to cope with such unrest.

It is certainly too soon to conclude that Algeria's democratic experiment has been aborted. It is entirely possible that both presidential and legislative elections will yet be held in 1991. Conceivably a new president might be able to secure a fresh degree of legitimacy for Algeria's fledging democracy. But a great deal will depend on the ability of the FLN to remake itself in such a way as to hold some appeal to the frustrated youth of Algeria's cities and attract them away from the Islamist formula. After the arrest of Madani and Belhadj, that Islamist project was disrupted.

Conclusion

The Gulf crisis was a major challenge to Algeria's audacious attempt to conduct a smooth and peaceful transition to democracy. It constituted an immense complication of an already extremely complex political situation, and, by making necessary the postponement of the National Assembly elections, it deferred the resolution of the national political crisis which began in October 1988. It thereby forced Algeria to limp along without an authoritative government for at least six months longer than previously anticipated, in difficult and steadily deteriorating economic and social conditions.

The danger in these circumstances was that the Gulf crisis would constitute a new and explosive bone of contention among Algeria's political parties and especially between the Islamist movement and the Chadli administration. While there were differences and these were vigorously expressed, there also appeared to be an impressive degree of national unity on the fundamental aspects of this question. Even the most militant positions, notably those of the FIS from early January 1991, were consistently articulated within the procedures and institutions of the 1989 constitution, through meetings and demonstrations, many of them of massive size, but nearly all of them orderly and peaceful.

In short, the Gulf crisis failed to subvert the 1989 constitution and, while it prolonged the transition to democracy, it did not abort it. The possibility that popular anger and bitterness at the outcome of the war would burst the bounds of the existing political institutions could not be dismissed, but the evidence suggests that the various political parties, and the Islamist parties in particular, had become extremely adept at remaining abreast of public opinion and at channelling it. As a rule, the maneuvers which they performed in doing so were carefully calculated and were executed with an eye on the likely reaction of the authorities, and with a tacit understanding of what the Chadli regime could accept. While criticism of President Chadli's handling of the crisis, and in particular his refusal to countenance the training of Algerian volunteers for the war, was vented on several occasions, there was no solid evidence that the Islamist movement in general or the FIS in particular were disposed at the time to subvert Chadli's position as the necessary arbiter of the political system.

Events since the end of the Gulf war have not refuted this analysis. The major political crisis which erupted in May and which, after an apparent settlement in early June, broke out again and culminated on 30 June with Madani's and Belhadj's arrest, was not a direct consequence of the Gulf crisis. The trial of strength in which the FIS and the state were engaged was provoked by the enactment of what was widely perceived as an unfair electoral law,[36] accompanied by numerous other minor forms of harassment. The strategy of confrontation was thus not an unprompted initiative on the FIS's part, and was conducted entirely peacefully at first.[37] But in late June, when the army took control of the conflict, the FIS leaders realized that the days of a negotiated understanding with the civilian government were over. The available alternatives being capitulation or defiance, the various elements in the FIS's leadership made their respective choices, and Madani and Belhadj, remaining true to themselves and their supporters, preferred to go to jail than disavow their words.

The Gulf crisis gave a renewed relevance to the FLN's traditional nationalist vision, and especially to its preoccupation with the question of Algeria's national sovereignty. The Algerian army, commanded by strongly nationalist officers, obviously decided that the preservation of Algeria's national sovereignty could not be entrusted to a government of Islamists, for whom the "nation" is a secondary consideration at best.

Endnotes to Chapter 7

1. Hugh Roberts, "Radical Islamism and the Dilemma of Algerian Nationalism," *Third World Quarterly* 10 (2) (April 1988): 556–89; see also François Burgat, *L'Islamisme au Maghreb: La Voix du Sud* (*Islamism in the Maghreb: The Voice of the South*) (Paris: Karthala, 1988).

2. Notably in Ben Bella's speech on his return to Algeria, Reuters, 27 September 1990.

3. This first became apparent following the major earthquake in the Tipaza district west of Algiers on 29 October 1989, when it was the FIS, not the government, which took charge of the relief operations.

4. The FIS officially polled 33.73 percent of the electorate in the communal elections and 35.20 percent in the wilaya elections. See Jacques Fontaine, "Les élections locales algériennes du 12 juin 1990" ("The Local Algerian Elections of 12 June 1990"), *Maghreb-Mashrek*, July-September 1990, pp. 124–40.

5. Official spokesmen initially credited the FLN with control of 14 wilaya; in fact, it won overall control of only six, with a plurality in a further four: Ibid., p.126.

6. Jon Marks, "Algeria: The Long Election Trail," *Middle East Economic Digest,* 31 May 1991.

7. Abassi Madani is usually referred to simply as Madani in media coverage of Algeria, as though Madani were his surname. In fact, Madani is his given name and Abassi his family name. The reversal of the order of the names is a relic from the practice of French-run schools in the colonial period and frequently misleads foreign journalists in respect of Algerian politicians.

8. *El-Moudjahid* (official daily paper of the FLN), 16–17 November 1990.

9. Ernest Gellner, "The Unknown Apollo of Biskra: The Social Base of Algerian Puritanism," in Ernest Gellner, *Muslim Society* (Cambridge: Cambridge University Press, 1981), pp. 149–73.

10. *Jeune Afrique (Young African),* no. 1555, 17–23 October 1990.

11. Ibid.

12. Ibid.

13. See report of Radiodiffusion-Television Algerienne, Algiers, 13 September 1990, in BBC, *Summary of World Broadcasts,* ME/0870/A8–9, 15 September 1990.

14. Reuters, 27 September 1990; see also *Le Monde,* 30 September–1 October 1990.

15. Information from interviews with members of the Algerian Islamist movement.

16. An index of popular feeling was the demonstration in Constantine, the capital of eastern Algeria, on 18 January, when the French consulate was attacked and set on fire.

17. Reuters, 23 January 1991.

18. *The Times,* 1 February 1991.

19. *The Guardian,* 1 February 1991.

20. Information from personal sources in Algeria.

21. See the article "La Tourmente des Frères" ("The Torment of the Brothers") in *Algérie-Actualité* (*Algeria Today*) no. 1320, 31 January–6 February 1991.

22. George Marion, "Silence embarrassé et repli sur soi à Alger" ("Embarrassed Silence and Withdrawal in Algiers") in *Le Monde,* 28 February 1991.

23. According to the *Middle East Economic Digest* of 24 May 1991, an opinion poll published by *Algérie-Actualité* estimated that the FIS would win only 206 seats (38 percent) to the FLN's 244 (45 percent), with minor parties taking the remaining 97 (17 percent).

24. *Le Monde,* 3 April 1991; *El-Moudjahid,* 3 April 1991. For example, the heavily populated northern wilaya of Blida, an Islamist stronghold in 1990, was given the same number of seats in the new Assembly as the huge but very thinly populated wilaya of Tamanrasset in the far south of the Sahara, which the FLN carried in 1990. See "Economist Intelligence Unit," *Country Report on Algeria,* no. 2, April–June 1990.

25. *Le Monde,* 9 April 1991.

26. *Arab News,* 26 March 1991.

27. *Le Monde,* 9 June 1991.

28. Its demand for a presidential election had been only partially conceded, since it had stipulated that this should be held before or during, not after, the legislative elections. But this demand is unlikely to have reflected the FIS's true priorities. It had been tacked onto its main grievance about the electoral law, as a way of putting pressure on President Chadli directly and also in order to outflank other parties which had also begun to raise this demand, notably the Algerian Movement for Justice and Development (Mouvement Algerian pour la Justice et le Developpement, MAJD) of former Prime Minister Kasdi Merbah.

29. Chadli's decision was announced at the meeting of the FLN's Central Committee on 28 June but reportedly taken on 10 June. See *Le Monde,* 30 June-1 July 1991.

30. This announcement was made by the FLN's General Secretary, a close ally and relative of President Chadli, in remarks to the Algerian weekly *L'-Observateur,* according to the Moroccan News Agency as reported by *SWB,* ME/1109/i, 27 June 1991, and confirmed from other sources. The discreet character of this announcement suggests that it was for internal consumption and it should be read cautiously.

31. These included arrests of armed militants in various places in eastern and western Algeria, some of whom reportedly belong to a fringe group, Takfir

wa'l-Hijra (Society of Excommunication and Emigration), an Algerian extension or, more likely, imitation of the Egyptian group of the same name, and thus well outside the ambit of the FIS. See *Middle East Economic Digest,* 21 June 1991, page 10. Madani's conciliatory attitude at this time was made clear when he wished success to Prime Minister Sid Ahmad Ghozali's new government on 18 June and declared that "the country is heading toward the return of peace and a way out of the political crisis." Quoted in *Le Monde,* 2 July 1991.

32. Ibid., 27 June 1991.

33. He was widely reported as having called for jihad. In fact, what he said was that the FIS "had not called for jihad nor ordered the use of arms" but added "we have the right to do so if the army does not return to its barracks." See Ibid., 30 June-1 July 1991.

34. Ibid., 2 July 1991.

35. *International Herald Tribune,* 2 July 1991.

36. That this law was obviously unfair was the view of many Algerians; the FIS was by no means alone on this point. See the interview of Mar Zerguine, an Algerian lawyer, in *Le Figaro,* 6 June 1991, and especially the interview of Hocine Ait Ahmed, leader of the main Kabyle-based movement, the Front des Forces Socialistes (and an inveterate opponent of the Islamist Movement) in *Le Figaro,* 7 June 1991.

37. It should be noted that Madani met Hamrouche in late May, before the protests had escalated into serious civil disobedience (let alone violence), and had sought a settlement, but Hamrouche had flatly refused to agree to a revision of the electoral law. See *Middle East Economic Digest*, 21 June 1991. Having made no concession to Madani, Hamrouche then received rivals of Madani within the FIS leadership who promptly, on their own initiative, issued a call for the general strike to be abandoned: *Le Monde,* 31 May 1991. This call was immediately disavowed by Madani and Ali Belhadj, and the confrontation escalated. It this appears that it was Hamrouche's intransigence towards Madani, combined with his attempt to manipulate the division within the FIS, which ensured that the situation deteriorated.

8

THE POLITICS OF WAR: ISLAMIC FUNDAMENTALISMS IN PAKISTAN

Mumtaz Ahmad

Since the beginning of the twentieth century, the commitment to universal Islamic brotherhood has been an important component of the South Asian Muslims' sense of identity. Occasionally romantic in its contents and orientations, this commitment to solidarity with the universal Muslim *umma* (community) "was nevertheless grounded in the pillars of the faith and made good political sense in the Indian context."[1] The Muslims were convinced that the integrity of their faith and the prospects of their political future were seriously threatened by both their Christian rulers and their Hindu compatriots. Their religious identity that led them to embrace pan-Islam as a means to counteract the European machinations to establish hegemony over *dar al-Islam* (the Islamic realm), and their political identity that culminated in the establishment of Pakistan as a means to offset their minority status, were thus "inextricably entwined."[2]

The first, and probably the most important, manifestation of the feeling of universal Islamic brotherhood on the part of South Asian Muslims was the Khilafat Movement of the 1920s that arose to save the Turkish caliphate from dismemberment in the wake of the post-World War I rearrangement of European and Middle Eastern state boundaries. Beginning with the Tripolitan and Balkan wars of 1911–12 to the end of World War I and the Treaty of

Sèvres—which put Syria, Palestine, and Mesopotamia (Iraq) under French and British mandates, gave the Turkish territories of Eastern Thrace and Smyrna to Greece and the Dodecanese Islands to Italy—Muslim public opinion in India was convinced that these developments were part of "a plot by the Christian powers of Europe . . . against the last great Muslim power."[3]

Since then major events in the international community that have had an impact upon Muslims, directly or indirectly, have triggered a massive reaction among activist Muslim groups in Pakistan. The Arab-Israeli wars of 1967 and 1973, the burning of al-Aqsa mosque in 1969, the Israeli invasion of Lebanon in 1982, the Soviet invasion of Afghanistan in 1979, and the American bombing of Libya in 1988 all had immense reverberations throughout Pakistan. The Gulf crisis of 1990–91 provided once again an instance of popular mobilization by Islamic groups in support of a member of dar al-Islam menaced by non-Muslim forces.

Contemporary Muslim Groups in Pakistan

Islamic groups in Pakistan can be divided into three broad categories: lay religiopolitical movements, the *ulama*-based religious organizations prominent in Pakistan's politics since the 1960s, and the non-political *da'wa*-type revivalist movements that are mainly concerned with improving the Islamic education of Muslims and their manner of conduct.[4]

In the first category, the Jamaat-i-Islami (The Islamic Group, JI), founded by Abul Ala Maududi in 1941 in British India, is the most important Islamic political movement in Muslim South Asia today. As one of the most effectively organized religiopolitical movements, the Jamaat has been active in politics since the creation of Pakistan in 1947 and has played a decisive role in shaping the nature and content of Islamic political discourse in Pakistan. Led primarily by lay, modern educated Muslims and supported by lower middle class Muslims from both the traditional and the modern sectors of Pakistani society, the Jamaat has pursued the goal of Islamic revival through the establishment of an Islamic state with the Qur'an and *Sunna* (the way of the Prophet) as its constitution and the *Shari'a* as its law. The political struggle of the Jamaat-i-Islami has been based on the assumption that Islamic change in society can only occur as a result of the change in the nature and direction of political power. The Jamaat has fought incessant battles against secular liberalism, Communism, Islamic modernism, and Islamic socialism and has emerged as the most effective and articulate voice of Islamic conservatism in contemporary Islam in Pakistan.

A movement of pan-Islamic orientation, the Jamaat has, over the years, established close ideological and organizational links with Islamic movements in other parts of the Muslim world and, as a consequence, has become a militant advocate of Muslim causes such as Kashmiri and Palestinian self-determination, *jihad* in Afghanistan, and religiopolitical rights of Muslim minorities in non-Muslim states. The Jamaat-i-Islami has about 4,000 organizational units in Pakistan with more than 6,000 "full members"—a select group that constitutes the core of the ideological purity and organizational strength of the movement—and about half a million workers and supporters. Recently, as a part of the Islamic Democratic Alliance, the ruling coalition, the Jamaat has been able to exercise considerable influence on the tone, if not the substance, of Pakistan's foreign policy.

In the second category, the ulama-led Islamic groups, four organizations have emerged as important actors in Pakistan's politics. First is the Jamiyat Ulama-i-Pakistan (The Society of Pakistani Ulama, JUP), which is led by Maulana Shah Ahmad Noorani. It enjoys a considerable following in the Urdu-speaking areas of urban Sind. However, its religious influence has been particularly strong in the rural areas and small towns of Punjab where the intellectual and doctrinal influence of Islamic orthodoxy has not penetrated very deeply. The JUP's religious ideology is based on folk Islam with an emphasis on Sufism, veneration of saints, idolization of the Prophet and one's spiritual preceptors, and popular and festive display of syncretic religious rituals. In politics, although the JUP has campaigned for the introduction of Shari'a, its major concern has been to safeguard the integrity of its own "denominational domain"— Muslim Family Laws, and religious shrines and endowments. As an organization led by the ulama, the JUP also enjoys a considerable following among the *madrasa*, or Islamic school, students. The JUP's patron saint is Abd al-Qadir al-Jilani (d. 561 A.H., 1161 A.D.), the celebrated saint and founder of the Qadiriyya order of Sufis. He is buried in Baghdad. With substantial financial support from the Memon business community of Karachi, and reportedly from Libya and Iraq as well, Maulana Noorani has been able to organize an extensive network of Islamic missionary activities in Africa, the Caribbean islands, and Great Britain. A splinter group of the JUP has recently joined the government of Prime Minister Nawaz Sharif.

The second group in this category is the Jamiyat Ulama-i-Islam (The Society of Muslim Ulama, JUI), an ultra-conservative religiopolitical party of the ulama who owe their doctrinal allegiance to the Islamic seminary of Deoband in India. This party represents the core of Islamic orthodoxy in its pure form. In their religious ideas, JUI members are uncompromisingly rigid and insist on the strict following of the rules of the Shari'a as interpreted by the founders of the four schools of classical Islamic law. They are irreconcilably opposed to the syncretic and eclectic kind of Islam as represented by the JUP and regard all innovations *(bida')* in religion—both Sufi and modern types—as a sin. In politics, their platform consists of the enforcement of Shari'a under the strict guidance of the "righteous ulama" who will have the ultimate authority to determine whether or not a law passed by the Parliament is in conformity with the Shari'a. They also demand the enforcement of the strict social and moral code of Islam, especially in gender relations, to save the Muslim society from "the evils of the West." The JUI, currently headed by Maulana Fazlur Rahman, enjoys solid support in the Pathan majority areas of Baluchistan and settled areas of the North West Frontier Province. The JUI controls the largest number of mosques and madrasas in Pakistan and has thus the strongest base in the madrasa student body in the country. During 1973–74, it was able to form governments of its own in the provinces of Baluchistan and the North West Frontier.

The third group in this category is the Jamiyat Ulama-i-Ahl-i-Hadith (The Society of Ulama of "the People of the Hadith," JUAH), the heir of the extreme right-wing theocratic particularism of Muhammad ibn Abd al-Wahhab, an eighteenth century Arab puritanical reformer and co-founder of the modern Saudi Arabian state. Because of this doctrinal lineage, the JUAH ulama are known as Wahhabis, especially among their opponents in the JUP. The JUAH preaches uncompromising monotheism, rejects the notion of intercession by one's spiritual mentors, and condemns visitation of Sufi shrines as polytheism. A major pillar of its religious ideology is its subordination of juridical opinions and decrees to the overarching discipline of *Hadith* (traditions of the Prophet) and its rejection of purely rational sciences such as philosophy, and even theology. The JUAH ulama are mostly known for their relentless crusade against the "religious excesses" of syncretic Islam that is the hallmark of the JUP and some Sufi orders. Although a follower of the Hanbali school of law, the JUAH does not accept its precepts as final and emphasizes that the Qur'an and Hadith constitute the only bases of Islamic law.

In politics, the JUAH has vehemently opposed Western democracy and its institutions such as universal suffrage, multiparty elections, and legislative authority of the Parliament. It described the election of Benazir Bhutto as Pakistan's Prime Minister as "a curse of Allah on the Muslim umma."[5] The JUAH has been very close to the Saudi government authorities and the Saudi religious establishment because of their doctrinal affinities and has fought rigorously against Shi'ism and the influence of the Iranian revolution on Pakistan. The majority of the Ahl-i-Hadith leaders and supporters are businessmen. The party has a limited following confined to business communities in Karachi and some cities in Punjab.

The fourth group in this category is a Shi'ite organization, Tahrik-i-Nifaz-i-Fiqh-i-Ja'afriya (Movement for the Enforcement of Ja'afiri Law—TNFJ). Organized ten years ago, it has since emerged as the sole spokesman for the political interests and religious concerns of the Shi'i minority in Pakistan. The TNFJ came into being as a Shi'ite reaction against the Sunni-oriented Islamization programs of General Zia ul-Haq in the early 1980s. Its political program includes the introduction of the Shi'ite Ja'afiri law for the Shi'ites, autonomy for the Shi'ite religious endowments, complete freedom for the public observance of the Shi'ite religious rites, close relations with Iran, and "an end to the American influence on Pakistan's foreign policy."[6] As a political off-shoot of the Islamic revolution in neighboring Iran, the TNFJ has maintained close relations with Iranian authorities and has generally followed the Iranian line in matters of foreign policy. Since there are few electoral constituencies in the country with a solid Shi'ite majority, the TNFJ failed to win even a single seat during the 1988 parliamentary elections which it contested under its own banner.

Among the nonpolitical da'wa-type revivalist movements, the most important is the Tablighi Jamaat (Association for the Propagation of Islam, TJ), a grassroots movement of lay Muslims from all sections of society that strives for the moral and spiritual renewal of individual believers. The Jamaat shuns politics and views religion as a personal and private affair of the individual. Since its inception in 1926, the Jamaat has remained aloof from political controversies and has focused on preaching the moral and religious precepts of Islam and reforming the socio-religious customs of South Asian Muslims in accordance with orthodox Islam. The itinerant-based da'wa methodology of the Jamaat has spread its activities to more than one hundred countries of the world. In Pakistan, the Jamaat has become an important training ground for thousands of aspiring laymen among the small town shopkeepers, school teachers, government clerks, and artisans and para-professionals in the private sector. Its annual conference in Raiwind near Lahore attracts more than one million Muslims from over ninety countries of the world.

Muslim Groups Respond to the Gulf Crisis

These diverse Pakistani Islamic movements shared at least one conviction concerning the Gulf war: it was part of an increasingly predictable pattern of Western disregard for Islamic integrity and self-determination. Two developments in particular inspired the Jamaat-i-Islami to take the lead as the severest critic of the United States during the Gulf conflict.

First, the United States' decision in October 1990 to cut off all economic and military aid because of Pakistan's clandestine nuclear program had already aroused widespread anti-American sentiment. The Jamaat-i-Islami and other religiopolitical groups are committed to pursuing a nuclear weapons program as a necessary deterrent against a potential Indian nuclear threat. These groups interpret the U.S. opposition to Pakistan's nuclear program "as a clear case of the anti-Islamic stance" of American policymakers who, in the words of the President of the Jamaat-i-Islami, "have shown no serious concern about the similar and much advanced nuclear weapons programs of Israel and India and have chosen to single out Pakistan for all kinds of restrictions and punishments. This only goes to prove that the U.S. does not want a Muslim country to possess nuclear weapons."[7]

The cut-off of American aid (which had amounted to $578 million annually) came at a time when thousands of Pakistani expatriate workers were returning home after losing their assets and life savings in Kuwait and Iraq. The Pakistani government had dispatched 5,000 troops to Saudi Arabia and was preparing another armored brigade to join the U.S.-led international alliance against Iraq when the news of the American aid cut-off was reported in the Pakistan newspapers in October. A common reaction to the news was expressed by a Jamaat-i-Islami senator during a foreign policy debate in the Pakistani Senate: "While the Egyptians have got their $7 billion in *bakhsheesh*, what did Pakistan get in return for supporting U.S. policies in the Gulf? A slap in the face?"[8]

A second development in 1990 had already intensified the anti-Western attitudes of the Jamaat-i-Islami and other groups. The Jamaat-i-Islami was openly resentful of what it described as "a joint U.S.-Soviet conspiracy" to deprive the Islamic forces among the Afghan Mujahidin of an ultimate victory. The Jamaat-i-Islami had supported the jihad in Afghanistan throughout the 1980s, working vigorously to mobilize domestic and international support for the success of Hizb-i-Islami (The Islamic Party), a fundamentalist Afghan resistance group headed by the uncompromising Gulbadin Hikmatyar. After the Geneva accord and the withdrawal of the Soviet troops in February 1989, the United States and Saudi Arabia were no longer willing to provide significant financial, diplomatic, and military assistance to an anti-Western fundamentalist group such as Hizb-i-Islami. The Jamaat-i-Islami had hoped for the establishment of an Islamic state in Kabul by its ideological protégé and was bitterly disappointed at this uncertain outcome. The President of the Jamaat, Qazi Hussein Ahmad, had been the sole figure in charge of the Jamaat's Afghan policy. He became convinced that by their support of the so-called moderate groups among the Afghan resistance, the United States and Saudi Arabia were mainly responsible for aborting the prospects of victory for the Islamic forces. "If it was not for the American machinations, Islamic forces would have defeated Najibullah a long time ago," he told a public gathering in Peshawar.[9]

During the early phase of the Gulf crisis, the Jamaat-i-Islami led the other religiopolitical groups in Pakistan in condemning the Iraqi invasion of Kuwait as unjustified and demanding that Iraq withdraw immediately and unconditionally from Kuwait. (Even the JUP, which has close links with the Iraqi government, did not endorse the Iraqi invasion of Kuwait at this time.) The consensus among all the major Islamic religiopolitical parties was that Iraq had committed an aggression against "a brotherly Muslim country" and had thus created a dangerous precedent for the conduct of relations between the Muslim states. But these parties also insisted that the problem was essentially an Islamic one and that the foreign powers, especially the West, should not be allowed to take advantage of the Iraqi invasion and create a foothold for its permanent hegemony in the religious heartland of Islam. They suggested that after the withdrawal of the Iraqi forces, the disputes between Iraq and Kuwait should be resolved with the help of a conciliation committee formed under the auspices of either the Organization of the Islamic Conference (OIC) or the Arab League.

At first, then, there was little support for President Saddam Hussein among the religious political parties and the masses. In fact, until the middle of October, attention in Pakistan was primarily focused on the suffering of the Pakistanis returning from Kuwait and Iraq, and on the impact of the Gulf crisis on Pakistan's already faltering economy. In mid-October the JUAH even staged a public rally and a protest march in Lahore against the Iraqi invasion of Kuwait and the potential Iraqi threat to the security of Saudi Arabia—and to the holy shrines of Mecca and Medina. The Youth Force of the Ahl-i-Hadith ulama were joined in this anti-Iraq rally by the Pakistani returnees from Kuwait and by the Kuwaiti and Saudi students in Pakistan. At the end of the rally, workers of the JUAH Youth Force burned Saddam Hussein in effigy and declared that they were ready to go to Saudi Arabia and fight against his "anti-Islamic" forces in order to defend the *haramain sharifain* (the two holy shrines in Mecca and Medina). Significantly, there was no opposition from the Islamic political parties when the Pakistani government announced its decision to contribute 5,000 troops for the security of Saudi Arabia; on the contrary, there was a sense of pride that Pakistan was fulfilling its religious obligation to defend the holy places of Islam.

At this time the Jamaat-i-Islami organized a delegation of major Islamic movements representing Jordan, Sudan, Turkey, Malayasia, Tunisia, Algeria, Morocco, Egypt, and Pakistan. Qazi Hussein Ahmad represented the Jamaat-i-Islami in this delegation, which met with Saddam Hussein, King Hussein of Jordan, King Fahd of Saudi Arabia, the exiled Emir of Kuwait, and leaders of North African Muslim countries. The delegation asked these leaders not to allow the United States and other Western countries to station their troops in the region and called for the resolution of the issue through the good offices of the OIC. The delegation asked Saddam to withdraw his troops from Kuwait so as to "deprive the United States of an excuse to establish a permanent control over the Arab oil resources."[10]

By the middle of November 1990, however, the massive deployment of the American troops in the region convinced the Islamic movements in Pakistan that the United States was planning for a war and was not serious about seeking a peaceful, negotiated settlement. The attitudes of Islamic fundamentalists toward the crisis, as reflected in their rhetoric, shifted significantly. Among Islamic politicians the perception of a double standard in U. S. policy toward the Middle East was strengthened amid growing suspicions that the real agenda of the Gulf crisis was the further aggrandizement of American and Israeli power in the region.

Saddam Hussein successfully played upon this suspicion by offering to withdraw from Kuwait if Israel would withdraw from the occupied Arab territories. Subsequently the Jamaat-i-Islami's Qazi Hussein Ahmad argued that the frequent and exaggerated references in the American media and in Washington circles to Saddam's "awful military machine" demonstrated that "the real aim of American deployment is neither the defense of Saudi Arabia nor the liberation of Kuwait; rather, the real aim is to destroy the military power of an Arab Muslim nation in order to ensure the hegemony of Israel in the region."[11]

This suspicion about "the true meaning of the conflict" attained the status of doctrine once the war began. The war was seen as the culminating act in "the sinister design aimed at reintroducing imperialism through crushing the Muslim's balance of power in the region by snatching their oil wealth and, at the same time, strengthening the hands of Zionists."[12] Professor Khurshid Ahmad, a prominent Jamaat-i-Islami intellectual and a member of the Pakistani Senate, noted that the United Nations never showed as much haste to have its resolutions on Kashmir and Palestine implemented as it did in the case of Kuwait. In a Senate speech Ahmad claimed that the American government, apprehensive of the emerging economic power of Germany and Japan, desperately wanted control of "Muslim wealth in the garb of a war for liberation of Kuwait." He also advanced an increasingly popular theory—namely, that Iraq had acted on the advice of the United States in using force against Kuwait. "The trap," he said, "was to entangle Iraq in war so that it could provide the United States with a chance to interfere and advance its sinister designs—to give an edge to Israel in the region and to control the Muslim oil."[13]

This theory that the war was "a clear manifestation of the anti-Muslim forces at work at the behest of Israel and the Zionist lobby in the United States" was repeated by many influential figures in Pakistan, including the Army Chief of Staff, General Mirza Aslam Beg.[14] Qazi Hussein Ahmad termed it "the war between the Jews, the worst enemy of Islam, and the Muslims."[15] Senator Javed Jabbar, a secularly-oriented Pakistan People's Party (PPP) leader from Karachi who had been Minister for Information in Benazir Bhutto's cabinet, demanded that the government of Pakistan "desist from becoming a party to a design in which Israel is a co-host and which is meant primarily to weaken a Muslim nation."[16]

After 17 January 1991, then, whatever Pakistani Islamic concern remained over the Iraqi occupation of Kuwait was quickly displaced by concern over "the massacre of thousands of helpless Iraqi people by the Americans and a systematic destruction of the socioeconomic infrastructure and military capability of Iraq by the infidels."[17] Having returned from a meeting of religious scholars in Baghdad and an audience with President Saddam, the JUP chief, Shah Ahmad Noorani, led a propaganda barrage against the "joint Christian-Jewish assault against Islam. . . . [this] war between Islam and *kufr* [unbelief]." Noorani characterized Saddam as a modern-day Saladin and predicted that he would defeat the forces of evil and liberate Jerusalem for the Palestinians and Muslims. "We love Saddam Hussein," he told a mass rally in Hyderabad in southern Pakistan, "because he burnt midnight oil and toiled around the clock to make Iraq invincible while the rulers of Saudi Arabia and Kuwait have their cozy and [grand] palaces in European countries with taps of gold in them. We love him because he talks of the liberation of al-Quds al-Sharif [Jerusalem] and the elimination of Israel from the face of this earth. We love him because he has already made good on his promises by pounding Tel Aviv with his Scud missiles. Who else, among all the Arab leaders, has ever been able to do this to Israel?"[18]

The JUP was also deeply concerned about the safety of the shrine of its patron saint, Abd al-Qadir al-Jilani, in the wake of the massive bombing by the allied forces on and around Baghdad. The JUP established "recruiting centers" in about twenty cities of Pakistan to recruit volunteers to go to Iraq "in order to fight against the infidels and to protect the holy shrine of Ghows-i-Azam [the Great Saint] in Baghdad."[19] JUP sources claim that by the middle of February, 110,000 people had signed up for this voluntary force.[20]

The government, however, took a different view. In response to the mass demonstrations in support of Saddam and the establishment of roadside "recruitment centers" to register volunteers for Iraq, the government expelled a senior Iraqi diplomat based in Islamabad for "distributing money to recruit mercenaries to fight against the allied forces in the Persian Gulf, organizing mass demonstrations through local agents, inciting people to engage in anti-state activities, and paying money for printing pro-Saddam posters and Saddam portraits." Both the JUP and Jamaat-i-Islami claimed that the decision to expel the Iraqi diplomat was made in Washington and not in Islamabad. Instead of expelling a diplomat of a brother Muslim country, Qazi Hussein Ahmad said, "the government should have expelled the U.S. ambassador Robert Oakley as a protest against the genocide of Iraqi Muslims by the United States."[21]

The support for Iraq gained momentum as the war continued. Hundreds of thousands of Pakistanis supportive of the Islamic movements embraced the notion that the war was actually a major conflict between Islam and unbelief as represented by the Western powers fighting against Iraq. Demonstrators of the students' wing of the Jamaat-i-Islami and the JUP burned effigies of George Bush and attacked American diplomatic facilities in Lahore, Islamabad, and Karachi.[22] Protest demonstrations demanding immediate cessation of the hostilities and the withdrawal of U.S. troops from the vicinity of Islam's holy shrines were organized everywhere in Pakistan by the workers of the Jamaat-i-Islami, the JUP, and the People's Party. The Jamaat-i-Islami organized fifty-seven "jihad" rallies and two dozen "coffin-clad" rallies to emphasize that its workers were ready for martyrdom in the jihad against the anti-Islamic forces of the West. Jamiyat-i-Tulaba (The Society of Students), the student wing of the Jamaat-i-Islami, organized 338 rallies and public meetings throughout the various cities and towns of Pakistan.[23]

While almost all posters and slogans in the Jamaat-i-Islami sponsored rallies and public meetings were directed

167

against the United States and Israel, there were few posters in favor of Saddam. The JUP rallies, however, featured poster-size pictures of Saddam in Islamic prayer posture and with background pictures of the Ka'ba (the square building in Mecca that is the focus of the pilgrimage), the mosque of the Prophet in Medina, and a Scud missile falling on Tel Aviv. The poster pictures of Saddam Hussein seen on trucks, trains, rickshaws, and on the walls of alleys and bazaars in Pakistan were printed and distributed by the JUP. The government claimed that the funding for this massive publicity campaign came from the Iraqi embassy in Islamabad.

The Jamiyat Ulama-i-Islam was also an active participant in the pro-Saddam and anti-American mass rallies. A Karachi faction of the movement had been closely allied with Iraq during the Iran-Iraq war and reportedly received substantial financial contributions from the Iraqi authorities during its anti-Shi'ite campaign in 1983. In the second week of the air war the head of the Karachi branch of the JUI denounced the "open aggression against the Muslim umma," argued that an "internal Arab-Muslim affair" provided no justification for the United States to attack Iraq, and demanded that the Kuwaiti issue be brought before the OIC and the Arab League.[24] Subsequently the JUI rhetoric escalated. Responding to a resolution presented by his party workers for an immediate ceasefire, Maulana Fazlur Rahman said: "The time for hoisting white flags of peace and cease-fire has long passed. The time now is to prepare for a long drawn-out war, a war that will continue until we succeed in kicking the Americans out of the Middle East and the Israelis out of Palestine."[25] Referring to a statement by Prime Minister Sharif that joining the U.S.-led alliance did not mean that Pakistani troops would be siding with Israel, the JUI chief told a Lahore rally: "Let the Pakistani government know that the people of Pakistan make no distinction between Israel and the United States. They know that the real aim of this war is to crush the Muslim military power so that Israel could feel safe and implement its hegemonic designs in the

Arab world. If Iraq is defeated, there will be no power left in the Arab world to save the holy places of Islam in Saudi Arabia from falling in the dirty hands of the Israelis."[26]

The Shi'ite organization, TNFJ, had condemned the Iraqi invasion of Kuwait and reminded the people that the world had remained completely silent and indifferent when Saddam Hussein had committed aggression against Iran in 1980. "It was the Saudis, the Kuwaitis, and the Americans who had fed and armed this dictator in the first place to fight against the Islamic revolutionary forces in Iran and elsewhere and hence they are equally responsible for his recent aggression," a TNFJ leader told a public meeting in Lahore in September.[27] Later, when the American forces had been deployed in large numbers in Saudi Arabia, the TNFJ accused the Saudis of "handing over the holiest places of Islam in the care of the Great Satan." After the outbreak of hostilities, the massive American bombing of Iraq incited concerns about the destruction of the Shi'ite holy places in Najaf and Karbala. A leader of the TNFJ threatened that "American interests will never be safe anywhere in the world if anything happens to the holy sanctuaries in Karbala and Najaf."[28] When the Iranian Ayatollah Sayyid Ali Khamanei declared that "fighting against the Western forces to expel them from the Arabian Peninsula is a jihad,"[29] the Pakistani Shi'ite organization joined its Sunni counterparts with full vigor and unfolded its favorite *"Marg ber America"* ("Death to America") banners and posters which had been saved from its earlier rallies during the Iran-Iraq war.

The reaction of the Tablighi Jamaat leaders and followers was typical of their overall apolitical religious orientation and philosophy. They urged the faithful "to bow down before Allah Almighty in this time of great affliction and tribulation for Muslims" and "seek repentance for your sins." *Imams* (prayer leaders) and *khatibs* (preachers) of mosques affiliated with the Tabligh movement asked their congregations "to offer special prayers for ending the Gulf war and for the safety of Muslims."[30] The predominant theme in their sermons was that Muslims have no one to blame for this "misfortune" except themselves. A Tablighi Jamaat religious leader told a Friday prayer congregation in Karachi that this war of Muslim against Muslim which has "dragged non-Muslim forces in to the vicinity of Islam's holiest shrines is a clear sign of Allah's wrath against the misdeeds and sinful actions of the Muslim rulers and masses everywhere in the Islamic world."[31] He also interpreted the earthquake in northern Pakistan that killed more than two hundred people as another sign of God's displeasure with the state of affairs of Muslim societies.

The most interesting and theologically significant formulation on the Gulf crisis also came from the Tablighi Jamaat and was based on the notion of *fitna* (sedition, commotion, strife), a term especially used for the disorder that, according to some unauthentic traditions of the Prophet, will precede the end of the world and the Resurrection. Like some Armageddon Christian theologians in the United States, the Tablighi Jamaat ulama believed that the Gulf conflict represented the beginning of the end (in this case, as predicted in the Hadith literature). One Hadith that these ulama quoted frequently in their Friday sermons stated that the Prophet Muhammad told his companions: "There will be caliphs after me that will not go the straight road in which I have gone; nor will they follow my example. But in those times there will be the hearts of devils in the bodies of men." A companion asked, "O Prophet, what shall I do if I live to see those days"? And the Prophet said, "Obey him who has authority over you, even though he flogs your back and takes your money."

The pacifist message of this Hadith is reinforced by many other similar traditions in this genre that became the basis of the Tablighi Jamaat's policy of "withdrawal" and "repentance" during the Gulf crisis. The thrust of these traditions refers to the post-Prophetic time, "which is not far away," when "a great strife will encircle the entire Arab world," and "all those killed in the strife will go to hell-fire." To speak out during this strife will be more dangerous than taking up the sword, the Prophet is reported to have said. Another tradition states that there will be great strife between two major groups before the end of the world. There will be a great deal of killing between those two groups (of Muslims) and both will claim that they are fighting for Islam. In other traditions, the Prophet is reported to have advised the faithful to stay aloof from this strife and take no sides. "A person who is sitting will be better than the one who is standing" during this strife. Another Hadith also quoted by some Tablighi ulama referred to "the final battle between the Jews and Muslims" in which the Christians will fight on the side of Muslims. During the height of the scorched-earth bombing and the lightning attacks on Iraq by the allied forces in Saudi Arabia, a Tablighi *alim* (religious official) quoted this Hadith to his congregation: "The day of Resurrection will not be instituted until (you witness) a great fire coming out of Hijaz [i.e., Mecca and Medina] that will light up even the necks of the camels of Basra."[32]

For Tablighi leaders and workers, this genre of fitna traditions led to an interpretation of the Gulf crisis as an event fulfilling part of the prophesies about internal strife between Muslims. In this interpretation the crisis was seen as symptomatic of the moral and spiritual degeneration of Muslims. During such a time of great stress and tribulation, the best policy for the faithful was not to take sides but to "withdraw," "repent," and pray for an early end of the situation.

Channels of Islamic Mobilization

The mosque and the madrasa were the primary organizational and institutional channels by which the various Islamic parties sought to mobilize the masses behind their interpretation of the Gulf war. The JUP, JUI, and JUAH all enjoy a strong following among the madrasa students. In fact, leaders of these three parties control over ninety percent of all madrasas in Pakistan. These students provided a highly disciplined and loyal corps of "the soldiers of Islam" who were brought to the streets for rallies, processions, and protest demonstrations at any time that their religious mentors wanted them. Being dependent entirely on their senior ulama for their education, food, clothing, and shelter, these madrasa students, in a sense, constitute "the bonded workers" for the ulama-led political parties. On the day of the national strike to express sympathy with the people of Iraq and to protest against the brutality of American bombing, for example, an estimated 80,000 students from madrasas—most of them under the JUI's control—were freed from their classes by the management of their madrasas and were asked to join the protest rallies. Their *akaabar* (elders) in the madrasas had convinced them that this was indeed a war between Islam and kufr and that it was their religious obligation to take part in efforts to mobilize the people against the American infidels.

Since the entire thrust of the anti-American agitation by the Islamic parties was couched in religious idioms and symbols, the mosques provided an appropriate and convenient forum for the religiopolitical protest as well as a sanctuary from the reprisals of the police. Throughout the war, major protest meetings were held in the mosques and most processions were started from there after the Friday congregation prayers. The local imams and khatibs delivered ravaging criticisms of America's double standards on Kuwait and Palestine, and on its bombing of Iraqi cities and yet indifference to the Kashmiri Muslims under Indian occupation. Much of the mobilization of mass protest was carried out through the pulpits of about 200,000 mosques throughout the country. The ulama's control of and access to such an important forum of mass contact on a daily basis is a great political asset for the ulama-led political parties. This is especially significant in the context of Pakistan where, unlike many other Muslim countries, the mosques and madrasas largely remain independent of state control.[33]

Another institutional channel that proved extremely effective in mobilizing the masses during the Gulf war consisted of local-level voluntary Islamic associations and societies. There has been a mushroom growth of such associations in Pakistan in recent years.[34] Proliferation of religiously-based associations is evidence of not only the pervasive influence of religion on society, but also the attempt by the religiopolitical groups to increase that influence. A sample survey that I conducted recently revealed the existence of 216 Islamic associations in the twin cities of Rawalpindi and Islamabad alone. The majority of these associations are local level political or religious off-shoots of the major religiopolitical parties such as the JI, JUP, JUI, JUAH, and TNFJ and tend to follow their leads on important national and international issues. These associations are used by the religiopolitical parties to mobilize mass support and to "test the political waters," to give an aura of nonpartisanship to their essentially political agenda, and to seek public reaction on controversial issues.

International connections and contacts were also used extensively during the Gulf conflict by the Islamic parties in Pakistan. We have already mentioned the initiative taken by the Jamaat-i-Islami to organize an international delegation of prominent Islamic activists from various parts of the Muslim world. This delegation met with the rulers of many Muslim states and presented its proposals for "an Islamic solution" to the conflict.[35] Regardless of the outcome of their efforts, the meetings of the Jamaat leaders with the kings, presidents, and prime ministers of Muslim states gave them a great publicity boost in Pakistan. These international diplomatic efforts won the Islamic movements an added measure of legitimacy in Pakistan by demonstrating the seriousness of their endeavors to act as mediators in intra-Islamic disputes—and the possibility that these endeavors could prove fruitful.

Another notable dimension of the Jamaat's international connections is its relationship to Saudi Arabia. There was no love lost between the Jamaat-i-Islami and Saddam Hussein. In fact, before the Gulf crisis, the Jamaat had described Saddam Hussein as a "ruthless dictator" and "an enemy of Islam" and enjoyed excellent relations with the Saudi governmental and religious authorities. Some of its prominent leaders are also the founding members of many of the international Islamic organizations formed directly or indirectly by the Saudis. Both Maulana Maududi, the founder of the Jamaat, and Professor Khurshid Ahmad, the current Vice-President of the Jamaat, are the recipients of the prestigious King Faisal award as a recognition by the Saudi authorities of their services to Islam.

In view of this relationship, one would not have predicted that the Jamaat would take such an aggressively anti-Saudi stance during the Gulf war. What seemed to have contributed to the significant change in its attitude were its growing contacts with the Islamic movements in Sudan, Jordan, the occupied West Bank and Gaza, Tunisia, and Algeria. The anti-American and anti-Saudi orientations of the movements in Jordan, as Beverley Milton-Edwards describes in her chapter, and in the Gaza Strip, as Jean François Legrain explains in his chapter, had a great influence on the Jamaat's thinking.

Another kind of international contact also played a significant role in influencing the reaction of some Islamic groups in Pakistan. During the Iran-Iraq war, the Iraqi government, through its diplomats in Pakistan, had been able to establish a strong foothold in the Pakistani Sunni establishment. The Iraqis, through financial contributions to some Sunni madrasas, used the already existing anti-Shi'ite sentiments of the sectarian-oriented ulama of the JUI to gain sympathy in their war with Shi'ite Iran. Similar contributions were made to the JUP establishment and its leaders were invited to visit Iraq as state guests. The Iranian government, although much more cautious and subtle than the Iraqis, has also been cultivating support among its natural allies, the Shi'ite organizations, without jeopardizing its relationship with its Sunni sympathizers. The Ahl-i-Hadith group has developed similarly close contacts with the Saudi authorities and has been a recipient of many rewards and privileges from the kingdom.[36] These contacts between Pakistan's religiopolitical parties with foreign governments, although couched in Islamic terms, have added a new dimension to the interaction between Pakistan's domestic politics and international Islamic developments.

The use of religious symbolism also played an important role in defining the Gulf conflict in Islamic historical terms. While the daily newspaper headlines about the massive bombings and destruction of Iraqi cities caused widespread resentment against the United States and an outpouring of sympathy for beleaguered Saddam, fighting alone against the mightiest powers of the world, the Islamic political parties invoked the powerful Islamic historical symbolism of the tragedy of Karbala, the seventh-century battle in which Imam Hussein, the grandson of the Prophet Muhammad, and his companions, including children, were massacred by a much larger army of the Umayyad Caliph Yazid in Karbala, now in modern-day Iraq. When Maulana Noorani of the JUP told a mass rally in Hyderabad that "the tragedy of Karbala is being reenacted in Iraq today," he sent a powerful message to his followers. The Chief of the Pakistan Army Staff, General Beg, was the first to use the Karbala analogy while addressing the General Headquarters Garrison officers in Islamabad on 28 January.[37]

Finally, we may also note another important recent development in Pakistan, Jordan, Sudan, and Algeria. Islamic movements in these countries are now part of the state apparatus and are in a position to influence the foreign policies of their countries. The deterioration of relations with the United States and the suspension or interruption of American aid to the governments of Sudan, Jordan, and Pakistan are likely to augment the influence of the Islamic groups on the domestic and foreign policies of these governments. In Pakistan, the Jamaat-i-Islami, the JUI, and the JUP are all part of the ruling coalition under the leadership of Prime Minister Sharif. All parliamentary decisions require their approval. Professor Abdul Ghafoor Ahmad, a prominent leader of the Jamaat-i-Islami from Karachi, is the Secretary General of the ruling coalition, the Islamic Democratic Alliance. When the head of the Jamaat, Qazi Hussein Ahmad, accused Foreign Minister Sahibzada Yaqub Khan of "pursuing American interests" during the Gulf crisis and launched a full-fledged campaign for his removal, the Prime Minister had no option but to seek the Foreign Minister's resignation. It was also the pressure built by the religious parties among his allies that sent Prime Minister Sharif on a "peace mission" to seven Muslim countries with a proposal for an immediate ceasefire and the simultaneous withdrawal of Iraqi troops from Kuwait and foreign (Western) troops from Saudi Arabia. Like their counterparts in Jordan, the Islamists in Pakistan used the Parliament and Cabinet chambers as effectively as they used public rallies and street demonstrations.[38]

Developments After the Ceasefire

Rhetoric and slogans aside, the Pakistani Islamic groups knew from the very beginning of the conflict that Saddam Hussein could not win against the powerful American-led international coalition. The use of the Karbala analogy itself signalled their anticipation that the crisis would end in defeat for the forces of good. Saddam Hussein's cryptic and incompetent handling of the war, his eleventh-hour retreat from his demand for linkage of the Gulf crisis to the Palestinian question, and his decision not to offer himself for martyrdom deprived his supporters among the Islamic parties of even a modicum of symbolic victory. The denouement of the war, with the humiliating scenes of mass surrenders of the Iraqi soldiers, did not even provide a worthy occasion for Saddam's Pakistani supporters to recite Muhammad Iqbal's famous line, *"Islam Zinda hota ha har Karbala key ba'ad"* ("Islam emerges stronger after every Karbala").

When the ceasefire came into effect, there was grief for the suffering of the people of Iraq but anger and resentment against Saddam Hussein for causing this humiliating defeat in what most Islamic groups thought was a war between Islam and unbelief. Protest demonstrations against the United States stopped; "recruiting centers" for raising an "Islamic legion" were dismantled; and Saddam's posters were removed from all public places. After a few days, there was business as usual in Pakistan—ethnic riots in Karachi, political bickering against the ruling coalition, "horse-trading" in the Senate elections—and the usual rumors about a change of government.

Prime Minister Nawaz Sharif issued a scathing criticism of the Islamic groups accusing them of "exploiting the sentiments of the people" in the name of Islam in order "to boost their own political fortunes." Referring to the leaders of Islamic parties who led pro-Saddam rallies on almost a daily basis, he asked: "Why are our politicians now hiding in their homes when the Iraqi people need their support and sympathy? They seem to be in a dire state of shock—not because of their grief over the destruction of the people of Iraq, but because of their utter failure in their petty political designs."[39] Other government spokesmen also claimed that the public rallies organized by the JUP, the JUI, and the PPP during the Gulf war were intended neither to demonstrate love of Saddam Hussein nor to express resentment against the United States; rather, these rallies were primarily intended to express opposition to the government of Prime Minister Sharif.[40]

Maulana Shah Ahmad Noorani and other leaders of the JUP, the most enthusiastic and ardent supporters of Saddam during the war, became conspicuously silent after the ceasefire. A lower level JUP leader argued, however, that Saddam's withdrawal from Kuwait was a "tactical move" and that he would strike again against "the forces of evil" at an

177

appropriate time.[41] The JUI leaders, as usual, saw a "Shi'ite conspiracy" in this debacle and attributed Saddam's defeat to the betrayal of Shi'ite soldiers in the Iraqi army. The TNFJ, the Shi'ite political organization that had joined its Sunni counterparts in support of Iraq, now saw the toppling of Saddam Hussein as fair game for Iran.

Yet the Jamaat-i-Islami, which had been careful enough not to glorify Saddam as an Islamic hero and had organized its jihad rallies primarily around the theme of anti-Americanism, continued its rhetorical crusade against the United States even after the war was over. "Regardless of what they [the government] think of our policy, we will continue to oppose America," Qazi Hussein Ahmad, the leader of the Jamaat told journalists in the Parliament House cafeteria on 16 March 1991. "If the New World Order is meant to bring the whole world under American control, we will never accept this."[42]

Some observers see the Gulf war as another important milestone in the growing radicalization of the Jamaat-i-Islami in Pakistan. This process began with the Islamic revolution in neighboring Iran in 1979. The impact of the Iranian revolution on the rank and file of the Jamaat, however, remained subdued because of the conservative, bureaucratic, and pro-Saudi leadership of Mian Tufail Muhammad, then leader of the Jamaat. The most important development that legitimized the Jamaat's appropriation of the revolutionary rhetoric of the Iranian revolution by the Jamaat was the Soviet invasion of Afghanistan; the Jamaat was now involved in nothing less than a jihad against the Marxist infidels. Later, the change of leadership from Mian Tufail to Qazi Hussein Ahmad, who had started his Islamic activist career in the student wing of the Jamaat and had close contacts with the Afghan Islamic movement, further strengthened this process of radicalization. The need to mobilize international Muslim support for jihad in Afghanistan brought the Jamaat-i-Islami even closer to the Islamic movements in the Arab world.

Given the fact that the majority of the Arab Islamic movements have an anti-American bias because of the American policies toward the problem of Palestine and the Arab-Israeli conflict, the internationalization of the political agenda of the Jamaat further contributed to its radicalization. By 1989, the Palestinian intifada, the Afghan jihad, and the Kashmiri struggle for freedom were seen by these Islamic movements as powerful manifestations of a radical resurgent Islam. It is in this context that one should understand their reaction to the massive show and use of force by the United States in and around the Islamic heartlands.

But the anti-American and anti-Saudi stance of the Jamaat under the leadership of Qazi Hussein Ahmad during the Gulf war did not go unchallenged. There was dissension within the Jamaat. Some party leaders thought that Ahmad had gone far beyond the original party mandate as approved by its central consultative committee. The party old guards feared that the new leadership of the Jamaat was influenced more by the mob than by reason and logic. They thought that populism and demagogy were not befitting an Islamic movement. *Takbeer* and *Zindagi*, the two most popular pro-Jamaat weekly newsmagazines, were highly critical of the anti-Saudi and anti-American politics of the Jamaat during the war and described it as "irresponsible," "irrational," and "sheer opportunism."[43] The most devastating public criticism of the Jamaat's Gulf policy came, however, from its former leader, Mian Tufail Muhammad, who described it as "unreasonable" and "unjustifiable." He attacked Saddam Hussein for his anti-Islamic activities throughout his political career and castigated the Jamaat for supporting "such an enemy of Islam and a ruthless dictator" who was "responsible for the killing of hundreds of thousands of Muslims." Mian Tufail said it was Saddam himself who was primarily responsible for bringing misery to his people, not the Saudis and the Americans.[44]

It is also important to note that the anti-American and anti-Saudi rhetoric of the Jamaat-i-Islami in Pakistan was not echoed by its sister organizations elsewhere. The Jamaat in India and Bangladesh repeatedly condemned the Iraqi invasion of Kuwait and held Saddam squarely responsible for the war. They condemned the massive American bombing of Iraq but remained considerably restrained in their anti-American rhetoric. The Jamaat-i-Islami in Kashmir, on the other hand, took a clearly anti-Saddam position and supported the U.N.-sanctioned action against Iraq to preserve Kuwait's right to self-determination. It believed that this new, more active role for the United Nations would bode well for the Kashmiris' case of self-determination supported by U.N. Security Council resolutions. The Kashmiri Jamaat also noted that while Saudi Arabia had always supported this cause, "Iraq and the PLO had lobbied for India." One of its leaders regretted that "Pakistanis who were well-mobilized during the Gulf crisis have been less vocal on Kashmir."[45]

Another related development was the introduction of the Shari'a Bill in Pakistan. The political mobilization of the masses during the Gulf conflict by the Islamic parties brought added pressure on the already beleaguered government of Prime Minister Sharif to prove the genuineness of its Islamic credentials. Believing that the general political climate was further "Islamized" by the upsurge of popular sentiment during the Gulf crisis and fearing a massive onslaught by the newly formed United Shari'a Front—a coalition of religious parties—with its demand for a radical Shari'a Bill, Nawaz Sharif introduced in Parliament on 10 April his own, moderate version of the bill. It is a package of legislative and administrative measures to Islamize education, the mass media, economy, bureaucracy, and the legal system. A miscellany of pious hopes and noble intentions ("The state shall take . . . measures to eliminate bribery, corruption and malpractices. . ."), the Shari'a Bill can be considered, at best, a symbolic gesture of plausible Islamic commitment by the Sharif government.[46] By and large, it consists of promises to establish a series of commissions to recommend "the ways, means, and strategy . . . measures and steps" to bring the social, economic, legal, administrative, and educational structures in line with the teachings of the Shari'a. Given the nature of the coalition government in Pakistan, however, one can argue that the mobilization of the Islamic constituency occasioned by the Gulf crisis hastened, but did not cause, the introduction of the bill.

Conclusion

Although Pakistan's own political problem with the United States—the opposition to Pakistan's nuclear program, the suspension of aid, the lack of support for Pakistan's position on the Kashmir problem—played a crucial role in influencing the reaction of the Islamic political groups in Pakistan to the Gulf war, one can also attribute motives of political expediency to the Jamaat-i-Islami and the JUP. Their anti-American agitational politics was intended all along to gain mass support for their organizations, especially in Karachi where both had suffered humiliating defeats during the 1988 and 1990 general elections. The Gulf crisis provided an irresistible opportunity to seize the day with a new and virulent round of anti-American rhetoric. It paid off in part in political capital in April 1991 when Prime Minister Sharif introduced the Shari'a bill.

The primary basis of the Islamists' reaction to the war, however, was religious and related to the notion of Islamic solidarity. The Islamic movements were genuinely concerned about the safety and integrity of Islamic holy places in both Saudi Arabia and Iraq. They considered the presence of close to half a million non-Muslim troops in the vicinity of Mecca and Medina as "blasphemous." They were also deeply concerned about the deaths of thousands of Muslims in Iraq and the massive destruction of Iraqi civilian and military facilities—notwithstanding the fact that all of them had earlier categorically disapproved of the Iraqi invasion and occupation of Kuwait. None of them was convinced, however, of the moral legitimacy of the American government's claim that it was implementing U.N. Security Council resolutions.

Sympathy for Iraq also grew with the general perception of all the religiopolitical groups—and, in fact, of secular groups such as the Pakistan People's Party, Tahrik-i-Istiqlal (The Independence Movement), and the Awami National Party as well—that the war was primarily a concerted military campaign against a potentially powerful Muslim state for the purpose of establishing Israeli hegemony over the Arab world. It was widely believed by the religious groups that the main beneficiary of this war would be Israel. "The Americans were driven to this war by Israeli interests," declared a Jamaat-i-Islami leader of Karachi, who pointed out that the resolution authorizing the President to use force against Iraq was sponsored by Rep. Stephen Solarz of New York. Because the Islamic groups in Pakistan were convinced that the interests of Israel and the United States in this particular war were indistinguishable, religious discourse was especially pointed and popular in its appeal. The Islamic groups argued, in effect, that the war against Iraq was the result of a conspiracy of Jews and Christians in the West to destroy a powerful Muslim country in the Middle East so that Israel could establish unchallenged hegemony in the region. This argument was taken seriously by significant numbers of Pakistanis.

Endnotes to Chapter 8

1. Gail Minault, *The Khilafat Movement: Religious Symbolism and Political Mobilization in India.* (New York: Columbia University Press, 1982), p. 57.

2. Ibid.

3. Ibid., p. 22. The British Prime Minister, Lloyd George added to these perceptions by describing the British conquest of Jerusalem as "the last and most triumphant of the crusades" (Quoted in Minault, p. 52).

4. For more extensive treatment of Islamic groups in the first and third categories, see my chapter, "Islamic Fundamentalisms in South Asia: The Jamaat-i-Islami and the Tablighi Jamaat" in Martin E. Marty and R. Scott Appleby, eds., *Fundamentalisms Observed* (Chicago: University of Chicago Press, 1991).

5. *Muhaddith*, February 1989.

6. *Manifesto of Tahrik-i-Nifaz-i-Fiqh-i-Ja'afriya,* (Lahore, n.d.), p. 11.

7. *Jang* (Karachi), 15 October 1990.

8. *Jamaat-i-Islami Press Release,* Publicity Department, Jamaat-i-Islami Pakistan, 19 January 1991.

9. *Jang* (Karachi), 25 January 1991; and *Zindagi,* 26 January–1 February 1991.

10. *Asia,* 9 December 1990.

11. Ibid.

12. *Pakistan Times Overseas Weekly,* 25 January 1991, p. 9.

13. Ibid.

14. *Dawn,* 29 January 1991; and *Muslim,* 30 January 1991.

15. *Pakistan Times Overseas Weekly,* 1 February 1991, p. 7.

16. Ibid., 25 January 1991, p. 9.

17. Statement of Sayyid Munawar Hasan, leader of the Jamaat-i-Islami branch in Karachi, as quoted in *Jamaat-i-Islami Press Release,* Publicity Department, Jamaat-i-Islami, Karachi, 20 January 1991.

18. *Jang* (Karachi), 31 January 1991.

19. Ibid., 16 February 1991.

20. Of course, none of these 110,000 volunteers actually left Pakistan to join Saddam Hussein's forces in Iraq. The whole exercise of recruiting volunteers was more of a symbolic show of solidarity with Iraq than a serious move to go to Iraq and fight.

21. *Jasarat,* 2 February 1991.

22. The police arrested more than 400 student workers of the JI in Karachi, Lahore, and Islamabad to prevent damage to the American diplomatic facilities.

23. The "officially approved" slogans given to the workers for these rallies and protest meetings included: "Crush America"; "Death to America"; "No to America"; "Allah is the only Superpower"; "America—Get out from the Gulf"; "America—the Greatest Enemy of Islam"; "Our war will continue until the total destruction of America and Israel"; "O you Jews! Muhammad's armies are advancing on Tel Aviv"; "Arabian Desert: the graveyard of America"; and "OIC—the only way to solve the Gulf problem." *Hamqadam,* February 1991, p. 40.

24. *Muslim,* 29 January 1991.

25. *Jang* (Rawalpindi), 5 February 1991.

26. *Jang* (Karachi), 3 February 1991.

27. *Nawa-i-Waqt,* 16 September 1990.

28. *Jang* (Karachi), 3 February 1991.

29. *Crescent International,* 16-28 February 1991, p. 1.

30. *Pakistan Times Overseas Weekly,* 1 February 1991 and author's telephone interviews with the Tablighi Jamaat leaders and workers.

31. Author's interviews; see also *Jang* (Karachi), 1 February 1991.

32. This Hadith is narrated by Abu Huraira and is included in the collection of both al-Bukhari (d. 256 A.H./870 A.D.) and "Muslim" (d. 261 A.H./875 A.D.), the two most widely accepted collections of the Prophetic traditions.

33. Hafiz Nazar Ahmad, "Jaiza Madaris-i-Arabiya Pakistan" (Lahore: Muslim Academy, 1971), reprinted in *Religion and Societies: Asia and the Middle East* (Berlin: Mouton, 1982), pp. 278–79.

34. Mumtaz Ahmad, "Class, Religion and Power: Some Aspects of Islamic Revivalism in Pakistan," (Ph.D. Dissertation, University of Chicago, 1990), pp. 26–29.

35. The Jamaat-i-Islami also convened a meeting of international Islamic movements in Lahore in early March. The meeting was attended by representatives of the Muslim Brotherhood from Egypt, Syria, Sudan and Jordan; Tunisia's Nahda party; Malaysia's Islamic party; three Afghan Islamic parties; and the JI Pakistan and JI Bangladesh. A statement issued after the two-day meeting accused the West of waging "a war . . . against Islam and its civilization" and said "an alliance of crusaders and Zionists" was seeking to control Muslim lands and wealth. Participants of the meeting met with the Pakistani President Ghulam Ishaq Khan under the leadership of Dr. Hasan al-Turabi of the Sudanese Muslim Brotherhood and demanded that Pakistan recall its 11,000 troops from the multinational force in Saudi Arabia and back Iraq "in its steadfastness. . . ." See *The Message International*, March 1991, p. 15.

36. The Ahl-i-Hadith establishment remained consistent in its support of Saudi Arabia and Kuwait throughout the Gulf crisis. While the Ahl-i-Hadith journals, *Tarjuman-al-Hadith, Tarjuman-as-Sunnah, Sahifa Ahl-i-Hadith, Al-Ihtisam,* and *Ahl-i-Hadith* pleaded for a diplomatic solution of the Gulf crisis before the beginning of hostilities, they were all unhesitant in their support for the Saudis' decision to go to war after 17 January. They held Saddam Hussein responsible for the bloodshed and carnage of the war *(Ahl-i-Hadith,* 1 March 1991; *Al-Ihtisam,* 15 March 1991; *Tarjuman-al-Hadith,* February 1991). At a time when pro-Saddam and anti-American emotions were running high throughout the country, the main spokesman of the Ahl-i-Hadith ulama wrote in its editorial: "Inshallah, Saddam will be defeated in his nefarious designs and will be remembered in the annals of human history as a butcher of Muslims." Ironically, the magazine employed the same sentimental Karbala analogy that pro-Saddam forces were employing, but dramatically reversed its application: "The Iraqis are once again reenacting the tragedy of Karbala in Kuwait by killing innocent and helpless Muslims." *(Ahl-i-Hadith,* 1 March 1991).

37. *Dawn,* 29 January 1991. Referring to the Karbala analogy frequently employed by the Pakistanis during the Gulf war, a Shi'ite scholar based in Washington remarked, in a caustic twist, that "The irony of the present conflict was that there were Yazids on both sides of the battlefield." Yazid was the Umayyad leader who killed the Prophet's grandson and supporters at Karbala.

38. For Jordan, Tunisia, and Algeria, see Walid Khalidi, *The Gulf Crisis: Origins and Consequences* (Washington, D.C.: Institute for Palestine Studies, 1990), pp. 16–19. Also see Milton-Edwards in this volume on Jordan and Roberts in this volume on Algeria.

39. *Jang* (Karachi), 18 March 1991.

40. Ibid., 11, 13, and 17 March 1991.

41. Ibid., 15 March 1991.

42. Ibid., 17 March 1991.

43. See *Takbeer,* 26 January 1991 and *Zindagi,* 7 March 1991. The editor of *Takbeer,* Muhammad Salahuddin, is a member of the Jamaat and is a former editor of the Jamaat's official daily newspaper, *Jasarat.* The editor of *Zindagi,* Murjib Shami, is also one of the most prominent pro-Jamaat journalists in Pakistan.

44. *Zindagi,* 7 March 1991.

45. *Eastern Times,* March 1991, p. 19.

46. The following dialogue between the Minister of State for Law, who formally moved the Shari'a Bill in the Parliament, and a Pakistani journalist is indicative of the "seriousness" with which the government is taking its new Islamic legislation:

Journalist: What difference will the Bill make in my life, practically? Give me one or two examples.

Minister: Let me go through the Bill and I will point them out. (He started sifting through the copy.) Yes, we will start teaching Shari'a and give training to students of law.

Journalist: But I am not a student of law. What difference will it make to me?

Minister: It will make you a better Muslim. The environment would change.

Journalist: How can a Bill make me a better Muslim if I do not want to become one? Where would the Bill come into play?

Minister: (Going through the copy further.) It will provide you a framework to remove interest from the economy.

Journalist: But for that ... Islamic banking has already been introduced in the country. Where does the Shari'a Bill come in?

Minister: (Going through the copy.) It will improve law and order, curb corruption, change the life of citizens, provide them security and safety.

Journalist: But it is already the duty of the government to provide security to every citizen. Is the government not doing its duty?

Minister: I am a simple man of few words. That is why I do not go out and confront the press.

(*Dawn,* 12 April 1991)

9

ISLAMIC FUNDAMENTALISM, DEMOCRACY, AND THE GULF WAR

Daniel Brumberg

> The war . . . [has] . . . exposed the mindless clichés about the Arab world that the experts had propagated. These are clichés . . . proclaiming . . . the power of . . . Islamic slogans to mobilize the Arab street. . . . The Arab street is a creation of intellectuals who want the West to believe that the radical agenda is the Arab agenda and the West must bend to it. In fact, in the Arab world public opinion—the street—is tightly controlled by regimes. . . . The street is largely an echo of the palace.[1]

The above writer has it half right. The representation of the Arab world advanced by some critics of the 1991 Gulf war was indeed constructed in part to undermine public and elite support of American policy. Yet to suggest that the "Arab world" is a place "tightly controlled by regimes," where the "street is largely an echo of the palace," is to replace one political misrepresentation with another. Was the Arab response to the Gulf crisis shaped by a widespread Islamic sensibility that fundamentalists exploited to advance their agendas? Or did the Arab "palace," or some other essential form of "Arab politics," determine the policies of each state with little regard for the expectations and desires of the Arab populations?

The chapters in this volume concerned with Arab populations grapple with these two difficult questions and conclude that neither question appropriately conveys the complex array of social, political, and economic factors that shaped the various responses of Arab peoples and nation-states. The Arab world is not defined solely by authoritarian dictates from above, or popular hysteria from below. In three of the cases examined in this volume, for example, a growing if fragile trend toward democratization and political pluralism provided the context in which Islamic groups responded to the Gulf crisis. The chapters on Egypt, Algeria, and Jordan are concerned in part with the diverse and paradoxical consequences of this inchoate democratization for the political fortunes of Islamic groups. While possibly strengthening what I will call the "pragmatic" Islamic groups, or pragmatic elements within these groups, the selective opening of civil societies has also created dilemmas and constraints. Thrown in sharp relief by the Gulf crisis, these may serve eventually to undermine the political and ideological influence of the "radical" fundamentalists.

In the past few years democratic reform has provided Islamic groups in Egypt, Jordan, and Algeria with an expanded political arena in which to solidify and enlarge their constituencies. To date the programs of democratization have been modest and cannot yet be described as a trend. Yet the Gulf crisis, coming on the heels of this development, offered a unique opportunity for the fledgling "democrats" to test their ability to mobilize their supporters according to democratic procedures. It also enabled the fundamentalists temporarily to bury the ideological rifts that had divided their own ranks — and that had separated fundamentalists from other groups.

However, while the Islamic groups benefited from these developments in the short term, the crisis also exposed the difficulties inherent in the fundamentalist program in rendering Islam an ideological system—that is, in translating religious law and Qur'anic precept into a coherent modern political vision capable of inspiring the formulation of effective solutions for difficult or even intractable problems. By exposing the ambiguities of Islamic fundamentalism's political and social project, the Gulf war may have thereby weakened the Islamic movement in those Arab countries in which the formidable task of democratization is a genuine prospect.

The Dilemma of Democratization

Democratization has come to parts of the Arab world largely as an elite initiative, by rulers seeking solutions to economic crises that could not be easily resolved through the use of brute force or through recourse to the old "ruling bargain." This "ruling bargain" was fashioned through an arrangement by which Arab rulers promised social welfare and job security in return for the populace's pledge not to engage in autonomous political action. This authoritarian social contract was secured by creating huge, inefficient public sectors, or by relying on foreign debt or workers' remittances earned in the Arab Gulf.[2]

In the 1980s these sources ran out. Unable to buy political passivity, reformers proposed a new "democratic bargain": in return for popular support of painful economic reforms, they opened up their political systems to more independent forms of political participation. They did so at a time in history when the levels of education and literacy were rising significantly in such urban population centers as Cairo, Amman, and Algiers.[3]

In Egypt and Tunisia this process unfolded through increased political liberalization rather than genuine democratization. Officially recognized opposition parties and syndicates were allowed to organize openly and to publish, but Islamic groups such as the Muslim Brotherhood and the Mouvement de Tendance Islamique (Islamic Tendency Movement, MTI) were not allowed to contest seats on their own platforms and elections were not conducted independently of government control. For example, parliamentary elections in Egypt (1987) and in Tunisia (1989) allowed for a relatively greater degree of multiparty participation, but were nonetheless skewed in favor of the incumbent regimes of Presidents Mubarak and Ben Ali. Subsequently both governments tried to fashion a rough accommodation with the opposition parties and professional associations regarding the limits of political and economic reform. Elsewhere, in Algeria and to some extent Jordan, the rulers made a more determined effort to open up the democratic system. The 1989 parliamentary elections in Jordan, and the June 1990 provincial and municipal elections in Algeria, both indicated a serious move toward substantive democratization.

However, political change brought new dilemmas. Precisely because the impetus for reform came initially from "above" and in circumstances of economic crisis, it was not cushioned by changes from "below." Secular democratic forces lacked the institutional and economic resources by which to mobilize mass followings. By contrast, the Islamic fundamentalist groups were able to use, and to an extent transform, their traditional institutions—mosques, charitable networks, schools, and hospitals—to address social and economic needs unmet by the centralized and heavily bureaucratized government. These institutions became in effect local political centers—channels through which Islamic fundamentalists were able to amass popular support in provincial, municipal, and national elections.[4]

Everywhere the result was the same: the Islamic groups, many of which advocated authoritarian goals, were the first to profit from democratic reforms. Egypt's Muslim Brotherhood won the largest bloc of opposition seats in the 1987 People's Assembly elections by entering into an electoral alliance with the Labor Party and the smaller Liberal Party.[5] Subsequently, Muslim Brothers won positions in councils of the professional syndicates and the "Professors' Clubs."[6] Beverley Milton-Edwards explains in her chapter that, in the November 1989 elections in Jordan, Islamic fundamentalists won 34 out of 80 seats in the House of Representatives, the lower house of Parliament. Most dramatically, as Hugh Roberts points out in this volume, Algeria's Islamic Salvation

Front or the FIS won two-thirds of the 48 provincial assemblies and 55 percent of the municipal councils during the June 1990 elections.[7]

The Facade of Unity

One of the factors that contributed to the successes of the Islamic movement within each of these countries was its apparent ideological and political unity. In contrast to the leftists, liberals, and Arab nationalists of varying stripes, the Islamists seemed devoted to a common vision. However, this facade of solidarity seemed to mask a reality of discord and difference as the Islamic groups moved from the realm of opposition and entered the arena of competitive politics. In each country, cleavages within the ranks of the Islamic movement surfaced in the months following its initial electoral victories. These Islamic movements in Algeria, Jordan, and Egypt may generally be described as "fundamentalist" in the sense in which the authors of this volume use the term—to characterize those Muslims who are actively committed to the establishment of a state on the basis of Islamic law. But beyond this basic commitment, the movements encompass a variety of viewpoints on the character of the envisioned Islamic state and society, as well as on a number of particular issues.

In general, however, the fundamentalist movements tend to split into two broad and at times overlapping camps: the authoritarian "radicals" and their more open-minded "pragmatist" competitors. The radicals favor an organic view of society in which the values of solidarity and moral unity take precedence over—but do not necessarily negate—the values of individual freedom. For them the early community of the Prophet Muhammad and his companions serves as a paradigm from which to deduce the guidelines for this religious form of corporatist ideology. The pragmatists, while starting from the premise that contemporary society must be based on "authentic" Islamic values, argue that the interpretation of Islam should be in keeping with the values of human rights, individual freedom, and even competitive democracy.[8]

As articulated during the past few years, these two visions have appealed to different social classes. Pragmatists spoke to the desire of middle class professionals, intellectuals, and entrepreneurs to synthesize Islamic tradition with modern political and social ideas. They also reinforced these middle class groups' support for economic reforms after decades of state-run development. The radicals' greater emphasis upon spiritual unity, political solidarity, and social justice articulated the distress of intermediate groups such as students, underemployed public sector employees, and elements of the petty bourgeoisie—groups which suffered from the inflation, corruption, and food shortages that accompanied economic reform in the Arab world. A myriad of other issues also helped to promote latent but potent divisions within the ranks of the fundamentalists, as well as between them and potential allies such as Arab nationalists.

During their political campaigns, Islamic fundamentalist strategists in Jordan, Algeria, and Egypt tried to obfuscate these differences by directing vague slogans ("Islam is the Solution") towards the widest possible coalition of social classes and ideological forces. Utopian visions and simplistic political slogans were propagated not only to unite the Islamists, but also to attract Arab nationalists, many of whom shared with the Islamists a deep suspicion of Western cultural influence.

During Egypt's 1987 elections, for example, the Muslim Brothers forged an "Islamic Alliance" with the Labor Party, a populist party which, despite its evocation of Islamic themes, did not share the Brothers' unyielding commitment to the application of Islamic law. Similarly, in Jordan the fundamentalists joined forces with Arab nationalists to form a parliamentary coalition. Led by the moderate Dr. Abd al-Latif Arabiyyat, the coalition boasted 40 members—just one vote short of a majority in the House of Representatives. In Algeria, the FIS leader Dr. Abassi Madani, a professor of education who favored a pragmatic position, joined forces with his fiery, fundamentalist deputy, Ali Belhadj, in a bid to galvanize support from both the lower class youth and the middle class professionals and small businessmen.

The Facade Breaks Down

By early 1991, however, just weeks prior to the outbreak of the Gulf war, these alliances and the fundamentalist slogans that helped to sustain them began to wear thin under the pressure of the crisis. This development was pronounced in Jordan and Algeria, where democratic reform had offered the Islamists substantial opportunities to exercise political power. Seeking to divide the opposition, King Hussein in January 1991 offered the Muslim Brotherhood five cabinet positions, including the Ministries of Health, Social Development, and Education. Acceptance of his offer immediately led to the collapse of the parliamentary coalition, whose Arab nationalist members, fearing (with some justification) that it would enable the King to coopt the Islamists, objected to the initiative. Several of the radical fundamentalists also objected. Unlike Arabiyyat and his more moderate colleagues, they insisted that no deal should be cut with the regime that could undermine the long-term quest to establish an "Islamic state" through democratic means.

In Algeria the situation was more complex. In the wake of the FIS's June 1990 victory, Madani had insisted that the FIS would respect the rights of other Islamic parties. "We are not Islam itself. . . . We do not monopolize religion," he declared.[9] But such tolerance reflected, at least in part, the pragmatic calculation that the FIS faced no serious competitors in the Islamic field. This began to change in the autumn of 1990, as Roberts explains. Responding to soaring middle class criticism of the FIS's authoritarian and sometimes violent control over the municipalities, Shaikh Mah-foud Nahnah, leader of the pragmatist Movement for Guidance and Reform, with the support of 300 Islamic associations, proposed an "Islamic Alliance." Madani promptly denounced this initiative, insisting that "anyone who wants unity should join our ranks for establishing the Islamic state." Initially Madani's remonstrations proved ineffective. Nahnah's proposal led to the creation of the Hamas organization, which spoke for those Islamic parties more supportive of a pragmatist orientation.[10] Subsequently, Shaikh Abdullah Djaballah threw his Movement of the Islamic Renaissance into the arena. This movement was closer to the FIS in that it insisted on an Islamic state. But it rejected the FIS's attempt to speak for the entire Algerian Islamic movement.[11]

As the Islamic movement fragmented and pressure grew on the Islamic parties to define their positions on economic and political reform, a complex struggle ensued to define the terms of a political alliance. Madani demanded that the other Islamic parties join one FIS list—a demand which they resisted. At the same time his relationship with Belhadj became tense. Madani implied the possibility of reaching an accommodation with President Chadli Benjedid, who was then holding discussions with the opposition leaders regarding the elections for the National Assembly, which he had promised to hold in the winter or spring of 1991. But Belhadj, rejecting Madani's position, insisted that the FIS press for the immediate creation of an Islamic state and the imposition of Islamic law.

In Egypt the way in which the democratization process had unfolded created a somewhat different situation for the Islamic groups such as the Muslim Brotherhood. The Egyptian government under Mubarak had led the way in fostering a fledgling democracy, but only on the conditions of the unwritten social contract which Gehad Auda discusses; by this contract, for example, the relatively unfettered parties and press are limited in several important ways, not least of which is in their freedom to criticize and mount opposition to

Egyptian foreign policy. And, since the opposition parties had little chance to share real power with the ruling National Democratic Party, much less replace it through elections, Islamist politicians were not compelled to define specific or detailed positions regarding domestic policy. On the other hand, Egypt's civil society was more developed by comparison to Algeria and Jordan. Its professional syndicates, "faculty clubs," student unions, and political parties offered a network of institutions through which Islamists could articulate and pursue political goals.[12]

Until the Gulf crisis the Islamic fundamentalists in Egypt had primarily devoted their energies to protesting the arrest of radical Islamic activists. But with Iraq's invasion of Kuwait they turned their attention to the Gulf. In early autumn the Muslim Brotherhood leader Ma'mun al-Hudaibi insisted that the invasion contravened Islam:

> We do not approve of an attack and a military invasion that one Arab country carries out against its Arab neighbor. . . . We are advocates of unity, but this unity must be achieved by mutual consent. Everyone must believe in that unity, and everyone must feel a sense of common interest. God Almighty says, "Believers are a band of brothers" (Qur'an, 49:10).[13]

However, the Brotherhood's major partner in the Islamic Alliance—the Labor Party —viewed Iraq's invasion through the prism of Arab nationalism rather than pan-Islam. As the Gulf crisis escalated, Labor Party spokesmen began to portray Saddam Hussein as a defender of Arab nationalism. This divergence of views created tension within the Alliance and eventually led to an open revolt within the Labor Party. In the People's Assembly, Labor Party deputies "almost lost their senses when they saw that the Labor Party leadership . . . blindly endorsed . . . a stance that contradicts logic."[14]

In short, by the mid-point of the Gulf crisis, the Islamic fundamentalists of Algeria, Jordan, and Egypt were unable to agree upon and articulate even the outline of a shared Islamic political critique of the situation, much less a set of constructive policy proposals on either common domestic or international issues. Fundamentalist dogma, which had served to conceal profound socioeconomic, political, and ideological ruptures within the Islamic movement, gave way to competing voices and claims, a trend which was reinforced by the political liberalization and democratization of Arab societies.

The Gulf War: A Temporary Respite

For the Islamic fundamentalists, then, the Gulf war came at an opportune time. James Piscatori in this volume discusses the rich repertoire of symbols and images that fundamentalist leaders—as well as the "situational fundamentalist" Saddam Hussein— drew upon to build a common Islamic discourse to counter that of the American-led coalition. This effort did prove strikingly effective for a time, mitigating conflicts among Islamic opposition groups as well as those between Islamists and Arab nationalists or leftists. But it was ultimately unable to conceal the fundamentalists' own difficulty in providing practical answers to difficult problems at the very moment that the exigencies of democratic reform demanded coherent policies. At times the rich Islamic discourse seemed to be reduced to a simplistic series of anti-imperialist and anti-Jewish diatribes; ideological slogans took the place of substantive political platforms.

For example, Jordan's Muslim Brotherhood, as Milton-Edwards reports in this volume, wasted no time in fusing Islamic, Arab, and anti-Western slogans into a formula designed to whip up popular support. The Brotherhood spokesman in the House of Representatives, Dr. Arabiyyat, denounced "Jewish rabbis and clergymen in the sacred lands."[15] A week later, after street protests in Amman, fundamentalist deputies told a public rally that "our first objective is . . . to liberate the Islamic world from any foreign tutelage. . . . This holy land will not tolerate infidels setting foot on it."[16] To accentuate its populist credentials, the House of Representatives declared that "resistance to the imperialist invasion . . . is a pan-Arab, Islamic, and universal responsibility."[17]

As the utility of the Gulf crisis became clear, all of Jordan's political parties and professional associations jumped on the anti-imperialist bandwagon. This trend facilitated cooperation between leftist-Palestinians and Islamists, groups which had previously shared little other than a profound antagonism toward the West.[18] United by this sentiment, the leftist People's Democratic Party, the Islamic Jihad, and the Muslim Brotherhood denounced the United States' "barbaric invasion of the Gulf," and appealed to Muslims "not to bow to Bush or anyone else among the enemies of Islam."[19] The Jordanian Pharmacists' Association, a group dominated by Arab-Palestinian nationalists and leftists, joined Islamic fundamentalists in Amman's "Professional Association Center" in denouncing the United States.[20] Academics then held a rally which condemned the allied air campaign as "reminiscent of the crusading spirit of the Middle Ages, which can only ignite the spirit of jihad in self defense."[21] Although these events often followed or paralleled spontaneous protests, such protests were relatively insignificant by comparison with the zealous initiative shown by the professional associations, political parties, labor federations, and especially the House of Representatives.[22]

As the Gulf crisis distracted Jordan's fledgling civil society, issues of political, economic, and social reform fell to the wayside. The parameters of reform were defined in a new "National Charter," a draft of which was submitted for public debate in December 1990. A good part of the Charter dealt with the relationship between Arabism, Islam, and Palestinian nationalisms.[23] But when events on the ground—and in the air—took over, the contentious debate over national identity was postponed until June 1991, when King Hussein proposed a new charter that affirmed pluralism in the political system and seemed by its wording to reject the hopes for an Islamic fundamentalist state in Jordan.[24]

In Algeria, the Gulf war created a climate in which FIS leader Madani found himself compelled to compete with the demagogic appeals of his deputy, Belhadj. Similarly, by radicalizing the political arena the war made it difficult for other Islamic parties such as Hamas and the Movement of the Islamic Renaissance to resist the demand that they subordinate themselves to the FIS's will. In the beginning of the crisis Madani adopted a moderate position. "We are for a peaceful solution that is decided by the Arabs themselves," he declared in late November 1990. "The presence of these [foreign] forces will not contribute to the solution, but will further complicate the issue."[25] Madani at first did not attend the FIS's anti-war rallies, where he would have been pressed to compete with Belhadj's inflammatory rhetoric. However, he was soon pressed to take a more radical stand. As prospects of war loomed in January, attendance at the FIS rallies increased to embrace a wide spectrum of Algerians, many of whom did not "share the FIS version of Islamic law . . . but all [of whom] . . . wanted to say that between Bush and Saddam they have made their choice."[26] Simultaneously, the other political parties (some 30 in all by January), professional syndicates, and labor unions organized their own rallies at which they declared "solidarity with the Iraq people."[27]

Responding to these events, Madani began playing to the masses. On 12 January 1991, in a Friday sermon, he and Belhadj urged a congregation of some 6,000 worshippers to "attack U.S. and Jewish interests anywhere in the world."[28] Several days later Madani insisted that the government mobilize "one million reservists . . . and all sons of Algeria" in order to "prepare ourselves for war." He also took the occasion to argue that the popular mobilization in support of Iraq was not a fluke but could be sustained for domestic economic goals. "The second point is that the country needs harmony and cooperation, particularly at the level of the economic apparatus, " he said. "We must open spheres for more production, mobilize the people. . . . We must produce [commodities]

... and store them so that we will not ... [be] faced with the catastrophe of a boycott ... or merely scarcity of commodities brought about by this war."[29]

The strategy of depicting the popular response to the Gulf crisis as a victory for democratization guided by Islamic principles was quickly imitated by the other Algerian Islamic parties. Even before the ground war, the leaders of the Movement of the Islamic Renaissance and Hamas indicated that they might consider joining a FIS list in the upcoming yet still to be scheduled elections. In addition, several Hamas leaders were beginning to compete with the FIS's radical rhetoric. Some observers of Algerian politics wondered whether this turn of events demonstrated that Hamas's relatively "liberal voice" had been a facade all along.[30]

In Egypt a similar pattern could be detected. The divisions between the Muslim Brotherhood and Arab nationalists in the Labor Party, which had been pronounced at the start of the war, began to narrow as both groups adopted a pan-Islamic/Arab discourse directed first and foremost against the United States. However, there were two key differences between Egypt's experience and that of Jordan and Algeria. First, Egypt was an official and active member of the anti-Iraqi alliance. Support for Mubarak, at least at the outset of the crisis, was widespread because of the resentment that many Egyptians harbored against Saddam Hussein's regime, and Saddam in particular. After all, his regime had for years mistreated Egyptian soldiers and civilians living in Iraq, while Saddam himself had humiliated Mubarak by promising not to invade Kuwait two days before his tanks rolled into Kuwait City. Second, and more importantly, Egypt's participation in the alliance enhanced the saliency of the military in domestic politics. Extended and exposed in the Gulf, the military feared that the fundamentalists would exploit the Gulf crisis to advance their interests. Furthermore, its concerns about a "popular" reaction were heightened by pressures on the Egyptian government from the International Monetary Fund to initiate substantive but painful economic reforms. Coming in the wake of the Gulf crisis, such a situation could spark a popular uprising similar to the 1977 "food riots" that had shaken Sadat's regime.

For these reasons Mubarak's government, and particularly the military, was not keen to advance the democratic process any further. On the contrary, when the High Court in November 1990 ruled that the previous People's Assembly had been elected illegally in 1987, the regime passed a new election law, the modalities of which predictably played into the hands of the ruling National Democratic Party.[31] In turn, the opposition parties, with the exception of the small leftist National Progressive Unionist Group, boycotted the November elections.[32]

Against this backdrop of rising government authoritarianism, both Brotherhood and Arab-nationalist leaders of the "Islamic Alliance" found it expedient to flog the regime with the Gulf crisis. But this policy did nothing to hide the previous failure of all the political parties, including the Islamic ones, to build party structures that could mobilize the populace. Only by exploiting crises could the Islamic fundamentalists spark Egypt's desperate yet largely apathetic youth—many of whom had grown weary of the personal disputes that characterized opposition politics in Egypt.

The Limits of Fundamentalist Ideology

With the close of the Gulf crisis and the return of Egyptian troops in May 1991, the realities and demands of domestic politics returned quickly to the center of public consciousness. The democratic agenda, interrupted in Jordan and Algeria, was once again on the table; in Egypt, the fundamentalists pondered their next move in light of the fact that the regime had arrested some of their leaders and had efficiently quelled student protests against the war in March. As Auda characterizes it, this was indeed a moment of uncertainty.

In Jordan the resumption of domestic politics did not overshadow discussions of regional and international issues.

Indeed it could not, since in Amman, as in Jerusalem, domestic politics and foreign policy were barely separable. Accordingly, the Muslim Brotherhood continued to invoke the Gulf crisis as yet another episode in which weak Arab and Muslim leaders had capitulated to the ruthless West. However, as the extent of Saddam's defeat became clear, and as he turned his guns against the Kurds in the north and the Shi'ites in the south, the Brotherhood discovered that the value of the crisis had depreciated. On 6 April, it attracted a crowd of no more than 15,000 protestors during a rally outside Amman —far less than the 50,000 people expected. Despite this low turnout, the spokesman for the Brotherhood parliamentary bloc, Deputy Ahmad Qutaish al-Azayida, told his audience that the rally was held "to prove that campaigns undermining the movement's popularity are false."[33] Whether in fact the Brotherhood's popularity had dropped, as this statement might suggest, was unclear. No polls were taken, nor was Jordan approaching an election that could test public opinion.

Nevertheless, the Brotherhood could not deny political realities. The contentious issue of political identity, which had been raised in the draft National Charter in December 1990, was now back on the domestic political agenda. King Hussein addressed this question in late April 1991, when he urged "further dialogue among diverse tendencies and minds in the spirit that permeated the deliberation of the National Charter Committee, which has led to increased understanding and closeness of ranks and has laid foundations that may be consolidated before endorsing the National Charter and organizing political activity."[34] Whether the ideological ranks have closed to the extent that King Hussein suggested is doubtful. The resumption of "dialogue" is now confronting Arab nationalists, Hashimites, liberals, and fundamentalists alike with daunting tasks that will likely revive the ideological, social, and political cleavages that had originally divided them. Indeed the postwar activities of the Islamic fundamentalists have caused some people to question their level of tolerance. For example, the Ministry of Education, controlled by the Muslim Brotherhood, has caused a national controversy by banning fathers from watching their daughters play at sports, and by introducing daily prayers in the schools that condemn both the United States and Israel. In the face of such impolitic behavior King Hussein apparently judged that the fundamentalists had not proven themselves reliable partners in the delicate game of political moderation that the Jordanian government must play. The new National Charter which he proposed on 9 June 1991 advanced the democratization process by "allowing a multiparty system, providing for greater rights for women, and enhancing the freedom of the press," as Milton-Edwards reports, but it may simultaneously have the effect of circumscribing "the power of the Islamic fundamentalists."

In Algeria the resumption of democratic reform has revived ideological divisions within the Islamic movement, and between Islamists and their secular opponents. In fact, recent events, including the postponement of national elections, suggests that the FIS, by overplaying its hand during the Gulf crisis, not only pushed the smaller non-Islamic parties toward the FLN, but also drove potential Islamic allies such as Hamas toward the other opposition parties. The FIS's troubles came about as a result of the resort to violence and intimidation by its more zealous members, who in March disrupted a number of artistic and musical events in Algiers and other cities; and as a result of Madani's increasingly violent and even irrational rhetoric, which, despite widespread and genuine sympathy for Iraq, alienated many Algerians.

The government responded to Madani by employing both its coercive and its political assets. On 31 January 1991, for example, it brought in anti-riot commandos to prevent the FIS protestors from attacking pro-alliance foreign embassies, as they had threatened to do. As it turned out, attendance at the rally was reported to be "highly disappointing," while "a large portion of the population approved the president's firm handling of matters."[35] President Chadli subsequently exploited the growing backlash against the FIS by having the FLN-controlled Assembly pass new electoral legislation designed to limit the FIS's influence in any upcoming election. The new legislation, passed in April, banned campaigning in mosques, forbade "proxy" voting, and most importantly, divided Algeria into over 500 constituencies to be elected through unified, nominal lists. This initiative was promptly welcomed by several of the smaller, liberal parties. But Madani denounced it and then escalated his war of words with the government by demanding the annulment of the legislation and immediate presidential elections. This attack on Chadli, who despite the FLN's declining fortunes had gained wide popular support, further isolated the FIS.

Equally if not more important, Madani's behavior helped to revive cleavages that had set his movement apart from other Islamic groups before the Gulf war. With the government's announcement that the first round of National Assembly elections was to be held on 27 June, FIS's Islamic competitors began jockeying for position. The most pronounced rift was between the FIS and Hamas. Shaikh Nahnah, Hamas's leader, issued a moderate political program in which he called for an "Islamic society" to be achieved "by steps" on the basis of "a dialogue and far from violence." "Islam," he explained, "calls for Muslim fraternity and charity."[36] Several weeks later, he insisted that "a one-party system with an Islamic party would be a dictatorship. The antidote to sclerosis of the mind is a multi-party system."[37] After repeating this moderate line in interviews and once on the (Algerian) television program "Meet the Press," Nahnah was approached by several leaders of the smaller, non-Islamic parties, including the Rally for Culture and Democracy, a Berber group which was the sole party to have called explicitly for a "secular" republic. In the ensuing months, to the FIS's dismay, Nahnah suggested that his party might consider joining a coalition government with other pro-democratic parties—including the FLN.[38]

Whether this development corroborates the claim that "Saddam's defeat has turned the Algerian political situation upside down, leaving the FIS in the worst position of all," remains to be seen.[39] Hugh Roberts (see chapter 7) does not agree that the postponement of the June 1991 elections supports this view; to the contrary, he sees Chadli's suspension of the elections after two weeks of rioting by Islamists as a victory for the FIS, and by extension, a triumph for the forces of democracy. In Robert's view, the supporters of the FIS were compelled to take to the streets in order to oppose the regime's "unjust" election laws. Thus the subsequent arrest of Belhadj and Madani was a clear indication that the regime, and particularly the military, had no intention of permitting a genuine experiment in democratic reform.

However, while there is no doubt that elements within the regime were looking for an excuse to clamp down on the FIS, it is possible to interpret the events of late June 1991 in a different light. FIS's claim that it was only defending democracy may have been somewhat disingenuous; indeed, Madani's intolerant reaction to the aspirations of other Islamic parties suggested a rather narrow view of any process which would not guarantee FIS its "rightful" victory. This intolerance turned into outrage with the passage of new election laws that made it more difficult for the FIS to usher in an Islamic State under "democratic" auspices.

In any case, the violent confrontations between the Algerian army and Islamists in June 1991 demonstrated how difficult it is to advance democratic reform in the absence of a strong political center of established and time-tested civil institutions and procedures capable of absorbing the shocks that inevitably accompany a transition from one-party rule to political pluralism. This is not to suggest, however, that Algeria's authoritarian past condemns it to an authoritarian future. The prospects for democracy will depend, in part, on how Algeria's middle classes—and particularly the more moderate elements within the Islamic movement—interpret and respond to the crisis in the Algerian public order that followed closely upon the heels of the crisis in the Persian Gulf.

In the case of Egypt, as I have noted above, the Islamic political parties and professional associations were largely excluded from the political arena during the Gulf crisis. Combined with the structural weakness of the fledgling Egyptian civil society, this exclusion from prominence in the public debate meant that the failure of Egypt's mainline Islamists to move beyond slogans and diatribes was not immediately damaging. But, as Auda suggests in his chapter, neither does it augur well for their ambitions for a more expansive and central role in Egyptain political life. Egyptians are well aware that when push came to shove, the Islamic groups were not in a position to prevent the regime from altering the rules of the election process. Nor could they deter the regime from backing the anti-Saddam alliance in the Gulf. And most telling of all, the fundamentalists have had relatively little to say regarding the regime's decision to go ahead with a rigorous International Monetary Fund economic austerity package.

The weakness of Egypt's principal Islamic groups is not solely of their own making. The institutions in which they have gained a foothold—particularly the professional syndicates—have thus far had more experience in making particular demands of the state than in addressing and mobilizing civil society. Lacking social constituencies, these institutions have focused their attention on either stridently opposing ruling elites, or when the occasion presents itself, on stirring up a usually apathetic constituency. Under these conditions there has been little incentive to move beyond slogans and diatribes. Yet even in those rare cases where Islamic fundamentalists have struck deeper roots in civil institutions, they have not translated these gains into effective political outcomes. The "faculty clubs" are a case in point. By drawing on the universities' huge student and teaching staff population, Islamic fundamentalists turned the clubs into centers of opposition. But there was little consensus within their own ranks as to what the relationship was between Islam and the myriad of professional issues that affected students and academics. Lacking answers to these difficult issues, the fundamentalists found it easier to exploit whatever crises came their way—including the Gulf crisis.

Conclusion

Asked in January 1991 whether he was shocked by the Jordanian Parliament's declaration in which it described the United States as the "great Satan," Crown Prince Hasan of Jordan remarked: "This Islamic feeling has been growing fast since the 1989 elections . . . In this part of the world, there is a long list of burning . . . crises . . . [which] . . . produce fundamentalist . . . movements."[40] In the "old days," such movements in the Arab world had two choices. They could remain underground; or they could "rally the masses" through street demonstrations that would be either violently suppressed by fearful regimes, or demagogically embraced by populist leaders seeking to exploit the masses. Today, however, Arab civil societies have increasingly opened up to the play of pluralistic politics, in large part because authoritarian governments can no longer manage economic and political challenges through authoritarian dictate. In Algeria and Jordan, and to a limited extent Egypt, nascent professional syndicates and political parties absorbed and even reshaped the popular pressures provoked by the Gulf crisis. At the same time they exploited this crisis in a bid to extend their ideological reach.

Ironically, this strategy played into the hands of ruling regimes. By tolerating debate and free assembly, Chadli Benjedid and King Hussein deflected public opinion away from their regimes while appearing to champion democracy. This approach did entail risks; at times both leaders found themselves echoing popular concerns regarding the Gulf war—concerns which Chadli and King Hussein no doubt shared.[41] Yet political liberalization offered, for the most part, a safe alternative to the use of force. Moreover, it created an arena in which the diverse and often conflicting claims of the Islamists were submitted to the verdict of popular opinion. This verdict is by no means in. But many in the Arab world are now wondering how the Islamic movement—and in particular the radical fundamentalists among them—can articulate a practical vision which effectively links Islamic values to the trying tasks of political and economic reform.

Endnotes to Chapter 9

1. Charles Krauthammer, "On Getting It Wrong," *Time,* 15 April 1991, p. 70.

2. The "democratic bargain" is discussed in greater detail in Daniel Brumberg, "The Prospects for a Democratic Bargain in the Middle East," a paper prepared for the National Endowment for Democracy (unpublished, 1991).

3. Muhammad Muslih and Augustus Richard Norton, "The Need for Arab Democracy," *Foreign Policy* 83 (Summer 1991): 12.

4. For a discussion of this development in Egypt, see John O. Voll, "Sunni Arab Fundamentalism: Egypt and the Sudan" in Martin E. Marty and R. Scott Appleby, eds., *Fundamentalisms Observed* (Chicago: University of Chicago Press, 1991).

5. Still, it should be emphasized, Mubarak's National Democratic Party won 60 percent of the 448 seats in the People's Assembly.

6. See Gehad Auda's discussion of interest groups in the *1989 Arab Strategic Report* (Cairo: Al-Ahram Center, 1990) (In Arabic). Auda contrasts, in particular, the experience of the Lawyers' Syndicate, with that of the Syndicate of Journalists.

7. Daniel Brumberg, "Islam, Elections and Reform in Algeria," *Journal of Democracy* 2 (1) (Winter 1991): 58–71.

8. On these divisions, see Leonard Binder, *Islamic Liberalism* (Chicago: University of Chicago Press, 1988); and, Issa J. Boullata, *Trends and Issues in Contemporary Arab Thought* (New York: State University of New York Press, 1989). We should be careful, however, not to equate Islamic pragmatism with liberalism. Islamic pragmatists also have an essentially corporatist vision in mind. Yet they would like to rebuild society and recover its essential unity, not through the coercive imposition of an "Islamic state" from above, but through the individual "reform" of free men. This vision shares certain affinities with liberalism but is not equal to it.

9. See "Islamic Front Outlines Plans," an interview with Abassi Madani, in *Al-Watan (The Nation),* 22 June 1990. Translated in *Foreign Broadcast Information Service* [hereafter, *FBIS*], NES 90–124, 27 June 1990.

10. Not to be confused with the West Bank Gaza Palestinian organization "Hamas," which is discussed in detail in Jean François Legrain's contribution to this volume.

11. See interview with Djaballah in *El-Moudjahid,* p. 24. Translated in *Joint Publications Research Service* [hereafter, *JPRS*], NEA 91-008, 25 January 1991, pp. 14–15.

12. For an extended discussion of the role of these syndicates and political clubs in the democratization process, see Daniel Brumberg, "The University Intelligentsia and the Struggle for Democracy in Contemporary Egypt," (Ph. D. dissertation, University of Chicago, 1991).

13. See "Islamic Scholars Discuss Iraqi Invasion," *Akhir Sa'a (Another Hour)*, 8 August 1990, translated in *JPRS*, NEA 90-050, 14 September 1990, pp. 4–8.

14. See "Labor Party Members Condemn Leadership in Gulf," *FBIS*, NES 90-183, 23 September 1990, p. 10. Liberal Party members also opposed the Labor Party's support for Saddam Hussein, arguing that such a stand would hurt the party's chances in the parliamentary elections scheduled for December. See "Some Egyptian Labor Party Leaders Freeze Their Membership," *Al-Sharq al-Awsat (The Middle East)*, 20 September 1990, in *FBIS*, NES 90-186, 25 September 1990, p. 10.

15. See "Muslim Brotherhood Welcomes Call for Jihad," in *FBIS*, NES 90-184, 21 September 1990.

16. See *Al-Ra'i (The Opinion)*, 30 September 1990, in *FBIS*, NES 90-191, 2 October 1990, pp. 47–48.

17. The statement took the form of a joint declaration issued in conjunction with Iraq's National Assembly. See "Joint Statement Issues on Gulf" in *FBIS*, NES 90-197, 11 October 1990, p. 43.

18. During the 1989 elections the Islamic fundamentalists established an alliance with Arab nationalists and leftists. But this alliance quickly broke down, in part because the fundamentalists rejected the nationalists' and leftists' call for a two-state solution to the Palestinian problem.

19. *Al-Dustur (The Constitution)*, 23 November 1990, in *FBIS*, NES 90-226, 23 November 1990, p. 46.

20. See *Jordan Times*, 13 January 1991, in *FBIS*, NES 91-009, 14 January 1991, p. 74.

21. See *Jordan Times*, 2 February 1991, in *FBIS*, NES 91-023, 4 February 1991, p. 73.

22. For example, some 10,000 protestors—at the very most—marched in Amman several days before the meeting of Jordanian professors. The size of public protests in the ensuing months, even after the ground war began, did not more than double this number. See *Jordan Times*, 31 January–1 February 1991, in *FBIS*, NES 91-021, 31 January 1991, p. 40.

23. See "Draft National Charter," *Al-Dustur*, 30 December 1990, in *JPRS*, NES 91-018, 15 March 1991, pp. 16–25.

24. See Beverley Milton-Edwards' chapter in this volume.

25. See "Islamic Front Denies Change in Position on Gulf" in *FBIS*, NES 90-229, 28 November 1990, p. 1.

26. See "FIS Holds Pro-Iraqi Demonstrations" in *FBIS*, NES 91-014, 22 January 1991. The report refers to a rally held in Algeria's Harcha hall on 21 January, at which "One absence was noticeable—that of FIS leader Abassi Madani."

27. See "Rallies Held in Solidarity with Iraqis" and "Marches Held in Support of the Iraqi People," *FBIS*, NES 91-107, 25 January 1991, pp. 3–4. No figures are given for the numbers of participants in the marches.

28. See "Attack on U.S. Jewish Interests Worldwide Urged," *FBIS*, NES 91-009, 14 January 1991, p. 14. It should be noted that the quotes in this report appear to be those of Belhadj rather than Madani.

29. "Fundamentalist Leader on Military Training," *FBIS, NES 91-019, 29 January 1991, p. 3.*

30. See Bouziane Ahmed Khoda, "FIS-HAMAS: A Semblance of Divorce" in *Revolution Africaine (African Revolution)*, 10 January 1991 in *JPRS*, NES 91-014, 22 February 1991, pp. 9–11.

31. One leftist Egyptian friend complained to me in November 1990: "If there is war in the Gulf, we'll never get rid of Mubarak."

32. The newly elected Peoples Assembly declared on 26 January its "full support for His Excellency President Muhammad Husni Mubarak in all his efforts . . . to tackle the crisis . . . (and) salutes our valiant Armed Forces, the immune shield of the nation, who are ready to defend Arab security and dignity . . . " See "People's Assembly Declares Support for Gulf Policy," *FBIS*, NES 91-018, 28 January 1991.

33. See *Jordan Times*, 6 April 1991, in *FBIS*, NES-91 069, 10 April 1991, p. 34.

34. See "King Addresses Cabinet on Local Arab Issues," *FBIS*, NES 91-182, 29 April 1991, p. 30.

35. See Pierre Devoluy, "Algeria Grapples with the Truth," in *L'Express*, 22 March 1991.

36. See "HAMAS Movement Presents Political Program," *FBIS*, NES 91-063, 2 April 1991. Nahnah's made these pronouncements on 30 March.

37. See *L'Express,* 22 March 1991.

38. As for the leaders of the Nahda Party, while they stated their willingness to run on a ticket with FIS, they also indicated this electoral alliance would have to "to represent Islam and not the parties." See "Political Parties Criticize Election Law Changes," *FBIS*, NES 91-059, 27 March 1991.

39. See *L'Express* , 22 March 1991.

40. See *Le Monde,* 23 January 1991, in *FBIS,* NES 90-016, 14 January 1991, p. 44.

41. See, for example, King Hussein's speech to "the Arab and Islamic nation" in Amman on 6 February, during which he stated: "When Arab and Islamic territory is presented as a base for the armies of the allies to destroy the Iraq of Arabism and Islam. . . . I say . . . any Arab or Muslim can imagine the size of the crime committed against his religion and nation. . . . As for our people in Iraq . . . to those kinsfolk, we extend all love . . . while they are defending us all and raising high the banner saying God is great, the banner of Arabism and Islam." *FBIS*, NES 91-026, 7 February 1991, pp. 27–29. During the war King Hussein and President Chadli regularly consulted opposition party leaders.

CHRONOLOGY

A Chronology of the Gulf Crisis

1990

16 July Tariq Aziz, Foreign Minister of Iraq, in a letter to Arab League, accuses Kuwait of having stolen 2.4 million dollars worth of oil from the Rumaila fields in the early stages of Iran-Iraq war, of erecting military installations on Iraq's territory, and of reducing Iraq's oil income by keeping oil prices low through overproduction. Aziz complains that the United Arab Emirates (UAE) had exceeded its oil production quotas, and that both it and Kuwait refused to cancel Iraq's war debts.

17 July Saddam Hussein, blaming the production policies of Kuwait and UAE on American influence designed to undermine Arab interests, threatens force to make Arab oil exporters keep to production quotas.

18 July Kuwait convenes emergency session of its National Council and sends emissaries to Arab states to discuss Iraqi accusations.

19 July Kuwait informs Arab League that Iraq is drilling for oil in Kuwaiti territory, and sends message to Perez de Cuellar, Secretary General of the United Nations, about relations with Iraq. Richard Cheney, American Secretary of Defense, states that the United States is committed to defend Kuwait in case of attack.

21 July 30,000 elite Iraqi troops mass on border with Kuwait; by end of July number grows to 100,000.

25 July After meeting in Alexandria between President Hosni Mubarak of Egypt, King Hussein of Jordan, and Tariq Aziz, a statement is issued that Iraq has agreed to settle differences with Kuwait and the UAE, and that Kuwait has agreed to talks with Iraq to be held in Saudi Arabia to settle the border dispute.

31 July Representatives of Iraq and Kuwait hold talks in Jeddah which collapse on 1 August.

2 August On pretext of supporting a group of Kuwaiti revolutionaries opposed to the ruling Sabah family, Iraq invades Kuwait and occupies oil fields. The United Nations Security Council passes Resolution 660 which condemns Iraq's invasion and states that unless Iraq withdraws immediately and unconditionally, sanctions and military force would be used.

3 August Fourteen of the 21 Arab League foreign ministers meeting in Cairo condemn the Iraqi invasion but caution against any foreign intervention in Arab affairs. Jordan, Mauritania, Sudan, Yemen, and the Palestine Liberation Organization (PLO) abstain; Libya walks out of the meeting. The Gulf Cooperation Council (GCC) insists that the Arab League's rejection of foreign intervention does not apply to Security Council measures as Arab League Charter includes adherence to United Nations resolutions. In Moscow, James Baker, the United States Secretary of State, and Eduard Shevardnadze, the Soviet Foreign Minister, issue a joint statement condemning the Iraqi invasion and asking for a halt to arms deliveries to Iraq.

6 August United Nations Resolution 661 imposes economic sanctions on Iraq.

7 August Accepting the invitation of Saudi Arabia to reinforce defenses against Iraq, the United States launches "Operation Desert Shield" by sending paratroopers, an armored brigade, and jet fighters to Saudi Arabia to protect that country from an Iraqi invasion.

8 August Iraq proclaims the union of Iraq and Kuwait and says that it will not attack Saudi Arabia. On American television President Bush says that the sovereign independence of Saudi Arabia is of vital interest to the United States. Great Britain announces the dispatch of two fighter squadrons to the Middle East, and the strengthening of its naval patrol in the Gulf. France also announces strengthening of its naval presence in Gulf.

9 August Resolution 662 is unanimously adopted by the Security Council: Iraq's annexation of Kuwait is declared to be null and void; a special committee is established to monitor compliance with trade sanctions.

10 August Twelve of the 21 members of the Arab League, meeting in Cairo, vote to send troops to help defend Saudi Arabia and other Gulf states against Iraq. Libya and PLO support Iraq. Jordan, Mauritania, and Sudan support the resolution but with reservations. Algeria and Yemen abstain. Tunisia is not present.

11 August Syria announces that it will send troops to Saudi Arabia; Egyptian and Moroccan troops land in Saudi Arabia.

12 August Saddam Hussein links the withdrawal of Iraqi forces from Kuwait with Syrian withdrawal from Lebanon, and Israeli withdrawal from the Gaza Strip, the West Bank, the Golan Heights, and Lebanon. The "linkage" is rejected by American and Israeli governments. Hussein also demands that foreign troops in Saudi Arabia be replaced by Arab forces under United Nations auspices, that United Nations resolutions regarding the Syrian and Israeli situations be implemented, and those applied to Iraq after 2 August be discontinued. Bush orders United States forces to stop Iraq oil exports, and also all imports apart from food stuffs. Saddam's attempt to shift the focus of the Gulf crisis to the Arab-Israeli conflict engenders an immediate response in some quarters of the Muslim world. A preacher at al-Aqsa mosque in Jerusalem sharply condemns the Saudi leadership before a congregation of some 10,000 worshippers. In Jordan, the Muslim Brotherhood calls on Muslims "to purge the holy land of Palestine and Najd and Hijaz from the Zionists and imperialists."

14 August Iraqi opposition movements, including Shi'ite groups, act in unison and take a firm stand against a permanent Western presence in the Gulf region. In a collective communiqué they pledge that after the liberation of Iraq from the Ba'thist yoke the new regime will "fulfill its national duty by fighting imperialism and Zionism and their schemes."

211

15 August Iraq accepts Iran's peace terms for the ending of the Iran-Iraq war.

17 August Speaker of Iraq's Parliament, Sadi Mahdi Salih, announces that nationals of "aggressive nations" will be held while there is a threat of war against Iran.

18 August Iraqi officials announce that foreigners held in Iran and Kuwait will be moved to military bases and other strategic areas to serve as "human shields." Resolution 664 is unanimously adopted by the United Nations Security Council: "Iraq should permit and facilitate the immediate departure from Kuwait and Iraq" of foreign nationals.

18 August Unconfirmed reports that demonstrations by Syrians against the deployment of Syrian troops had taken place in Homs, Hama, and Golan Heights.

19 August The United States rejects an offer from Saddam Hussein to release Westerners if the United States withdraws its forces from Saudi Arabia, and the economic sanctions against Iraq are lifted.

23 August Televised meeting of Saddam Hussein with British hostages including children. Jordan, overwhelmed by refugees fleeing Iraq, temporarily closes its borders with Iraq.

28 August Saddam Hussein, in a decree, declares Kuwait the nineteenth province in Iraq's administrative structure. He also says that all foreign women and children detained in Iraq (presumably including Kuwait) will be able to leave.

September A representative of the Egyptian Muslim Brothers joins a 13-man delegation representing Islamic movements across the Islamic world, which travels to Jordan, Saudi Arabia, Iraq, and Iran to seek Iraqi withdrawal from Kuwait. Another visit, to Jordan, Yemen, Iran, Iraq, and Syria, follows in December. The Egyptian Labor Party, in tacit alliance with the Muslim Brotherhood, advocates the avoidance of war, Iraqi withdrawal linked to a settlement of the conflicting interests of Iraq and Kuwait, the right of Kuwaitis to manage their own domestic affairs, and resistance to American attempts to impose hegemony on the Arab world—but its leaders are snubbed by the Egyptian government.

1 September "Inconclusive" ending to two days of talks between Perez de Cuellar and Tariq Aziz in Amman. Around 700 foreign women and children are allowed to leave Iraq.

2 September Saudi Arabia announces that it is increasing its oil production by 2 million barrels per day.

7 September In Saudi Arabia the deposed Emir of Kuwait promises $5 billion toward the costs of the American military operation. Saudi Arabia and the United Arab Emirates also offer to contribute to the costs.

9 September At summit meeting in Helsinki Presidents Bush and Gorbachev warn Saddam Hussein that the Soviet Union and the United States are prepared to take further action consistent with the United Nations Charter and insist that nothing short of the implementation of all the United Nations Security Council resolutions concerning Iraq will be acceptable. Following an Iraqi withdrawal from Kuwait and the restoration of the government of Kuwait, as well as the release of hostages, Bush and Gorbachev agree, their countries' foreign ministers will be urged to "develop regional security structures and measures to promote peace and stability" in the area.

12 September Muslim World League in Jeddah endorses Saudi decision to invite non-Muslim forces to help defend the kingdom. It calls for the creation of pan-Islamic forces eventually to replace non-Muslims.

12 September President Al-Asad of Syria defends deployment of Syrian troops to the Gulf and says foreigners were in Arab lands only because of the Iraqi invasion.

13 September U.N. Security Council passes Resolution 666 imposing strict controls on food aid to Iraq.

13 September In Iran, Ayatollah Khamanei, Khomeini's successor as the Leader of the Islamic Republic, declares combat against the United States a jihad. A few days later 160 Majlis deputies issue a statement in support of Khamanei which demands the immediate withdrawal of the American (and Iraqi) troops.

14 September   Britain announces that it will send an armored brigade and 6,000 combat troops to the Gulf. Secretary of State Baker meets with al-Asad in Damascus. Syrians press for a political solution to the crisis but say they are willing to send more troops if necessary.

15 September   France agrees to send a further 4,000 troops and three army air regiments, giving France 13,000 men, 14 war ships and nearly 100 anti-tank helicopters. Against the background of Saddam's popularity in Jordan, King Hussein of Jordan allows George Habash of the Popular Front for the Liberation of Palestine, and Nayef Hawatmeh of the Democratic Front for the Liberation of Palestine, banned for twenty years, back into Jordan to attend a conference of Arab Popular Forces.

16 September   Egypt sends a further 15,000 troops, bringing its number of troops in Saudi Arabia to 20,000.

20 September   Britain and United States agree that British troops can be placed under American command in Saudi Arabia, but that military action will require consultation.

23 September   Saddam Hussein threatens to retaliate to the "stifling of the Iraqi people" by the destruction of oil fields in the Middle East and by attacks on Israel.

24 September   President Mitterand of France proposes an international conference on the Middle East to discuss the settlement of all sources of conflict in the region, once Iraq has withdrawn from Kuwait and freed the hostages. The price of oil reaches $40 a barrel.

25 September   At the conclusion of President al-Asad's visit to Tehran, Syria and Iran announce that they are fully in accord in their opposition to Iraq and with regard to deployment of American forces in the Gulf.

26 September   Turkish President Turgut Ozal says that Turkey will support U.N.-authorized military action against Iraq. But Turkey seeks a free-trad agreement with the United States to balance losses sustained in the crisis.

27 September   Britain and Iran agree to restore diplomatic links.

29 September   In his address to the General Assembly of the United Nations the Emir of Kuwait, Shaikh Jabir al-Ahmad al-Sabah, compares the Iraqi invasion of Kuwait with the Israeli occupation of the West Bank and southern Lebanon.

October The United States cuts off all economic and military aid to Pakistan because of the latter's clandestine nuclear program. The cut-off of U.S. aid (which had amounted to $578 million annually) comes at a time when thousands of Pakistani expatriate workers are returning home after losing their assets and life savings in Kuwait and Iraq. The Pakistani government had dispatched 5,000 troops to Saudi Arabia and was preparing another armored brigade to join the U.S.-led international alliance against Iraq. Subsequently the Jamaat-i-Islami's Qazi Hussein Ahmad argues that the frequent and exaggerated references in the American media and in Washington circles to Saddam's "awful military machine" demonstrates that "the real aim of American deployment is neither the defense of Saudi Arabia nor the liberation of Kuwait; rather, the real aim is to destroy the military power of an Arab Muslim nation in order to ensure the hegemony of Israel in the region." This suspicion about "the true meaning of the conflict" attains the status of doctrine once the Gulf war begins months later.

8 October Israeli security forces in Jerusalem kill twenty-one Palestinian demonstrators on Temple Mount (known to Muslims as al-Haram al-Sharif), near the historic site of Solomon's temple and the current site of al-Aqsa mosque. During the weeks that follow, curfews keep one million people in their homes and Israel refuses to accept a United Nations investigative commission. On the same day, before this news is reported, an electoral struggle between pragmatists and radicals in the Iranian Majlis is decided in favor of the pragmatists.

23 October In response to efforts made by Soviet Union and France there is an Iraqi announcement that French citizens are free to leave Iraq. George Bush and British Prime Minister Margaret Thatcher reiterate that there can be no compromise on the Iraqi withdrawal from Kuwait.

25 October President Ali Abdullah Salih accuses Saudi Arabia of damaging Yemen's economy by expelling around 500,000 Yemenis from Saudi Arabia.

29 October Resolution 674 adopted by Security Council holds Iraq liable for human rights abuses, economic losses since the occupation of Kuwait on 2 August, and war damages.

November In Egypt the Labor Party, in cooperation with all the major opposition parties except the leftist party, boycotts the parliamentary elections after the High Court rules that the previous People's Assembly had been elected illegally in 1987. The regime passes a new election law, the modalities of which play into the hands of the ruling National Democratic Party. In its propaganda campaign against the elections, the Labor Party links the boycott to its stand against foreign forces in the Gulf.

1 November General H. Norman Schwarzkopf, the American commander of the multinational forces in the Gulf, says that it may not be in the best interests of the United States and "a long-term balance of power in this region" to destroy Iraq.

4 November A 15,000-man Syrian armored division begins to arrive in Saudi Arabia.

8 November George Bush orders a further 150,000 American troops to the Gulf "to provide an adequate offensive military option" in order to force Iraq from Kuwait; this will raise United States troop strength in Gulf to over 380,000 by early 1991. Saddam Hussein dismisses his Chief of Staff, Lieutenant General Nazir al-Khazraji, who is thought to have opposed the invasion of Kuwait.

14 November Ayatollah Khamanei of Iran endorses the diplomatic efforts of the Iranian President and the Foreign Minister, who had recently concluded a round of negotiations with the President of Turkey.

18 November Saddam Hussein announces that all hostages will be released from Christmas Day onwards "unless something takes place that mars the atmosphere of peace." Release of hostages starts before that.

19 November Iraq's official news agency announces that Iraq is sending an additional 250,000 troops (including 150,000 reservists) to Kuwait to deter any attempt to retake Kuwait. Iraqi forces in southern Iraq and Kuwait are estimated at 700,000.

23 November President Bush meets Syrian President Hafiz al-Asad in Damascus and announces that al-Asad is lined up with the coalition with a commitment to use force in the Gulf.

26 November While in Moscow Tariq Aziz is told by Gorbachev that Iraq must leave Kuwait if it wants to avoid war.

28 November Britain restores diplomatic relations with Syria after a four-year break.

29 November Resolution 678 is passed by Security Council authorizing member states "to use all necessary means" to implement Resolution 660 and subsequent resolutions on Kuwait if Iraq failed to withdraw from Kuwait by 15 January.

30 November President Bush announces that he has invited Tariq Aziz to Washington, and is prepared to send James Baker to Baghdad for talks with Saddam Hussein between 15 December and 15 January "to discuss all aspects of the Gulf crisis," to go "the extra mile for peace."

December In Lebanon, as a result of President Hrawi's political reforms, the withdrawal of the various militias from greater Beirut is virtually complete, and the Lebanese army with Syrian support controls the capital. Before the militia's withdrawal from Beirut the leaderships of the rival Shi'ite factions, AMAL and Hizbullah, had signed a peace agreement, and with the withdrawal the militiamen move south toward the Israeli border. Israel responds with military incursions into south Lebanon. The Lebanese government starts a rebuilding program, and takes over the operation of Lebanon's principal ports. Hrawi follows Syria in opposing Saddam Hussein and so ensures aid from Saudi Arabia.

1 December The Iraqi Revolutionary Command Council accepts "the idea of the invitation and the meeting" (Bush's offer of direct talks) and says that Iraq "will call on representatives of countries and parties that are connected with unresolved disputes and issues to attend the meetings" and that the future of the Palestinians in the occupied territories will be high on the agenda.

2 December Secretary of State Baker says that Iraq's reward for withdrawing from Kuwait would be that there would not be a military attack by the United States, and that there should be no "linkage" between Kuwait and the Palestinian question.

3 December Richard Cheney, United States Secretary of Defense, says that Iraq could withstand impact of sanctions for a year or more and that the United States cannot wait indefinitely for sanctions to take effect.

4 December After declaring its support for the United Nations Security Council resolutions, Iran's First Deputy President, Hasan Habibi, declares that Iran is opposed to any concession by the West to Iraq.

5 December William Webster, director of the Central Intelligence Agency, testifies to United States House Armed Services Committee that continued economic sanctions against Iraq would mean that the Iraqi air force would lose its ability to fly regular missions within three months, and Iraq's ground forces would lose combat-readiness in nine months.

6 December Saddam Hussein asks Iraqi National Assembly to allow all foreigners to leave. He indicates that this has been prompted after consultations with Jordan, Yemen, Palestine, Sudan, and Arab Maghreb countries, and also from positive signals from some sources in the United States and Europe.

11 December President Chadli Bendjedid of Algeria contacts Libya and begins tour of Arab capitals and Tehran in an Arab peace initiative. He visits Baghdad on 12 December but is told by Saudi officials that a visit to Riyadh would be pointless. The Prime Minister of Israel, Yitzhak Shamir, after talks with Bush in the United States, says that he believes that the United States will not settle the Gulf crisis at Israel's expense.

16 December The British embassy in Kuwait, the last to stay open, is closed.

18 December Majority of members of the European Community (EC) (France, Italy, Spain, and Greece dissenting) decide to cancel meeting between EC Council President and Aziz, until the dispute over the timing of the United States-Iraq talks is settled.

20 December The United Nations Security Council, with American support, approves a resolution criticizing Israel for its deportation of four Palestinians from the Gaza Strip, and asks the Secretary General "to monitor and observe" the conditions of the Palestinians in the occupied territories.

27 December 110 Democratic members of the House of Representatives urge President Bush to allow more time for sanctions to work.

28 December Defense Secretary Cheney tells United States troops in Gulf that force will probably have to be used against Iraq, and that if war were to occur there had to be "absolute total victory."

1991

January In Egypt the Labor Party succeeds in building a front among political parties and forces that oppose the war. This front includes the Left, but excludes the Wafd Party which supported the international alliance.

January Shaikh Bin Baz of Saudi Arabia issues a fatwa (Islamic legal ruling) which sanctions the use of force against the Iraqis and declares the battle against Saddam a jihad. Non-Muslim soldiers, it proclaims, have an important role to play in defeating "the enemy of God."

1 January Against background of wide support for Saddam Hussein in Jordan King Hussein brings Islamic fundamentalist delegates into the Jordanian Cabinet: ministries controlled by fundamentalist Islamic delegates include Religious Affairs and Education.

4 January Tariq Aziz accepts an invitation to meet James Baker in Geneva on 9 January and stresses the need to deal with the Palestinian question.

6 January The United States Department of Defense announces that journalists reporting on a Gulf war will have to operate in "pools" under military supervision and submit all reports to a "security review."

7 January Both Baker, and the new British Prime Minister, John Major, announce that there can be no extension of the United Nations deadline for Iraq to leave Kuwait.

9 January In Geneva Baker and Aziz fail to reach any agreement. In Egypt John Major says that an international peace conference on the Palestinian issue should be held once the Gulf crisis is over.

12 January The United States Congress authorizes President Bush to use force in Iraq.

12 January In a Friday sermon in Algeria, FIS leaders Madani and Belhadj urge a congregation of some 6,000 worshippers to "attack U.S. and Jewish interests anywhere in the world." Several days later Madani insists that the government mobilize "one million reservists ... and all sons of Algeria" in order to "prepare ourselves for war."

13 January The United Nations Secretary General Perez de Cuellar, after meeting Saddam Hussein, indicated that he has failed to achieve a resolution. Saddam invites al-Asad to Baghdad in response to an appeal from Syria.

14 January The Iraqi National Assembly unanimously votes to allow Saddam Hussein to use "all jurisdiction and constitutional powers required in the showdown" against the multinational force in the Gulf. Warnings of terrorist attacks lead to increased security precautions at world's airports.

15 January The Turkish Foreign Minister says Turkey will not participate in any offensive against Iraq, but American planes may refuel at U.S. bases in Turkey as long as they rearm elsewhere. Perez de Cuellar makes a final appeal to stop a conflict that no one wants. The United Nations deadline for the Iraqi withdrawal from Kuwait expires at midnight New York time.

16 January Shortly before midnight Greenwich Mean Time, the multinational air attack on Kuwait and Baghdad, code-named "Operation Desert Storm," begins. In initial raids on Baghdad the Defense Ministry, the airport, oil refineries, a chemical plant and the presidential palace are hit.

17 January With the launch of Operation Desert Storm and the bombing of Kuwait and Iraq by the coalition, the Israeli army places some districts of East Jerusalem under curfew, and then the rest of the occupied territories. Palestinians in the Gaza Strip are already under a blanket curfew following the assassination in Tunis on 14 January of PLO leaders. Iraqi Republican Guard units on the border between Saudi Arabia and Kuwait are bombed. General Colin L. Powell, Chairman of the United States Joint Chiefs of Staff, announces that the success rate of the bombing raids is 80 percent.

17–18 January Seven Iraqi Scud missiles armed with conventional warheads land in Israel near Tel Aviv and Haifa. American Patriot missile destroys Iraqi missile aimed at the American air base in Saudi Arabia at Dhahran. Oil price falls from $30 to $18 a barrel on evidence of the overwhelming allied military strength. Oil price still below $20 at end of January, and around $18 at end of February.

19 January Patriot missiles air-lifted by United States to Israel.

20 January General Schwarzkopf announces that Iraqi nuclear research reactors have been thoroughly damaged, and that Iraqi factories manufacturing chemical and biological weapons have suffered "a considerable setback."

21 January A demonstration organized by the Society of Militant Clergy in Iran against the war proves an embarrassing failure, with no more than 3,000 participants.

22 January Against background of widespread support for Saddam Hussein amongst the people of Tunisia, Habib Toulares, the Tunisian Foreign Minister, says in a radio broadcast that the destruction of Iraq's industrial and economic capacity was being witnessed rather than the liberation of Kuwait. He suggests that this destruction would have grave consequences for the security and interests of the entire Arab nation.

24 January American forces capture the island of Qura off Kuwait.

24 January Japan increases contribution pledged to the multinational effort to $11 billion.

25 January United States and Saudi Arabia accuse Iraq of creating an oil slick in the Gulf about 9 miles long from oil spills from tankers anchored off Kuwait and from the offshore Sea Island Terminal.

26 January In the West there are widespread peace demonstrations, with 200,000 protestors in Bonn; 50,000 in Paris; 100,000 in Washington and 100,000 in San Francisco. "Smart bombs" from United States aircraft stem flow of oil from Sea Island Terminal.

26–28 January About 80 Iraqi war planes are flown to Iran; this constitutes about 10 percent of the Iraqi air force. Iran says that is will impound the planes and intern the pilots for the duration of the war.

29 January Iraqi troops capture Khafji, a small town in Saudi Arabia. The German government increases earlier pledge for war effort of $2.2 billion by another $5.5 billion.

31 January The Islamic Salvation Front (FIS) in Algeria stages a demonstration which mobilizes some 60,000–80,000 supporters. In addition to calling for "victory to Islam and the Muslims" in the war, a partial endorsement of Baghdad's call for jihad, the demonstrators also make clear the internal political issue at stake by calling for a date to be fixed for the National Assembly elections in Algeria.

31 January Allies recapture Khafji.

mid-late January Palestinian support for Saddam Hussein increases with the Iraqi Scud missile attacks on Israel which includes hits on Tel Aviv and Haifa. Saddam Hussein is seen as the first Arab leader to pay more than lip service to the Palestinian cause and to attack the heart of the Zionist state. The curfew in the occupied territories remains in force, and this hampers the distribution of gas masks to Palestinians. This had already been a matter of some controversy when, on 1 October 1990, the Israeli military had announced that it would distribute gas masks to Israeli citizens, residents, and visitors of Israel and that Palestinians in the occupied territories could buy gas masks when further supplies arrived. The underground leadership of the intifada cancels all strikes and for the first time since the start of the uprising does not urge attacks against Israeli soldiers and settlers.

February The government of Morocco allows Moroccan Islamist groups, for only the third time in their history, to take part in a huge public march to express their views. In Tunisia, the government begins to collect blood to send to the Iraqis.

February In the wake of the massive bombing by the allied forces on and around Baghdad, the Jamiyat Ulama-i-Pakistan (JUP) in Pakistan, concerned about the safety of the shrine in Iraq of its patron saint, Abd al-Qadir al-Jilani, establishes "recruiting centers" in about twenty cities of Pakistan to recruit volunteers to go to Iraq "in order to fight against the infidels and to protect the holy shrine of Ghows-i-Azam [the Great Saint] in Baghdad." JUP sources claim that by the middle of February, 110,000 people have signed up for this voluntary force.

2 February In response to the mass demonstrations in support of Saddam and the establishment of roadside "recruitment centers" to register volunteers for Iraq, the government of Pakistan expels a senior Iraqi diplomat based in Islamabad for "distributing money to recruit mercenaries to fight against the allied forces in the Persian Gulf, organizing mass demonstrations through local agents, inciting people to engage in anti-state activities, and paying money for printing pro-Saddam posters and Saddam portraits." Islamic fundamentalist groups claim that the decision to expel the Iraqi diplomat was made in Washington and not in Islamabad. In the days following, demonstrators of the students' wing of the Jamaat-i-Islami and the JUP burn effigies of George Bush and attack American diplomatic facilities in Lahore, Islamabad, and Karachi. Protest demonstrations, demanding immediate cessation of the hostilities and the withdrawal of U.S. troops from the vicinity of Islam's holy shrines, are organized everywhere in Pakistan by the workers of the Jamaat-i-Islami, the JUP, and the People's Party. Prime Minister Nawaz Sharif issues a scathing criticism of the Islamic groups accusing them of "exploiting the sentiments of the people" in the name of Islam in order "to boost their own political fortunes."

3 February The United States announces that seven of the eleven marines who died in the battle for Khafji were killed by friendly fire.

4 February President Hashemi Rafsanjani offers to meet personally with Saddam Hussein and to serve as a mediator with the United States.

5 February Curfew restrictions in the occupied territories are eased, but apart from a small number, Palestinians are not allowed to enter Israel, and the economic difficulties in the occupied territories increase. Pictures of Saddam Hussein and Yasser Arafat are plastered side by side all over the occupied territories. Support for the PLO in the West, enhanced by the intifada and the Temple Mount killings, diminishes. No alternative leadership to the PLO emerges. HAMAS (Harakat al-Muqawama al-Islamiyya, Movement of the Islamic Resistance) sees an opportunity to gain at the expense of the PLO: if Saddam Hussein loses the war, as seems likely, the PLO would be further weakened and support for Hamas increased.

6 February King Hussein of Jordan delivers a pro-Iraqi speech which earns a strong rebuke from President Bush. The American aid program to Jordan subsequently comes under review in Washington, and Congressional sentiment turns decisively against Jordan.

12 February Gorbachev's special envoy, Yevgeny Primakov, meets Saddam Hussein in Baghdad, and an announcement follows on Baghdad Radio that Iraq is prepared to negotiate a solution to the situation in the Gulf.

13 February   United States bombs destroy a structure in the al-Amiriyya residential district of Baghdad killing around 300 civilians. In response to Iraqi claim that the building was a bomb shelter, the United States Department of Defense insists that it was converted to a military command-and-control center in 1985.

15 February   Iraq announces that it is prepared to withdraw from Kuwait, but makes withdrawal conditional on comprehensive ceasefire and the recision of the United Nations resolutions on Iraq passed during 1990. Bush states that conditions are unacceptable.

17 February   The massive air bombardment of Iraq and the preparation for the ground offensive lead the Muslim Brotherhood of Egypt to join other Islamic groups in their second declaration from Pakistan in which the war is depicted as an assault against Islam and its civilization. The declaration calls upon Muslims to transcend local borders in an immediate unification of Islamic groups and peoples. It also urges the Muslim people to struggle for their rights of political participation.

19 February   Tariq Aziz meets Gorbachev, and then carries peace plan, details of which are not released, to Rafsanjani.

22 February   Back in Moscow, after second meeting with Gorbachev, Aziz accepts Moscow's peace plan. This entails a ceasefire, withdrawal of Iraqi forces from Kuwait on the second day of the ceasefire with the withdrawal to be completed within 21 days, followed by the recision of the United Nations resolutions on Iraq. Bush insists that Iraqi troops start leaving Kuwait on 23 February and their withdrawal be completed within a week. Soviets then announce a revised peace proposal shortening some of the times for the Iraqi withdrawal.

22–23 February   Iraq destroys Kuwaiti installations and sets fire to oil pumping stations.

23 February   The U.S. Ambassador to the United Nations, Thomas Pickering, says that the Soviet peace plans "fall short."

24 February   Ground offensive starts against Iraq: units of multinational force move toward Kuwait City and into southern Iraq.

25 February According to Baghdad Radio, Iraqi forces have been given the order to withdraw from Kuwait, to positions held before 1 August 1990. This is claimed to be in compliance with United Nations Resolution 660.

26 February Bush says that as Iraq does not accept all the United Nations Security Council resolutions the coalition forces will pursue the war. United States military announces that 517 of Kuwait's 950 oil wells have been set alight by Iraqi troops. Britain suffers its worst losses during the war when nine British soldiers are killed in a mistaken attack on their Warrior armored infantry vehicles by a United States A-10 "tankbuster" war plane.

26 February Sahbzada Yaqub Khan, the Foreign Minister of Pakistan who has held the office for five years, resigns while in Beijing on a visit accompanying the Pakistan Prime Minister, Nawaz Sharif. Khan, trusted in the West, had had difficulty in persuading the ruling Islamic Democratic Alliance MP's and the public that if Pakistan had allowed a pro-Iraqi policy, it would have been isolated in the international community. The resignation reflects the turmoil in Pakistan over the Gulf war: Sunni mullahs supported financially by the Saudis are calling King Fahd of Saudi Arabia a Zionist agent; Shi'ite mullahs, paid by Iran, are volunteering to fight for Iraq, previously their enemy; Benazir Bhutto, the former Prime Minister and leader of the Pakistan People's Party, is annoying her followers by her praise of President Bush; the generals in the army who had supported President Sharif's dispatch of 11,000 troops to support the coalition in the Gulf the previous August are accusing Bush of being the enemy of Islamic military might, and are suggesting that after conquering Iraq, the United States will concentrate on Iran and Pakistan.

27 February Arab and United States troops take Kuwait City and airport. American troops fight Iraq's Republican Guard 50 miles west of Basra. Bush declares on American television that Iraq's army is defeated and Kuwait is liberated; the coalition will cease hostilities at midnight Eastern Standard Time; and that Baker will undertake a tour of the Middle East. Schwarzkopf announces that the United States has lost 79 troops killed, 213 wounded, and 44 missing in action; Britain has lost 13; France, 2; the Arab countries, 13. There are no official figures given for the Iraqi losses, but later estimates range from 200,000 to 700,000.

28 February Bush announces that Iraqi military leaders have agreed to work out terms of the ceasefire with multinational force commanders.

1 March In a television address King Hussein of Jordan expresses sympathy for the Iraqi people but stresses that the people of Jordan rejoice with their "Kuwaiti brothers." The King asks that the same criteria be applied to the Palestine question as had been applied to Kuwait.

1 March There are first signs of popular revolt against Saddam Hussein when crowds demonstrate in Basra against the ruling Ba'th Party. Disturbances spread to other towns and cities in the south, including Nasiriyya, and the Shi'ite holy cities of Karbala and Najaf.

2 March Following the Iraqi defeat by allied forces in February 1991, a well-coordinated revolt erupts in at least a dozen towns in the Shi'ite south of Iraq. Basra, Najaf, Nasiriyya, Diwaniyya, Karbala, Samawa, Suq al-Shuyukh, Zubayr, and Kut are at its core. According to eye-witness reports, in Basra alone between four and five thousand people, civilian and army deserters, fight against government troops in the following days. Because the city is effectively cut off from the main body of Iraq by American troops, the central government's control over Basra is substantially weakened. The single most important organization behind the fighting is the Supreme Assembly for the Islamic Revolution in Iraq (SAIRI), and on 3 March 1991 its leader, Ayatollah al-Hakim, claims that he is directing the revolt in Basra and elsewhere.

2 March United Nations Security Council passes Resolution 686 which demands Iraqi acceptance of the previous 12 relevant resolutions, release of civilian detainees, and acceptance under international law of responsibility for the damage done to Kuwait.

3 March Iraq accepts Resolution 686 and de facto ceasefire goes into effect.

4 March Shaikh Saad al-Abdullah al-Sabah, the Crown Prince, returns to Kuwait as Prime Minister and administrator of martial law.

5 March Saddam Hussein's elite Republican Guard, using tanks and heavy artillery, is managing to suppress rebels.

5 March Iraq announces that Revolutionary Command Council has "annulled the annexation of Kuwait" and will comply with United Nations demands to return Kuwait's assets.

5 March Grand Ayatollah Abu'l-Qasim Khoi of Iraq issues the first of two important communiqués calling upon Shi'ites to "guard the territory of Islam," to "look after its holy places" and to guard the property of the people and preserve the public institutions of Iraq. The second communiqué, of 7 March, establishes a "Supreme Committee" under whose leadership the Shi'ites would preserve Iraq's security and stabilize public, religious, and social affairs.

6 March Saddam Hussein appoints his cousin, Al-Majid, as Minister of the Interior with instructions to suppress the rebellion. Ali Hasan al-Majid was thought to have used chemical weapons against the Kurds in 1988, and also oversaw the occupation of Kuwait. President Bush, in his speech celebrating victory in the Gulf war, refers to the principle of territory for peace and legitimate Palestinian rights.

8 March Iranian President Rafsanjani indicates his dissatisfaction with the ongoing diplomatic maneuvers by calling for the resignation of Saddam Hussein. This call indicates a hardening of Iran's position in the wake of the Damascus agreement of 6 March 1991 among eight Arab states, which excluded Iran.

9 March Statement from SAIRI, made in Beirut, claims that over 30,000 people have died during the uprising in the south.

12 March First meeting between an American Secretary of State and a wide-ranging Palestinian delegation when James

Baker sees ten Palestinian personalities in Jerusalem. Egypt radio announces that Egypt and Iran have decided to establish "interest offices" in each other's capital, as a preliminary move toward the establishment of full diplomatic relations.

13 March At a meeting in Beirut 23 Iraqi opposition groups agree to form a joint leadership to overthrow Saddam Hussein.

14 March Kurdish rebels claim they control parts of northern Iraq.

16 March At the same time as promising democratic reforms and a referendum on a new constitution when the rebellion is over, Saddam claims that his troops had suppressed the rebellion in the south, but admits that there is unrest in the Kurdish areas in the north.

18 March An Amnesty International report claims that soldiers and civilians in Kuwait are arbitrarily arresting and torturing Palestinians.

20 March Iran re-opens its embassy in Amman, Jordan.

22 March United States Congress passes a bill which halts the American aid program to Jordan. Early in February, following speeches by King Hussein which had been construed as being anti-American and supportive of Saddam Hussein, the aid program had been placed under review. After President Bush threatens to use his veto, Congress agrees to allow the President to restore the aid program provided that he could show that "the government of Jordan has taken steps to advance the peace process in the Middle East, or that furnishing assistance to Jordan would be beneficial to the peace process in the Middle East."

22 March In Pakistan, generals celebrate national day with an armed parade in defiance of government policy. General Aslam Beg, the Chief of Staff of the Army, in a speech, accuses the United States of deceiving Iraq into invading Kuwait as a way of enhancing Israel's security. The Pakistan government is concerned that the attitude of the military could endanger the loans from the United States on which Pakistan's economy depends.

229

22-23 March United States Air Force shoots down two Iraqi fighter-bombers flying in violation of the ceasefire agreement of 3 March. General Colin Powell says that United States forces will remain in Iraq until the arrival of an Arab regional security force.

23 March Saddam appoints Sa'dun Hamadi (of Shi'ite origin), as Prime Minister, and Tariq Aziz moves from being Foreign Minister to one of two Deputy Prime Ministers.

26 March The United States State Department confirms that the oil center of Kirkuk is under Kurdish control. Saudi Arabia and Iran resume diplomatic relations which had been broken off in 1987 after clashes in Mecca between the security forces of Saudi Arabia and the Iranian pilgrims during which over 400 pilgrims had been killed. On 1 April Iran opens its embassy in Riyadh.

28 March The Shi'ite leader, Hojjatulislam Muhammad Baqr al-Hakim, concedes that Saddam Hussein's forces have retaken Karbala and other southern Iraq towns.

31 March The Iraqi government announces that its forces have retaken Dohek and two other towns in northern Iraq, Arbil and Zakho, from Kurdish rebels. As hundreds of thousands of Iraqi Kurdish refugees cross into Iran, relations between Iraq and Iran deteriorate. By this time it is reported that only seven of the 571 oil-well fires in Kuwait have been extinguished.

16–31 March Within Israel itself arbitrary knife attacks by Palestinians result in at least seven Israeli deaths, but interrogation of the captured killers fails to link them to any Palestinian organization. Several are revenge killings for relatives killed by Israeli security forces, but one medical orderly, who had killed four unarmed women, says that "it was a message to Baker."

31 March Israeli government votes for extraordinary measures against Palestinians, including deportation.

1 April Against the background of claims that Iraqi forces have retaken Kirkuk, Masud Barzani, the leader of the Democratic Party of Kurdistan, claims that around 3 million Kurds have fled into the mountains to escape the Iraqi government's program of "genocide and torture." Barzani asks Britain, the United States, France, and Saudi Arabia to request intervention by the United Nations.

3 April Resolution 687 is passed by United Nations Security Council giving the terms for a permanent ceasefire in the Gulf: Iraq is required to submit information concerning chemical and biological weapons stocks by 17 April; to accept on-site inspection of the destruction of weapons of mass destruction; to renounce international terrorism; to pay war reparations from a fund, administered by the United Nations, created from a levy on Iraq's oil export earnings. Resolution 687 is accepted on 5 April by Iraq's Revolutionary Command Council, and on 6 April by the National Assembly.

4 April The Iraqi Revolutionary Command Council, chaired by Saddam Hussein, announces that Iraq has crushed sedition in the towns of Iraq, and offers an amnesty to all Kurds except those who had "committed murder, rape and looting during acts of riots and treason." This offer is refused by the Democratic Party of Kurdistan on 5 April.

5 April President Bush reiterates the United States government's policy of non-intervention in the internal affairs of Iraq and says that it was not an objective of the coalition to overthrow Saddam Hussein. Security Council passes Resolution 668 which condemns the "repression of the Iraqi civilian population in many parts of Iraq, including most recently in Kurdish populated areas, the consequences of which threaten international peace and security." But the resolution makes no provision for stopping Iraq's repressive activities.

5 April In the Friday sermon, Ayatollah Khamanei urges the Iraqi dissidents to continue their rebellion until the end, forewarning them of the most stern oppression by Saddam's regime if they failed to do so.

8 April John Major, the British Prime Minister, outlines a plan to the European Community leaders attending a summit meeting in Luxembourg for the creation of a United Nations "enclave" in northern Iraq to protect the Kurds. Major's plan is endorsed and the scheme becomes known as "safe havens" for the Kurds. An estimate by governor of south-eastern region of Turkey puts the number of Kurdish refugees in Turkey at 400,000.

9 April A United States spokesman says that United States has no position on "safe havens" for the Kurds.

10 April The United States orders Iraq to stop all military activity north of the 36th parallel, an area passing just south of Mosul, but excluding Kirkuk, and extending to the Turkish border. The United States also warns Iraq that any military interference in the international relief effort mounted for the Kurds will be met by force.

10 April Believing that the general political climate has been further "Islamized" by the upsurge of popular sentiment during the Gulf crisis and fearing a massive onslaught by the newly formed United Shari'a Front—a coalition of religious parties—with its demand for a radical Shari'a Bill, Nawaz Sharif introduces in Parliament on his own a moderate version of the bill. It is package of legislative and administrative measures to Islamize education, the mass media, economy, bureaucracy, and the legal system. A miscellany of pious hopes and noble intentions ("The state shall take . . . measures to eliminate bribery, corruption and malpractices. . ."), the Shari'a Bill is a symbolic gesture of plausible Islamic commitment by the Sharif government.

13 April Heavy fighting between Kurdish guerrillas (Peshmerga) and Iraqi government troops is reported around the cities of Shaqlawa and Sulaimaniyya, as well as the capture by Kurdish guerrillas of the northern Iraqi town of Dukan.

19 April Amnesty International asks the Emir of Kuwait to intervene on behalf of those detained on suspicion of collaborating with the Iraqis. It is alleged that the detainees are being held in deplorable conditions.

20 April The Emir of Kuwait, Shaikh Jabir, names a new cabinet headed by the Crown Prince, Shaikh Saad. The new government includes technocrats but not members of the opposition or resistance movements. The Sabah family retains control of the Ministries of Defense, Foreign Affairs, and the Interior.

21 April Iran asks the United Nations to assume responsibility for the relief centers in the north of Iraq.

22 April Gush Emunim, the group of radical Zionists committed to settling Jews in the occupied territories, confirms that it is preparing to open two more sites for settlement on the West Bank.

24 April Jalal Talabani, the leader of the Patriotic Union of Kurdistan, announces that Saddam Hussein has agreed in principle to grant the Kurds a measure of autonomy, and appeals to Kurds to return to their homes.

26 April Number of Iraqi refugees in Iran estimated to be over 1 million, of which around 50,000 are Shi'ites from southern Iraq and the rest are Kurds.

28 April– June American efforts to set up an international peace conference are frustrated by Shamir who dislikes the possibility that such a forum could force Israel to trade captured Arab lands for peace. The Israeli Prime Minister prefers separate negotiations with the Arab states.

1–7 May According to *The Observer* (London, 19 May 1991), meetings occur between Richard Haass, United States Special Assistant for National Security Affairs in the Near East and Southeast Asia, and Majid, son of the Grand Ayatollah Khoi. This follows overtures made in the second week of March by Ayatollah Khoi for a meeting between Majid and General Norman Schwarzkopf. The initial meeting planned for 18 March was cancelled by the Americans, and later in April Majid met low-level officials from the French Ministry of the Interior in Paris. But through a fringe Islamic group, Jund al-Imam (The Imam's Army), which had links to the Central Intelligence Agency, Majid had been invited to Washington to meet the National Security Council. Majid is told by National Security Council officials that the Shi'ites should avoid escalating their insurgency in the south of Iraq so as to avoid endangering a coup the United States was planning with Iraqi officers to overthrow Saddam Hussein. *The Observer* reports that at this time Iran has indicated that it will support Iraqi Shi'ites, and military camps have been set up on the Iran-Iraq border to house around 30,000 Iraqi volunteers who have been equipped with captured arms. But Iran insists that all fighting must be under the control of Muhammad Baqr al-Hakim who heads SAIRI. This disturbs many Shi'ites, who are apparently aiming for a democratic regime in Iraq and who see control by al-Hakim as a retrogressive sectarian move.

8 May Egypt announces that it is withdrawing all its forces (30-35,000 men) from Kuwait and Saudi Arabia. The forces had been supposed to stay on and be reinforced to provide, along with the Syrians, the military potential for the proposed Mutual Defense Organization (MDO) that the United States and its allies hoped to establish. Egyptians are reported to be upset that the Kuwaitis and the Americans had agreed that the force to be stationed in Kuwait would be an American brigade, and that there had been no mention of Egyptian or Syrian troops playing a role in the Emirate. Furthermore, Egypt felt that it had not received sufficient economic benefits from its participation in the Gulf war: $14 billion of Egyptian had been cancelled but that left $30 billion outstanding. Egypt also felt that it was not getting its fair share of Kuwait and Saudi Arabian reconstruction contracts, and resented that the 1 million Egyptian laborers who had fled were not being reemployed.

11 May Saddam Hussein tells meeting of Iraqi journalists that they can write what they like.

13 May United Nations send eight food trucks through to Dahuk in northern Iraq, under the aegis of the agreement secured by United Nations envoy Prince Sadruddin Agha Khan on 18 March to set up humanitarian, non-military centers to assist displaced Iraqis. This establishes a United Nations presence in Dahuk. The United States military also hand over the administration of the Zakho refugee camp to the United Nations. The Foreign Minister of Iraq rejects outright the suggestion that Security Council Resolution 668, which offered limited protection to the Kurds, could be used to establish a United Nations police force in northern Iraq.

18 May A number of ulama in Saudi Arabia give a detailed memorandum to the King outlining a comprehensive program of reform and calling for the creation of a *majlis al-shura* or consultative assembly whose members would be chosen according to competence, and not according to rank or sex; "Islamization" of the judiciary, military, economy, and media; and abstention from all "non-Islamic pacts and treaties."

19 May Trials start in Kuwait of 628 people, mainly Palestinian and Iraqi, who are accused of aiding the Iraqi forces during the invasion of Kuwait. The "unceremonious" treatment by the martial law courts of the first 22 suspects, who are mainly Iraqis and Palestinians, leads to expressions of concern from the United States State Department, and a request to show compassion from President Bush.

20 May Security Council adopts Resolution 678. This, alongside the Secretary General's report of 2 May, initiates the creation of a fund to come from Iraq's oil revenues to be used to meet the claims of foreign governments, nationals and corporations for loss and damage, including environmental damage, resulting from Iraq's occupation of Kuwait.

20–24 May United States forces move into the provisional capital of northwest Iraq, Dahuk; the Iraqi military leaves. An American military spokesman insists that this is not an extension of the 75 by 30 mile Security Zone, and is just a temporary measure agreed with the Iraqi command.

22 May Treaty of Brotherhood, Cooperation, and Coordination signed by Lebanese and Syrian presidents in Damascus. Syria formally acknowledges Lebanon's independence. Under clause three, Lebanon agrees that it will not be a source of threat to Syria's security, and it will not be a corridor or springboard for any force, state or organization hostile to Syria. Over the previous few days Israeli artillery had pounded Shi'ite villages in southern Lebanon, and on 21 May Israeli tanks had crossed the border into Lebanon and had taken up positions along the security zone. On 21 May the pro-Israeli South Lebanon Army militia had complained that the treaty between Syria and Lebanon would both infringe Lebanon's sovereignty and independence and encourage Israel to resist pressure to withdraw from its self-proclaimed security zone in south Lebanon. Syrian move probably assisted by an American indulgence following President al-Asad's support of the coalition during the Gulf war. The pro-Iranian Lebanese Shi'ite Muslim group, Hizbullah, announces that it has elected a new Secretary General, Shaikh Abbas al-Musawi. Al-Musawi, who had led the political arm of Hizbullah, is regarded as a hard-liner. Another hard-liner, Shaikh Ibrahim al-Amin, is elected Deputy Secretary General.

23 May Brent Bernandet, the United Nations Secretary General's representative in Baghdad, signs an agreement with the Iraqis to allow between 100 and 500 United Nations security guards to move into northern Iraq to protect United Nations civilian workers and equipment. This is very different from the British proposal for a United Nations police force to protect the Kurds.

May–June The Islamic Salvation Front (FIS) in Algeria precipitates public demonstrations against the National Liberation Front (FLN) dominated government. On 12 June 1990 the FIS, under the guidance of Abbasi Madani, had won first multiparty elections in Algeria since independence, taking approximately 55 percent of the votes in local and provincial elections, and dealing a stunning blow to the ruling—and secular—FLN. The demonstrations starting in May 1991 are mainly in response to new electoral law which had been promulgated earlier in the year. This law is widely seen as being biassed in favor of the FLN and is resented by the FIS. The Islamic opposition, principally the FIS, had been expected to win the majority of seats in the projected June 1991 election. In response to civil unrest, President Chadli Benjedid dismisses the FLN Prime Minister.

2 June The Emir of Kuwait, Shaikh Jabir, makes concessions to opposition demands and announces a timetable for general elections to the National Assembly which had been suspended in 1986. The election date is set for October 1992 and there are immediate protests that by that time the ruling al-Sabah family would have been able to take the key decisions about the future of Kuwait. The Emir gives assurances that the Advisory National Council would be revived to operate for the intervening sixteen months. But this offer is thought to have little credibility with politically-concerned Kuwaitis.

3 June Eighteen senior ulama, including Shaikh Bin Baz, issue a statement which condemns the public manner in which the memorandum of 18 May was presented to the king, and pointedly remind Saudis of the "bounty of security, stability, [and] unanimity" which the Saudi regime has provided.

4 June Hamas, Islamic Jihad, and the PLO attempt a truce to end rival factional fighting that has broken out in Nablus and Gaza. It is estimated that support for the Islamic underground groups is around 10 percent whereas in Gaza it is put at between 30 and 40 percent of the 800,000 inhabitants. In Gaza, fighting had broken out over the issue of hijab, the dress code of Islam which, according to conservatives, requires women to wear a veil or a head scarf. A group of schoolgirls had broken the custom observed by most women in Gaza. The incident is seen as symptomatic of a major divergence between the fundamentalists and the PLO under Arafat over the approach to the United States and the envisaged peace conference. The fundamentalists regard the United States as an enemy.

5 June Foreign Minister of Saudi Arabia, Prince Saud al-Faisal, goes to Tehran. This is the first visit by a high-ranking Saudi official to Iran since 1979.

6 June Barzani, leader of the Kurdish Democratic Party, says that his delegation is nearing an agreement with the Iraqi government on Kurdish autonomy, based on the 1970 agreement which recognized the Kurds' cultural and national identity and gave them the right to run the three provinces of Iraq in which they were in a clear majority. There appears to be disagreement over the oil-rich Kirkuk province. The Iraqi government agrees, however, to allow Kurds back who had been displaced from villages on the Iranian border during the Iran-Iraq war, and the two sides also agree on "a legal body" to arbitrate disputes over the implementation of the future agreement.

7 June Britain and the United States renew their commitment to withdraw their troops from Iraq and reject calls from the Kurdish leaders (who fear reprisals from Saddam) for the troops to stay. This is at a time when the United Nations operation for the protection of the Kurds is facing a crisis: the United Nations Disaster Relief Coordinator's Office warns that lack of aid and an inability to recruit suitable guards could lead the returned refugees to flee from Iraq again. As the allied troops leave, all humanitarian functions in the 3,600 square mile Security Zone are handed over to the United Nations High Commissioner for Refugees.

9 June In the Security Zone in northern Iraq the number of allied troops declines from a peak of 21,700 on 21 May, to 17,400. It is understood that the rest of the troops will soon be gone.

9 June King Hussein, in an attempt to quiet domestic unrest— particularly among sections of the middle classes aroused by the application of Islamic principles— proclaims a National Charter calling for multiparty democracy, greater freedom for women, and greater press freedom. But he also calls for legislation to conform with Islamic law. King Hussein is admitted to hospital the following day with suspected heart trouble.

11 June President Ghulam Ishaq Khan of Pakistan uses constitutional prerogative to declare that Lieutenant-General Asif Nawaz Janjua, Chief of the General Staff, will take over as Army Chief of Staff on 16 August. This announcement ends rumors that the civilian government in Pakistan could be forced to extend General Beg's term of office. Beg had been criticized in the West and particularly the United States for his support of Saddam Hussein during the Gulf war, and for promoting Pakistan's nuclear weapons policy as a tactic of a hard-line foreign policy directed at India and the United States. On 9 June the Prime Minister of Pakistan, Nawaz Sharif, had threatened to bring charges of high treason against politicians supposedly sympathetic to General Beg who had called for martial law.

12 June The Ministry of the Interior in Kuwait announces that it has decided to allow Kuwaiti male citizens to teach certain female relatives to drive a car. These relatives must be "unmarriageable"—that is, according to Islamic law, too close to permit marriage between them. This, in effect, means that some women are to be allowed to learn to drive in Kuwait in certain circumstances.

12 June It appears that some of Egypt's troops, destined to be withdrawn after the announcement on 8 May, may stay in the Gulf area. This follows intense pressure from the West to make Egypt's Gulf allies more amenable to the idea of a permanent joint Arab defense force envisaged in the Damascus Declaration of March. Richard Cheney, the American Secretary of Defense, had assured Cairo that Kuwait had requested the presence of Egyptian peacekeeping troops. Kuwait had also tried to reassure Egypt over complaints concerning the treatment of Egyptians in Kuwait, and had stated that Egyptians with savings in Kuwaiti banks would soon be able to draw on them.

13 June Reports from Iran, suspected to be exaggerated, state that the Iraqi army has started to dislodge the Shi'ite rebels from their strongholds in the southern marshes.

15 June In Algeria, the leader of the Movement for Democracy, Ahmad Ben Bella, announces that he is to stand for President. He denies that he is in an alliance with FIS to solve the crisis in Algeria.

16 June According to the Islamic Republican News Agency, Kurdish Islamic groups of Iraq plan to form a united front to carry on the struggle against the Ba'thist rulers. The Kurdish Islamic Movement, the Kurdish Hizbullah, the

Kurdish Mujahidin, the Kurdish Ansar al-Islam, and others have been invited to join. The Kurdish Hizbullah, led by Adham Barzani, is opposed to the compromise moves evidenced by some Kurdish factions.

17 June The Hajj begins in Saudi Arabia, and for the first time since 1987 Iranian pilgrims take part. The Saudis hope to use the occasion to heal wounds in the Muslim world and to reaffirm the validity of their credentials as custodians of the Holy Places. The Iranian pilgrim quota is raised to 110,000. The Saudis also agree to allow limited Iranian demonstrations against "pagans" to take place during the period of the hajj. Approximately 4,700 pilgrims arrive from the Soviet Union—five times the number of previous years—and Afghans approved by the Kabul regime are allowed to attend for the first time since Marxist regime's takeover. Among other dignitaries, the Iranian Foreign Minister and the President of Indonesia attend.

17 June The Jordanian Prime Minister, Mudar Badran, resigns. King Hussein asks the Foreign Minister, Tahir al-Masri, to form a new government. Al-Masri is the first Prime Minister of Jordan of Palestinian origin to serve in twenty years.

17 June After a meeting of European Community foreign ministers Jacques Poos, the Foreign Minister of Luxembourg, announces that the negotiations between Saddam Hussein and the Kurds "are at a dead end and the Kurdish people who decided to return to their homes in the protection zones in the north of Iraq feel terribly insecure." Douglas Hurd, the British Foreign Secretary, says that the foreign ministers of Britain, France, the Netherlands, and Italy have agreed not to end their operations in northern Iraq so long as the Kurds are threatened by the Iraqi regime.

19 June The United States House of Representatives votes to cut off military aid to Jordan as a reprisal for its support of Saddam during the Persian Gulf war.

19 June Palestinians from the West Bank city of Hebron hold the first elections anywhere in the occupied territories in the last 15 years, and the Islamic fundamentalist candidates win. Of the 11 seats up for election in the local chamber of commerce, six are won by fundamentalists sympathetic to, or affiliated with, the Muslim fundamentalist movement Hamas. Four of the winners are allied with mainstream factions of the Palestine Liberation Organization, and one is an independent. The fact that many of these candidates are aligned with the Hamas movement renews concern among some Israeli officials that Islamic fundamentalists might win a much larger share of the vote than expected, if general elections were held in the West Bank one day. But some suggest that the businessmen and shopkeeper voters in this election had grown weary of the PLO's intifada strategy of closing shops and calling strikes.

19 June Demonstrations occur in Amman in a protest against the sentencing of Jordanian citizens (mainly Palestinians) to jail or death by Kuwait martial law court. They stand accused of collaboration with the Iraqi occupying authorities in Kuwait.

20 June The United States suspends its withdrawal of troops from northern Iraq pending discussions with its European allies on how to guarantee the security of the Kurdish safe havens in the future and pending the results of the autonomy talks between the Kurds and Saddam's government.

23 June In spite of its written agreement to uphold UN sanctions against Iraq, Jordan continues to support Saddam with goods and technology.

24 June A group calling itself The Islamic Liberation Front, ostensibly established three years previously in the West Bank, threatened to attack Kuwait interests around the world if Kuwait executes Jordanians jailed for collaboration with Iran. It also threatened to attack the emir himself.

25 June Fighting breaks out in several Algerian cities when the authorities attempt to remove Islamic slogans from the walls of public buildings. Three members of FIS Consultative Council appear on Algerian television. Calling for release of detainees and an end to the curfew, they also indicate willingness to enter into a dialogue with

241

the regime. One of the FIS leaders says members should ignore Abassi Madani—"a danger to Islam and to the FIS."

26 June The Kuwaiti government commutes the death sentences of 29 people convicted of collaboration with the Iraqis to life imprisonment. Martial law ends at midnight.

28 June After nearly a week of rioting in which 23 died, President Chadli resigns as head of FLN and says that he is "President of all Algerians." Prime Minister Ghozali seeks parliamentary approval for his new non-party government program. At Algiers' Kouba mosque, FIS leader Madani says that a jihad may be necessary if the state of emergency is not lifted.

26 June A new political party is accredited in Algeria, the 47th to be recognized. It is the Islamic and Modern Algeria Party (Hizb al-Jaza' ir al-Islamiyya al-Mu'asira)

28 June Saudi Arabia and Iran agree to exchange ambassadors, and the Saudi authorities also agree to permit an Iranian demonstration against "pagans and infidels" each year at the hajj.

30 June The Council of Ulama of Algiers declares that jihad is impermissible between Muslims. "Whoever kills a Muslim deliberately, no matter what his intention, [commits an act of] sedition. . . . All Algeria's people, praise be to God, are Muslims, so it is unimanginable for there to be a jihad or war amongst its sons and groups, who yesterday stood as one in a jihad against one enemy, that is, the enemy of their religion and homeland."

30 June FIS leaders Abassi Madani and Ali Belhadj are arrested by the authorities for allegedly fomenting civil unrest and undermining the state.

30 June Algerian Islamic party Hamas affirms its distance from FIS by calling on army to maintain public order and on FIS to disown radical elements inciting violence in the country. However, the army should not be at service of any one political party or group. Now that President Chadli has resigned as head of FLN, Hamas says, he should "comply with the request of the Algerian Muslim masses." Moreover, "the democrats should act in accordance with Islam and the Islamists should act on the basis of democracy." A new group, calling itself Organization for Combating Tyrants in Algeria (Munazzamat Muharabat al-Tughat fi'l-Jaza'ir), threatens violent activities if the government does not announce the date of presidential and parliamentary elections within 20 days.

30 June A United Nations delegation arrives in Baghdad to investigate Iraq's nuclear facilities. It had been denied access to the military base at al-Falluja on 28 June and earlier in the week to the Abu Gharib military complex. The Security Council had demanded that nuclear inspectors have free access to Iraqi military installations immediately or face "serious consequences." President Bush says that under U. N. resolutions passed during the Gulf crisis "the authority exists" for the use of force against suspected nuclear facilties.

1 July Army occupies the headquarters of the FIS in Algiers and continues to arrest Islamist activists, including six members of FIS's Consultative Council.

1 July In Kuwait opposition leaders announce that they will meet on 8 July, the day before the recall of the consultative body, the National Council. Seven main opposition groups will demand parliamentary elections without further delay.

7 July Algerian police arrest Muhammad Said at a news conference he called to announce he was taking over leadership of the FIS.

7 July In Jordan King Hussein cancels most of the provisions of martial law in effect since the 1967 Arab-Israeli war. He cites desire "to continue Jordan's liberalization process." Martial law had banned large public meetings and gave the government broad powers to restrict freedoms of speech and the press.

7 July Algerian League for Defense of Human Rights demands inquiry into state-of-emergency crackdown on Muslim fundamentalists, saying that the government has covered up scores of arrests and deaths. Cites figures showing 8,000 arrests and 300 deaths since 4 June as opposed to government figures of 1,367 arrests and 55 deaths).

List of Sources Consulted for Chronology

BBC Monitoring Service, *Summary of World Broadcasts*
Chicago Tribune
The Christian Science Monitor
Crisis in the Gulf; Transition to War? Aide Memoire III (London: Royal United Services Institute, 1991)
Current History
The Economist
The Guardian (London)
The Guardian Collection. Number One. *The Gulf Crisis: The First Sixty Days*
The Independent (London)
Israeli Mirror
Keesing's Record of World Events
Middle East International
The Middle East Journal
The New York Times
The Observer (London)
Time
The Times (London)

SELECT BIBLIOGRAPHY

Articles

Abdalla, Ahmed. "Mubarak's Gamble," *Middle East Report* 168 (January/February 1991): 18–21.

Ajami, Fouad, "The Summer of Arab Discontent," *Foreign Affairs* 69 (5) (Winter 1990–91): 1–20.

Akins, James. "Heading Towards War," *Journal of Palestine Studies* 20 (3) (Spring 1991): 16–30.

Baram, Amatzia. "Baathi Iraq and Hashimite Jordan: From Hostility to Alignment," *The Middle East Journal* 45 (1) (Winter 1991): 51–70.

Brenner, Robert. "Why is the United States at War with Iraq?" *New Left Review* 185 (January/February 1991): 122–37.

Chalabi, Ahmad. "Iraq: The Past as Prologue?" *Foreign Policy* 83 (Summer 1991): 20–29.

Chaudhry, Kiren Aziz. "On the Way to Market: Economic Liberalization and Iraq's Invasion," *Middle East Report* 170 (May/June 1991): 14–23.

Childers, Erskine B. "The Use and Abuse of the UN in the Gulf Crisis," *Middle East Report* 169 (March/April 1991): 5–7.

Eilts, Hermann Frederick. "The Persian Gulf Crisis: Perspectives and Prospects," *The Middle East Journal* 45 (1) (Winter 1991): 7–22.

Elon, Amos. "Report from Jerusalem," *The New Yorker,* 1 April 1991, pp. 80, 82–88.

Farouk-Sluglett, Marion and Peter Sluglett. "Iraq Since 1986: The Strengthening of Saddam," *Middle East Report* 167 (November/December 1990): 19–24.

Freedman, Lawrence. "The Gulf War and the New World Order." *Survival* 33 (3) (May/June 1991): 195–210.

Gigot, Paul A. "A Great American Screw-Up: The U.S. and Iraq, 1980–1990," *The National Interest* (Winter 1990–91): 3–10.

Glennon, Michael J. "The Gulf War and the Constitution," *Foreign Affairs* 70 (2) (Spring 1991): 84–101.

"The Gulf Crisis, the UN, and the New World Order" [interview with Ambassador Abdalla Saleh al-Ashtal, representative of Yemen to the United Nations], *Journal of Palestine Studies* 20 (3) (Spring 1991): 31–40.

Hallaj, Muhammad. "Taking Sides: Palestinians and the Gulf Crisis," *Journal of Palestine Studies* 20 (3) (Spring 1991): 41–47.

Halliday, Fred. "The Gulf War and Its Aftermath: First Reflections," *International Affairs* 67 (2) (April 1991): 223–34.

Hehir, J. Bryan. "The Pope's Perspective" ["The Gulf War in Retrospect: 5"], *The Tablet,* 22 June 1991, pp. 761–62.

Hippler, Jochen. "Iraq's Military Power: The German Connection," *Middle East Report* 168 (January/February 1991): 27–31.

Hitchens, Christopher. "Realpolitik in the Gulf," *New Left Review* 186 (March/April 1991): 89–101.

———. "Why We Are Stuck in the Sand; Realpolitik in the Gulf: A Game Gone Tilt," *Harper's,* January 1991, pp. 70–75, 78.

Howe, Jonathan T. "NATO and the Gulf Crisis," *Survival* 33 (3) (May/June): 246–59.

Hughes, Gerard J. "Let Slip the Dog of Faith" ["The Gulf War in Retrospect: 3"], *The Tablet,* 8 June 1991, pp. 701–02.

———. "Wise After the Event?" ["The Gulf War in Retrospect: 1"], *The Tablet,* 25 May 1991, pp. 634-35.

Judis, John. "Jews and the Gulf: Fallout from the Six-Week War," *Tikkun* 6(3) (May/June 1991): 9–17.

Kelly, Michael. "Rolls-Royce Revolutionaries; The Emir Looks to His Own House," *The New Republic,* 8 April 1991, pp. 22–24.

Khadduri, Majid. "Iraq's Claim to the Sovereignty of Kuwayt," *New York University Journal of International Law and Politics* 23(1)(Fall 1990): 5–34.

Khalidi, Rashid I. "The Palestinians and the Gulf Crisis," *Current History* (January 1991): 18–20, 37.

al-Khalil, Samir [pseudonym]. "Kuwait Rights Are the Issue," *Middle East Report* 168 (January/February 1991): 14–16.

Kuniholm, Bruce R. "Turkey and the West," *Foreign Affairs* 70 (2) (Spring 1991): 34–48.

Lalor, Paul. "Report from Baghdad," *Middle East Report* 169 (March/April 1991): 11–13, 36.

Landes, David. "Islam Dunk: The Wars of Muslim Resentment," *The New Republic*, 8 April 1991, pp. 15–18.

Layne, Christopher. "Why the Gulf War Was Not in the National Interest," *The Atlantic*, July 1991, pp. 55, 65–68, 70–71, 74, 76–81.

Lesch, Ann Mosely. "Contrasting Reactions to the Persian Gulf Crisis: Egypt, Syria, Jordan, and the Palestinians," *The Middle East Journal* 45 (1) (Winter 1991): 30–50.

Lewis, Bernard. "The Roots of Muslim Rage," *The Atlantic*, September 1990, pp. 47–60.

Mason, R. A. "The Air War in the Gulf," *Survival* 33 (3) (May/June 1991): 211–29.

"A Military Solution Will Destroy Kuwait" [interview with Ahmad al-Khatib, Kuwaiti opposition figure], *Middle East Report* 168 (January/February 1991): 8–9.

Muslih, Muhammad and Augustus Richard Norton. "The Need for Arab Democracy," *Foreign Policy* 83 (Summer 1991): 3–19.

Nicholl, Donald. "Useless Slaughter" ["The Gulf War in Retrospect: 2"], *The Tablet*, 1 June 1991, pp. 672–73.

Nye, Joseph S., Jr. "Why the Gulf War Served the National Interest," *The Atlantic*, July 1991, pp. 54, 56–57, 60–62, 64.

O'Donovan, Oliver. "Were We Right to Fight?" [The Gulf War in Retrospect: 4], *The Tablet*, 15 June 1991, pp. 733–34.

Pfaff, William. "Reflections: Islam and the West," *The New Yorker*, 28 January 1991, pp. 83–88.

Roberts, Hugh. "Beating About the Bush," and "Mubarak's Mixed Harvest," *South: Emerging World Review* 119 (February 1991): 51–53.

Rochlin, Gene I. and Chris D. Demachak. "The Gulf War: Technological and Organizational Implications," *Survival* 33 (3) (May/June 1991): 260–73.

Rodman, Peter W. "Middle East Diplomacy After the Gulf War," *Foreign Affairs* 70 (2) (Spring 1991): 1–18.

Rothstein, Robert L. "The Middle East After the War: Change and Continuity," *The Washington Quarterly* 14 (3) (Summer 1991): 139–60.

Rubenstein, Danny. "A Faith Betrayed," *Tikkun* 6(3) (May/June 1991): 17–21, 92–93.

Russett, Bruce and James S. Sutterlin. "The U.N. in a New World Order," *Foreign Affairs* 70 (2) (Spring 1991): 69–83.

Sadowski, Yahya. "Power, Poverty, and Petrodollars: Arab Economies after the Gulf War," *Middle East Report* 170 (May/June 1991): 4–10.

Saikal, Amin. "The Persian Gulf Crisis: Regional Implications," *Australian Journal of International Affairs* 44 (3) (December 1990: 237–46.

Schiff, Ze'ev. "Israel After the War," *Foreign Affairs* 70 (2) (Spring 1991): 19–33.

Segal, Jerome M. "The Gulf War and the Israeli-Palestinian Conflict: Another Chance for Peace," *World Policy Journal* 8 (2) (Spring 1991): 351–62.

Sid-Ahmed, Mohamed. "The Gulf Crisis and the New World Order," *Middle East Report* 168 (January/February 1991): 16–17.

Springborg, Robert. "Origins of the Gulf Crisis," *Australian Journal of International Affairs* 44 (3) (December 1990): 221–36.

Stein, Janice Gross. "The Challenge of the Persian Gulf Crisis," *Peace & Security* [Canadian Institute for International Peace and Security] (Winter 1990–91): 2–5.

Stork, Joe. "The Gulf War and the Arab World," *World Policy Journal* 8 (2) (Spring 1991): 365–74.

―――― and Ann M. Lesch. "Why War? Background to the Crisis," *Middle East Report,* 167 (November/December 1990): 4–10.

―――― and Martha Wenger. "From Rapid Deployment to Massive Deployment; The U.S. in the Persian Gulf," *Middle East Report* 168 (January/February 1991): 22–26.

"The Vatican and the Gulf War; Special Meeting of Patriarchs and Bishops," *Encounter (Documents for Muslim-Christian Un-*

derstanding) [Pontificio Istituto di Studi Arabi e d'Islamistica] 174 (April 1991): 1–14.

Viorst, Milton. "A Report at Large: The House of Hashem," *The New Yorker* 7 January 1991, pp. 32–37, 40–52.

Vuono, Carl E. "Desert Storm and the Future of Conventional Forces," *Foreign Affairs* 70 (2) (Spring 1991): 49–68.

Wohlstetter, Albert and Fred Hoffman. "The Bitter End; The Case for Re-Intervention in Iraq," *The New Republic,* 29 April 1991, pp. 20–24.

Wright, Robin. "Unexplored Realities of the Persian Gulf Crisis," *The Middle East Journal* 45 (1) (Winter 1991): 23–29.

Books and Monographs

Bulloch, John and Harvey Morris. *Saddam's War: The Origins of the Kuwait Conflict and the International Response.* London: Faber and Faber, 1991.

Crisis in the Gulf; Transition to War? [Aide Memoire III]. London: Royal United Services Institute, 1991.

Darwish, Adel and Gregory Alexander. *Unholy Babylon; The Secret History of Saddam's War.* New York: St. Martin's Press, 1991.

Desert Shield Fact Book. Bloomington: Game Designers' Workshop, Inc., 2nd ed., 1991.

Foster, Edward and Rosemary Hollis. *War in the Gulf: Sovereignty, Oil, and Security.* [Whitehall Paper Series, No. 8] London: Royal United Services Institute for Defense Studies, 1991.

Gresh, Alain and Dominique Vidal. *Golfe: Clefs Pour Une Guerre Annoncée (Gulf: Keys to a Declared War)* [Collection "La Memoire du Monde"]. Paris: Le Monde Editions, 1991.

The Gulf Crisis: The First Sixty Days. [The Guardian Collection, no. 1] London: The Guardian Newspaper, 1990.

The Gulf Crisis; Test Case for the New World Order ["Emergency Report"]. Bristol, England: Saferworld Foundation, September 1990.

Henderson, Simon. *Instant Empire: Saddam Hussein's Ambition for Iraq*. San Francisco: Mercury House, Inc., 1991.

Karsh, Efraim and Inari Rautsi. *Saddam Hussein: A Political Biography*. London: Brassey's, 1991.

Khalidi, Walid. *The Gulf Crisis: Origins and Consequences*. Washington, D.C.: Institute for Palestine Studies, 1990.

Lauterpacht, E., C.J. Greenwood, Marc Weller, and Daniel Bethlehem, eds., *The Kuwait Crisis: Basic Documents* [Cambridge International Documents Series, volume 1]. Cambridge: Grotius Publications Limited, 1991.

————, eds. *The Kuwait Crisis: Sanctions and Their Economic Consequences* [Cambridge International Documents Series, volume 2]. Cambridge: Grotius Publications Limited, 1991.

Miller, Judith and Laurie Mylroie. *Saddam Hussein and the Crisis in the Gulf*. New York: Times Books/Random House, 1990.

Moushabeck, Michel and Phyllis Bennis, eds., *Beyond the Storm: A Gulf Crisis Reader*. New York: Olive Branch, 1991.

Porter, Jadranka. *Under Siege in Kuwait: A Survivor's Story*. London: Victor Gollancz, LTD., 1991.

Salinger, Pierre (with Eric Laurent). *Secret Dossier: The Hidden Agenda behind the Gulf War*. London: Penguin, 1991.

Schofield, Richard. *Kuwait and Iraq: Historical Claims and Territorial Disputes*. London: The Royal Institute of International Affairs, 1991.

Sciolino, Elaine. *The Outlaw State: Saddam Hussein's Quest for Power and the Gulf Crisis*. John Wiley and Sons, 1991.

Sifry, Micah and Christopher Serf. *The Gulf War Reader*. New York: Times Books/Random House, 1991.

CONTRIBUTORS

MUMTAZ AHMAD is Associate Professor of Political Science at Hampton University, Hampton, Virginia. His publications include *Bureaucracy and Political Development in Pakistan, The Kashmir Dispute,* and *Studies in Rural Development and Local Government in Pakistan.*

SAID ARJOMAND is Professor of Sociology at the State University of New York at Stony Brook. A former fellow of the Institute for Advanced Study in Princeton, he is the author of several works, including *The Shadow of God and the Hidden Imam* and *The Turban for the Crown: The Islamic Revolution in Iran.*

GEHAD AUDA is Senior Researcher, Center for Political and Strategic Studies, Al-Ahram Foundation, Cairo. He also is a Senior Researcher at the National Center of Middle East Studies, Cairo and part-time Associate Professor in the American University in Cairo. He has written extensively in Arabic and English on contemporary political affairs in Egypt.

AMATZIA BARAM is Lecturer in Islamic History at the University of Haifa and the author of numerous works on Iraq and Shi'ite movements within Iraq. His most recent book is *Culture, History, and Ideology in the Formation of Ba'thist Iraq.*

DANIEL BRUMBERG is Assistant Professor of Political Science at Emory University and a Fellow of the Carter Center. Formerly a research associate and lecturer at the University of Chicago, he has written on political parties, syndicates, and the university intelligentsia in the Middle East.

JEAN-FRANÇOIS LEGRAIN is Researcher in Political Sciences at the Centre d'Etudes et de Documentation Economiques, Juridiques et Sociales (CEDEJ), Cairo. Formerly Professor of Islamology in the Institut Catholique de Paris, he has written extensively on Islamic movements and communities in Europe and the Middle East.

BEVERLEY MILTON-EDWARDS wrote her Ph.D. dissertation on "The Rise of Islamic Movements in the West Bank and Gaza Strip Since 1967" at Exeter University. She has contributed to various publications, such as *Middle East International* and *Review of Middle East Studies,* and to newspapers in Europe and the Middle East.

JAMES PISCATORI teaches at the University of Wales and is an Associate Fellow of the Royal Institute of International Affairs in London. He is the author of *Islam in a World of Nation-States* and the editor of *Islam in the Political Process* and (with Dale Eickelman) *Muslim Travellers: Pilgrimage, Migration, and the Religious Imagination.*

HUGH ROBERTS is the author of *Revolution and Resistance: Algerian Politics and the Kabyle Question* and writes for *South: Emerging World Review* in London. He has also taught at the University of East Anglia.

INDEX

87486 320.55
Is4